Workers' Struggle
in Puerto Rico

Workers' Struggle in Puerto Rico:

A Documentary History

by Angel Quintero Rivera

Translated by Cedric Belfrage

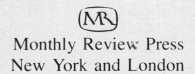

Monthly Review Press
New York and London

Library of Congress Cataloguing in Publication Data
Main entry under title:
Workers' Struggle in Puerto Rico.
    Translation of Lucha obrera en Puerto Rico.
    Bibliography: p. 215
1. Trade-unions—Puerto Rico—History—Sources.
2. Labor and laboring classes—Puerto Rico—History—
Sources.   I. Quintero Rivera, Angel.
HD6592.L813   331.88'097295   76-40343
ISBN 0-85345-342-6

Monthly Review Press
62 West 14th Street, New York, N.Y. 10011
21 Theobalds Road, London WC1X 8SL

First Printing   79 - 244

Manufactured in the United States of America

Contents

Preface

As we begin the task of grappling with Puerto Rican reality, we find that most interpretations of our society fail because they lack dynamic vision and because they do not position themselves in history. We want to break with these interpretations.

The history given us as ours is not our history but the mythology of a social class.

The problem goes further, for the interpretations based on history (books, remarks, declarations, courses we take as lower-school or university students) give a view of our reality that doesn't satisfy us. We face the problem that the history presented as ours is only part of our history. For the nineteenth century we are told more about the history of Spain in Puerto Rico than about the formation of our people under Spanish rule; for the nineteenth century till the present, the history taught us is a history (and a superficial one) of what we might call, stretching the term a little, the Puerto Rican bourgeoisie. One has but to look at the history-book names we know so well: Muñoz Rivera, Baldorioty, Betances, Ruíz-Belvis, De Diego, Barbosa, Matienzo Cintrón, Hostos, Barceló, Muñoz Marín—lawyers, doctors, sons of *hacendados*, or public officials. Not appearing in those books, and known to few of us, are Ramón Romero Rosa, Juan Vilar, Eugenio Sánchez López, Luisa Capetillo, José Ferrer y Ferrer, Eduardo Conde, Prudencio Rivera Martínez, Juan Sáez Corales—printers, tobacco workers, assorted artisans, and sugar-cane cutters.

So much for personalities. What of the history of the "history-less," the anonymous people who, in their collective acts, their work, daily lives, and fellowship, have forged our society through the centuries? What do our history books tell us about the men who twisted and the women who stripped tobacco, about the readings in cigar factories? About the Social Study Groups in this century's first decades (workers discussing Marx, Bakunin, Kropotkin, Reclus, the decisions of the Workers' International, British trade unionism)? About the Red Proletarian Theater Circle in Caguas around 1910, taking to the fields and villages allegories, poems, and songs about what they called the social question and the emancipation of the workers? Where in our history does one find the burnings of cane fields, strikes on the plantations, arrests and clubbings and massacres? Where are the emigrations to Hawaii of the years 1900 to 1904; the goings and comings of tobacco workers to and from Tampa and Santiago de Cuba; even the great emigrations of the 1940s and early 1950s? What do they tell us about the battles for workers' housing and the formation of the slums in San Juan de Cataño? Does anyone try to find out why there were republican workers and how they thought? Who dares to say that the organized public-transport chauffeurs did more campaigning at their work for the Partido Popular (PP—Popular Party) in 1940 than Muñoz Marín did on the platform? If the history books tell us nothing about these events and actions, what then about processes, developments, transformations?[1]

Our workers' history is missing from the history given us as ours. Recognizing this, the Centro de Estudios de la Realidad Puertorriquena (CEREP) initiates its publications on Puerto Rican reality with a historical work about the labor movement. Since none of us are now qualified to present a profound and rigorous analysis of this history, we prefer to publish a collection of its great documents—part of its flesh and blood. Not that it can be understood from the documents (reading them isn't enough). But they may destroy myths, create concern, awaken interest.

Some books deal summarily with our labor history, but from viewpoints depriving them of merit.

Examining the few books that touch on our working class, its processes and development, we find in their approach conceptions or views of Puerto Rican history which preclude, in our judgment, any real understanding of the subject.

One of these is what we call the "great-man view," which analyzes the changes and processes—all that has happened in Puerto Rico—as the product of actions by a few leaders and bigwigs.[2] Thus we get the history of Baldorioty, Muñoz Rivera, De Diego, Barbosa, etc., given as the history of Puerto Rico. Among these people a worker—Santiago Iglesias Pantín—makes an occasional appearance, so that our working-class history becomes the history of this labor leader. We are told, for example, that the labor movement began in Puerto Rico because Santiago Iglesias Pantin arrived on the island; that the movement took a trade-unionist position because of his relations with North American unions; that it was not at the outset independent because he was Spanish and hence didn't feel "the call of nationality"; that it (and its party) divided and faded out with Santiago Iglesias' death; and that, in more general terms, the emancipating labors of Santiago Iglesias made the Federación Libre de los Trabajadores (FLT—Free Workers' Federation) a movement for workers' demands (according to some) . . . or, according to others, the reactionary treason of Santiago Iglesias made it a reactionary movement.

One of our aims in publishing these documents is precisely to sow doubts about this "great-man view," which we consider simplistic and false, not only in terms of the working class but of Puerto Rican history in general. Santiago Iglesias appears in the documents included here a prominent figure but not as the moving power behind all that occurred. He appears, making history, but so do many others. The factors to be considered in an interpretative analysis are many.

Another common approach to our political history is to see it in terms of the internal ideological conflict around our colonial situation—that is, as the history of assimilationists, autonomists, and independentists. Into these categories the historical entities are either divided or placed, their actions explained in terms of their positions in that conflict. This approach, seeing as historical mover the struggles and positions regarding our "political status," ignores the possibility of historical research into the motives behind those positions. It doesn't seek an answer in history to the question of why independentists became independentists when they did, which would involve probing the country's socio-economic and cultural history for enlightenment as to why such-and-such groups of persons took such-and-such a "status" position at a given moment. That implies other "generators" in history, something this approach doesn't conceive of: hence, it resorts to static explanations of a psychological or ethical order. For example, some will say independentists are independentists because they are rebels or honest men, others because they are impatient or utopian. Some say autonomists are autonomists because they are moderate and realistic; others, because they are opportunists with no solid principles. Assimilationists are assimilationists because personal insecurity draws them to shelter behind another power . . . and so forth.[3] This is only one step removed from the "good guys-bad guys" theory of history.[4]

To show, in "flesh and blood," the limitations of this approach is one of our motives for publishing these documents. Puerto Rican labor history can't be categorized as above and can't be understood in such terms. Not that we wish to minimize or conceal the colonial problem, as some do: it appears as a basic problem in almost all the documents, but a problem wrapped in other series of conflicts and processes. For example, after reading "The Tyranny of the House of Delegates," none can describe the workers' petition for U.S. citizenship as one describing a position of assimilationist surrender. The document clearly shows it to be a weapon, a fulcrum, in a grim class struggle—their struggle against a bourgeoisie bent on total hegemony (control of an independent country). It is the class struggle that steers the workers, in that moment, into a specific "status" position, and not vice versa.

Another approach befogging comprehension of working-class actions is based on the so-called "theory of national personality." This conceives of the nation in terms of certain "behavioral traits" that shape a personality type. The Germans, for example, are methodical, harsh, authoritarian. History then becomes the formation of this set of characteristics or the manifestation of that personality type; in our case, the formation and manifestation of *lo puertorriqueño*. Since a series of characteristics shapes a personality type, *lo puertorriqueño* comes out as homogeneous and monolithic, personified, according to nearly all partisans of the theory, in Luis Muñoz Rivera, journalist, poet, politician from Barranquitas, "sap and blood of Puerto Rico."[5] Proud of his Spanish heritage, *hidalgo* and *caballero*, moderate, seeking a middle road between extremes, astute (*jaiba*), opportunistic, Catholic, liberal, reformist. How then do the founding leaders of the Free Workers' Federation get a place in our history? Eduardo Conde, for instance, the Puerta de Tierra house-painter, is shown as rabid against hispanism which he considers ' four centuries of ignorance and slavery,'"[6] hardnosed and foulmouthed,[7] revolutionary. Why is the *hacendado*'s wife, Mariana Bracetti, diligently sewing the Grito de Lares flag, *lo puertorriqueño*—and not the laundress Juana ("of Arc") Colón fighting the police with stones in the La Colectiva strike (as many tobacco strippers in that factory had to do), or raising high the red flag in the streets of Comerio, defying the flyblown local bourgeoisie and the talcumed old ladies on balconies with her *vivas* for the Partido Socialista Puertorriqueño (PSP—Puerto Rican Socialist Party)?[8]

The working man as identified in these historical works is the hinterland *jíbaro*, the peasant who is as *caballeroso*, Catholic, *jaiba* as the Creole *hacendado*; his Spanish heritage glows from him and he also votes for the Unionists (Puerto Rican Union Party) or the Partido Democrático Popular (PDP—Popular Democratic Party).[9] Among shapers of our personality one never finds the Puerto Rican who scared the Creoles by threatening their way of life, the mulatto of Puerta de Tierra, Carolina, or Playa de Ponce, the Socialist voter, the man whom Pedrera, his prejudices showing, labeled "the kinky-haired upstart." He is simply ignored.

We think that neither Eduardo Conde nor Muñoz Rivera, neither Juana Colón nor Mariana Bracetti, should be seen as *lo puertorriqueño*. We consider it mistaken to see our culture in terms of characteristics or personality types. To understand our national culture we must go to its marrow, not merely observe some of its manifestations.[10] The marrow of a culture is in life, in manners of behavior, and in forms of relations and interactions, whether they be forms of solidarity, aspiration, interfunction or conflict.[11] These are the springs of heterogeneity and dynamism, undeniable realities in our complex modern society.

One approach limiting labor history is seeing it as a history of movements or organizations, not of a social class.

As with general history books, the approach of the few investigative works on labor history makes the subject hard to understand. We refer to masters' theses presented in The University of Puerto Rico's Public Administration School or in U.S. universities. None has been published but they are available in UPR's library. Some are useful for the raw material they offer, for their factual discoveries. Yet an approach we consider limiting permeates them all: their concentration on workers' movements or organizations instead of on the history of the working class.[12] They offer short, more-or-less well-developed accounts of a movement. But they obscure our view of the processes behind the story, so as to allow us to see it in broader terms than as merely the actions of a few individuals. To see Puerto Rico's history through these works is extremely difficult.

Studying labor movements as institutional forms taken by the working class allows us the breadth.[13] We may then see the concept of a class not as a mere occupational category but as a historical formation, not as something that is but as something that occurs, not as a thing but as a relationship.

Like any other relationship, it is a fluency which evades analysis if we attempt to stop it dead at any given moment and anatomize its structure. The finest-meshed sociological net cannot give us a pure specimen of class, any more than it can give us one of deferences or of love. The relationship must always be embodied in real people and in a real context. Moreover, we cannot have two distinct classes, each with an independent being, and then bring them *into* relationship with each other. We cannot have love without lovers, nor deference without squires and laborers. And class happens when some men, as a result of common experiences (inherited or shared), feel and articulate the identity of their interests as between themselves, and as against other men whose interests are different from (and usually opposed to) theirs. The class experience is largely determined by the productive relations into which men are born—or enter involuntarily. Class consciousness is the way in which these experiences are handled in cultural terms: embodied in traditions, value systems, ideas, and institutional forms.[14]

We may say then that a social class, although rooted in certain experiences that an economic structure presents in terms of productive relations, is nevertheless a social and cultural formation.

This way of conceiving social classes has often been confused with the concept of subculture (or concepts like "the culture of poverty"), much used—or abused—by North American anthropologists in studying our society. But they are two different concepts and should not be confused in analysis.[15] By "subculture" we understand a system within a greater system; a class is, rather, an element in the relations that shape the broader system. In this sense a subculture is presented as understandable and analyzable in itself, while a class can neither be understood nor analyzed save in the context of the socio-economic structure, which is basic to experiences and relations with other classes in which it reveals its actions, reactions, and initiatives. Thus, to analyze the Puerto Rican working class's history is to study Puerto Rican history. The great labor documents we present are testimony to this. What they show is not the subculture of workers, but the actions of the working class; its aspirations, not with respect to its "sub-system" but to the living reality of Puerto Rico; its view of the world and of the island; its relations with other classes; and its struggles.

Nor, as we have said, must class be confused with occupational category. The latter merely represents a position within a structure, while the class concept implies the dialectic between social structure and human action: a type of social structure involving different experiences through which certain kinds of relations develop with repercussions, in turn, upon the structure and the experiences. This is why studying the history of the working class is more than studying its actions. It means examining also the history of the social and economic structures which are basic to those actions and upon which the actions leave their impact. Thus, collection of documents isn't enough, and we hope it will serve to stimulate deeper investigations.

CEREP and the Historical Analysis of Our Reality

*The great danger of reality is thinking
it will always remain reality.*

Everyone talks about "reality" and wants us to swallow the status quo under that label. But life, we have observed, isn't always routine and stationary. The world changes, we all change, types of social relationships, customs, and aspirations change. In general, the change isn't an obliteration that prefigures a new start: it preserves elements of the previous state of things, but with new significance, or within a new configuration or order. If our world is dynamic, it is a mistake to treat it as static. Yet that is what many who talk about reality seek to impose on us. This was the great concern that decided CEREP to initiate its publications on the reality of Puerto Rico with a work of dynamic reality, a work of historical character.

But there are those who go to history with the same astigmatism they apply to the present, asking, What's going on? What happened? . . . events, data, dates: a concern about those past moments and events in themselves.[16] We in CEREP aren't interested in what happened. It happened. What we want is to understand and make understood certain processes, formations, and transformations, certain developments arising from actions and happenings.

Others view history as the cause of the present and go to the past in search of cause and effect. This approach can sometimes yield valuable discoveries but, in general terms, seems to us erroneous. It involves two highly dangerous fallacies. One is the so-called fallacy of retrospective determinism which tries to depict the present situation as the necessary result of past events. Or, in tongue-twisting terminology: with a given present—what's happening now—the past happened because if it hadn't, what's happening now wouldn't be happening. An example may help illustrate this: Puerto Rico has a per capita income of X (present); Puerto Rico underwent such and such economic processes (past). Obviously, those economic processes are related to the present per capita income; the fallacy of retrospective determinism is in stating that Puerto Rico wouldn't have achieved that per capita income if it hadn't undergone those economic processes. In other words, it wouldn't have achieved that per capita income through other processes, other avenues of economic development. This approach limits a dynamic view of society by its causal determinism.

Seeing history as the cause of the present involves another and even graver fallacy: the assumption that the present is the mouth of the river of the past. This leads us to interpret certain processes, developments, formations, and transformations, begun in the past but still enveloping us now, as something finished and done with, as causes whose effects constitute the present. And it tends to make us—as it has made many students of society—recognize the dynamic of the past while analyzing the present statically. In the past, one sees changes, developments—history. In the present, "systems of functions and roles." Our concern with history is not to seek causes of a suddenly paralyzed present, but to find what can help us understand society in its dynamism.

Viewing society in its dynamism helps us perceive up to what point and in what way our actions conform with—or can transform—our society. We are all attempting this in one way or another. Voting or working in this or that political party, refusing or accepting military service, deciding on this or that occupation, even in such day-to-day matters as deciding to buy this or that product, and similarly in many moments of our lives.

Viewing society in its dynamism helps us in turn to see that much of our collective life is made for us, that much of it is shaped by previous generations or processes that they began.

To direct our actions with more precision in terms of the society we desire, and of the life we would like to share, we have to understand and be aware of the processes, developments, formations, and transformations in which our people are (or could be) involved.

CEREP begins its publications on Puerto Rican reality with a work of historical character not interested in the past, or because we seek causes for the present, but with deep concern for and commitment to the Puerto Rico that we are all going to build.

The Social Question
and Puerto Rico:
A Friendly Call to Intellectuals
R. del Romeral
(1904)

From the middle of the nineteenth century we see class consciousness growing among the artisans of Puerto Rico's main urban centers.* The economic structure, however, cramped the extension of this worker consciousness, and the political structure greatly limited its expression. Labor activity was concentrated in local associations and mutual-aid societies,[1] though we also find references to sporadic strikes.[2] Not until 1897 did a movement begin that was to create the first national union. Ramón Romero Rosa was one of this movement's chief leaders.

Romero, a printer, together with José Ferrer y Ferrer (another printer) and Fernando Gómez Acosta (a carpenter), founded the weekly *Ensayo Obrero* in which they began openly stating the need to transform society, and its prerequisite: a union of all the workers. It was this group that Santiago Iglesias joined immediately on

---

* We have included in the Appendix the ''Letter of an Artisan to His Newspaper'' (1874), in which this nascent class consciousness can be clearly noted. The letter is taken from the newspaper *El Artesano*—possibly the oldest workers' paper extant in Puerto Rico.—*Editor's note.*

arrival in Puerto Rico. Their weekly's slogan, "No Fatherland But the Workshop, No Religion But Work," showed how imbued they were with the ideas—mainly of the anarchist strain—of European workers of the period. *Ensayo Obrero* provided the spark for the Federación Regional de los Trabajadores (FRT—Regional Workers' Federation).[3]

As well as being a founding member of FRT (which had a brief life) and of its successor, Federación Libre de los Trabajadores (FLT—Free Workers' Federation), which dominated the labor scene up to the 1930s), Romero Rosa was president of the San Juan Printers' Union and was elected in 1904 and 1906 as a representative to the Puerto Rican House of Delegates.[4]

Under the pen name "R. del Romeral (Working Printer)," he wrote various books and pamphlets, differing in style and intention, but all concerned with "the social question." His first two works were propagandistic in tone: one, a defense of Santiago Iglesias (1901) with incisive criticisms of those bourgeois politicians who had denounced Spanish-born Iglesias as a foreigner intruding in the country's affairs; the other, an allegorical drama entitled *Emancipation of the Worker* (1903). He also wrote a social-criticism essay, "Testament of a Slave Progress" (1904), and a pamphlet admirably blending propaganda, social criticism, and his satirical view of Puerto Rican society, *¡April 16, 1905! Struggle Between Capital and Labor* (1905), part of which is reprinted in the Appendix. *Between Jest and Brink* (1906) follows the style of the previous pamphlet. He presented his view of Puerto Rico and his social philosophy in a series of satirical essays and allegories, and the same approach predominated in his post-*Ensayo Obrero* contributions to the workers' journals *El Porvenir Social* (1898-99), *La Miseria* (1901), and *El Pan del Pobre* (1901).

In 1904 he published *Musarañas*, one of his most interesting and valuable works. It is subtitled *Tract on Certain Concerns and Customs Which Hinder Puerto Rican Workers in Accepting the Lofty Goals of the World Labor Movement*. In it, he achieves a sharp sociological (as he refers to the new science of society) analysis of factors in the society's structure and culture which inhibit the development of class consciousness. In 1905 he published the *Social Catechism*, in which he explains to his class comrades the main concepts of socialism and the different socialist currents in Europe, and *The Social Question and Puerto Rico*.

In *The Social Question and Puerto Rico*, Ramón Romero Rosa concisely but systematically expounds his own social thinking (obviously within contemporary currents of socialistic thought) and interprets from a global viewpoint, in the light of that thinking, the society in which he lives. To facilitate reading, we have omitted some paragraphs of the Prologue and of Chapters 1 and 2. Otherwise we present the work as it was read and discussed by Puerto Rican workers at the beginning of our century.

It should be noted that when Romeral sounds a friendly call to intellectuals he isn't referring to bourgeois poets, but rather to a type of Puerto Rican (constituting an important group in the early 1900s) of artisan or worker stock who by education—often through his own efforts—achieved certain "intellectual offices," as they were sometimes called. These were people like Pedro C. Timothee, a mulatto of an artisan family in Naguabo, who, while working as a tailor, studied pharmacology at night and later distinguished himself as a schoolteacher; José de Jesús Tizol, of a San Juan family of musicians and artisans; Juan Carreras, of a tobacco-workers' family in Vega Baja, also a schoolteacher; Tomás Carrión Maduro, mulatto of Juana Díaz, journalist, secretary to political leaders, and professional orator; Norberto Escabí of Mayagüez, mulatto, journalist, writer and translator for the magazine *Pro Patria*. Romeral thought, with good reason, that due to their exceptional social position these intellectuals could as well lean toward the working class—in which case they would be of fundamental importance—as toward the values of the bourgeoisie. There were cases of both.

I ask your distinguished attention and invite you to put aside all romantic ideas and idle refinements.

For love of the piece of earth to which you owe all the emanations of your life, for love of this human concourse to which you owe your relative intelligence, I would have you enter fully into perception of the true Fatherland.

I call upon the inspired poet, the fertile writer—upon every intellectual who ingenuously identifies the Puerto Rican Fatherland with the blue sky, the charms of spring, the perfume of flowers, the luxuriant countryside, the soft breezes, the voluptuous nights, etc.—to change your illusions for an idea . . .

Everywhere Nature is one in its manifestations.

Wherever one may go there are sky, stars, breezes, flowers, perfumes, etc.

Nothing in the marvelous work of Creation of the Universe is Fatherland.

Fatherland is the humanity of people.

The Puerto Rican Fatherland is all Puerto Ricans.

Nature has placed us on this piece of earth, granting us at the same time the inalienable right to life.

And of this piece of earth all Puerto Ricans have the right of co-ownership; and from it we must wrest by our work enough to satisfy our legitimate needs and the pleasures inherent in life.

Puerto Rico cannot legally be the exclusive property of a few.

And the reason is that man did not make Earth on which he lives.

He has a right to the piece of earth where he is born or where he lives, but with the obligation of working it and making it fruitful.

The right to life is a sacred law dictated by Nature itself: "In the sweat of thy face shalt thou eat bread."

But the right of property is a predatory law dictated by man.

Nature stands above the laws of man.

Man cannot be more than Nature; nor can he ever become her equal, since he has created and can create nothing natural.

His power is limited: it consists solely in changing and combining the products of the earth.

The earth is what produces, and the workers are those who make it produce.

With all his intelligence, with all his profound but always limited knowledge, man is not capable of destroying so much as an atom of matter, nor of creating the atom with the components of matter.

These considerations, taught to the human being by healthy common sense, shape the beautiful concept of Fatherland, which means community of brothers.

And among brothers, by natural law, there can be no master.

Yet that is just what we have in abundance.

Masters who command us from without.

Masters who command us from within.

Masters of earth, water, light, in short of all that they have not conceived and often have not even worked to produce.

Masters of bread for the belly.

Masters of bread for the mind.

And because there are masters of everything, there are slaves for everything.

And where there are slaves there cannot be Fatherland, since the social basis—positive Liberty, whose precise condition is Equality leading us to its legitimate consequence Fraternity—doesn't exist.

Thus our people are degraded; thus they degenerate by anemia of the blood and brain.

Our peasant class, those who make sugar from cane—not "a lake of honey," as the poet sang, but a huge lake of gold—remains illiterate, naked, breadless, hygieneless: in short, in the same poverty in which Columbus found the aborigines.

Our workers, whose very appearance betrays their debilitation, build the steps of an altar to the glory of our drones, while they themselves live in pigsties, without light, air or health, short of bread, shelter, education, life.

Oh, intellectuals!

If you don't go to the masses to tear off the veil of their ignorance, don't call yourselves patriots.

Instruct the people.

But, instruct them, break away from all the formulas of humbug and hypocrisy.

Enough of lies!

R. del Romeral
Working Printer

PART ONE

Chapter 1

The religious lie—Natural poverty and artificial poverty—Yesterday and today—Pauperism

Our first ancestors lacked material and intellectual means by the natural order of things. Modern hypocrites make clever and malicious use of the religious lie about poverty, endlessly repeating to the ignorant and unhappy victims of exploitation that they must accept their privations because the poor are always with us.

And it is true, there has always been poverty; and there surely always will be until the solution of the great human problem which has been conclusively posed by the social question—that is, by modern socialism.

This primordially vital problem, blocking as it does nothing less than the relative happiness of all humanity, needs thorough analysis and clear exposition to remove hypocrites and swindlers from the field of modern rationalism and positive logic—to bring out the supreme truth from the murk of ignorance, and to enlighten the consciousness of the oppressed and exploited.

So to the task.

When man, in obedience no doubt to zoological laws, abandoned his animal-irrational life to enter the life of the spirit or intelligence, he began to feel all the woes of penury; and he has been hemmed in ever since by lack of bare necessities.

Thus poverty has always been with us.

But let us see how much of it is man's original invention.

Poverty embraces two periods, the one flowing into the other: natural poverty and artificial poverty.

The first, stretching from man's creation to the invention of machinery and discovery of steam, was due to the inadequacy of man's arm to produce enough for subsistence, given the emergencies of Nature. With physical effort limiting what could be produced by cultivation and industry, the smallest atmospheric casualty could suffice to bring hunger and privation to families or whole communities.

Not so with artificial poverty, created precisely by the super-abundance of products: that is, by the extraordinary overproduction thrown on the market by machinery installed under capitalist control, otherwise known as industrialism.

Modern poverty, more constricting than the old kind, is rooted in the sordid and despotic egoism of the wealthy class.

Yesterday, communities were scourged by hunger only when a hurricane or other seismic disturbance devastated the fields, or lack of water burned up the plantations.

Today, laborers die of hunger or cold, or for lack of some necessity of life, on the threshold of great stores of provisions and consumer goods. And they die not by hundreds but by millions.

Yes, there was always poverty, but we have to do some thinking about it and what causes it.

We will see how the aristocracy of blood, self-appointed as autocrats over slaves, knew, for better or worse, how to provide subsistence for its serfs. But today we see an aristocracy of money ruling the roost through political liberties which the proletariat helped to implant, using the marvelous power of the machine to make itself a dominant bourgeois class, and creating with its capitalist system a new feudalism much more despotic and inhuman than the system it overthrew in the Middle Ages. Not only does it not know how to maintain its proletarian slaves; it leaves them to die of hunger and cold at the very doors of its accumulations of food and manufactures.

Yesterday's serf, working individually with nothing but his empirical approach to agriculture and crafts, nothing but a wooden rake and a hand loom, could assure himself of bread and clothing.

Just when the revolutionary progress of production has filled us with awe of the men of science; just when economic sages are telling us that with present machinery seven men's work suffices to grow, reap, grind, and bake the wheat and bread needed by a thousand; this is when pauperism spreads more vigorously everywhere and the specter of hunger stalks through productive humanity.

Poverty, poverty everywhere.

But artificial poverty.

Poverty imposed by the capitalistic class.

Chapter 2

**The distraction of religion—Intelligence is the
spirit of Liberty—Past rebellions dignified the
worker—Humanity always the victim of religious
powers—The problem of Equality**

The hapless man whose mind has never been touched by
thoughts of Equality and emancipation is convinced that his lot in
life is something natural and inevitable.

And his case is much worse if his brain is preoccupied with the
dogmatic baggage of the religious lie, which tells him day after day
that he has to be poor and suffer privations in this vale of tears to
attain eternal life after he dies.

But this isn't the way honest and intelligent men think about
poverty. They can see that all religion has done is to school the
slave—that is, the poor—in meekness, to keep him ignorant so he
won't rebel against those who cause his artificial poverty, among
whom are the priests, potent allies of exploitative capitalism.

Religion knows that the spirit of positive Liberty is rooted in
human intelligence; but since religion derives its power from
dogged opposition to all that emanates from liberty, this explains
its enmity to all right and justice.

Yet while religion shows its enmity for liberty, it maintains its
ludicrous pretense of being the vehicle that leads humanity to
happiness through privation and penury.

Liberty is obtained through exercising the brain, which gives us
a precise awareness of its value.

The rebellions of eunuchs, Spartacists, and other slaves against
the masters of Sparta, Persia, Rome, Greece, etc. can only be
explained by the heightened awareness they achieved of liberty's
positive value.

And it is the beautiful concept of rebellion, forged in the slaves'
brains by the reasoning process that stimulates intelligence, that has
lent some dignity to the modern proletarian or worker, the
successor of the Sudras, helots, pariahs, villeins, serfs—in short, all
the slaves of the past, the products of animality and ignorance.

Meanwhile, religion, ever opposed to all intellectual evolutions, has consistently harried, oppressed, and mocked intelligence in the persons of the greatest geniuses.

Let Socrates, Savonarola, Galileo, Huss, Campanella, etc., speak. If necessary let Jesus Christ, slandered and reviled by men of religion, speak.

Consider in what depths of ignorance we would still remain if religion had been able, as it initially sought to do, to destroy that noble invention, the printing press.

If religion ever had a mission, it has been fulfilled: progress is a product of its victims.

And progress is what brings some happiness to man.

Efforts to block intellectual evolution are all in vain.

The world marches, as Felletan well says, and marches on the road of light.

For that reason, the problem of equality is on the agenda.

The social question has posed it.

Chapter 3

The social question exists only since socialism exists— The capitalist system—Socialism aims to transform society—The force of socialism—We must know how to fight

We must get it into our heads that the social question is a question of intelligence, of liberty, of right.

Not a question of hunger.

If it were, its problem would be resolved by silencing the groans of the belly, which can be done with bread or clubs.

The social question exists only since socialism exists. That is, since the natural poverty of old gave place to the modern, artificial poverty of industrialism.

The ideas peculiar to socialism were born when the invention of machinery and the discovery of steam created the division of labor and the manufacturing system with its competition to market its overproduction.

With replacement of the aristocracy of blood by the aristocracy of money—the bourgeoisie—the class war was openly declared everywhere.

The capitalist system was created to maintain harsh domination over every kind of physical and intellectual effort.

The same artificial poverty, produced by industrialism, that is suffered by workers in factories, mines, workshops, etc., is felt by poets, writers, scientists, and all who lack access to the means of becoming capitalists.

Poet, writer, craftsman, scientist, manufacturer, and laborer, equally crippled by poverty, all know there is no reason for such social injustice and contempt.

With the perfection of machinery and scientific advances in agriculture, four or six times what is needed to sustain everyone is produced today.

Socialism is an intelligent design for the transformation of society, that is, for abolishing artificial poverty and shaping a just, equalitarian society of free, honest, and intelligent workers.

And if only the hungry were socialist, as many have sought to tell us, the social question now on the agenda would be resolved with bread and clubs, as occurs each time that workers are ousted from factories by the excessive increase of production and, tormented by hunger, demand bread and jobs.

Socialism pursues the goal of human perfectibility, ever aspiring toward the reign of true justice in the world.

And can there be a greater and nobler ideal than to bring all men into participation in property, in the enjoyments and liberties and rights of life?

The power of socialism rests on the justice of its ideals.

And this power lies in the conquest of ignorance, mother of all the slaveries.

Its most potent inspiration is the desire and resolve for the socio-economic emancipation of Humanity by all intelligent means.

The class struggle furiously waged by humanity for countless centuries will not end as long as economic and political inequalities continue to divide men into exploiters and exploited.

But before these inequalities can disappear it is necessary to reconstruct rights, customs, and education from their foundations, raising the personality of the proletariat with constant instruction and propaganda in the ideals of socialism.

Socialism has therefore posed the social question, which is not one of hunger but of right, that is, liberty and justice.

And to the end that exploited humanity may one day triumph—as it surely will—and the social question be resolved, socialism, by the power of its ideals, calls on the proletariat to impregnate itself with this truth: that its interests as an exploited class is opposed to the exploiting class's interest, and so long as it lends direct or indirect support to that class it delays the coming of all humanity's socio-economic independence.

So it isn't enough to want to fight. We must know how to fight, for what human goal we fight, and against whom we fight.

Chapter 4

The economic problem—Knowing how, for what, and against whom we fight—Doom of the capitalist system—Yeast of rebellion

In old times the so-called economic problem didn't exist.

The most to which the slave could aspire was to be not less than an animal.

The economic problem begins with the disappearance of natural poverty upon the invention of machinery and the discovery of steam.

With this, artificial poverty was created and the economic problem posed.

And this problem, which at the outset was no more than the dispensation of steam-driven machinery's enormous production, hatched the bourgeois ideas and ambitions shaping the capitalist system.

With capitalism came the awakening of socialism, which is an accumulation of ideas already expressed in essence by ancient thinkers and philosophers.

And modern socialism has posed the social question whose solution must be all humanity's socio-economic emancipation.

But socialism, not being a question of hunger but of intelligence, stimulates the mind and offers a broad field for ideas about the struggle.

We must know how to fight.

And this necessity is the condition of knowing that present society, created by and for the capitalist system, keeps humanity divided into two classes: exploited and exploiter.

The exploited class—who are the many—consists of all the producers: mechanical, manual, and intellectual workers.

The exploiter class—who are the few—consists of all the nonproducers: the capitalists.

And we need to understand that the system on which this class bases its predominance is not merely useless but disruptive, for it has created artificial poverty by the filthy egoism of lucre.

But the exploiter class dominates because, apart from its exclusive ownership of all the means of production, it also owns the brains; so that everything is done for its interests and whims. It creates and maintains institutions, laws, and prisons to defend its exclusive privilege.

The great majority of the exploited class, on the other hand, succumbs to ignorance and the lowest kind of concerns, which is just the cause for it to remain indolent, enslaved, and oppressed by the capitalist class.

And this is what demonstrates the fact that socialism isn't a question of hunger but an intellectual question.

No ignoramus can be a socialist. He whose brain is untouched by thoughts of equality, emancipation, and justice cannot recognize his right to life, and hence doesn't know how he must fight and how to fight; for to know is to have an exact understanding of the ideas to be fought for.

Wanting to fight isn't enough. One must also know the human goal for which one fights.

The exploiting, capitalist class, master as it is of all means of production and disposing of state powers to defend its privileges, takes the lion's share of what the workers produce and leaves them only the bare necessities to enable them to continue producing.

Under this iniquitous system a minority of parasites lives in idle luxury, while those who work live in permanent insecurity, scarcity, and, more often than not, penury.

The human goals for which socialism fights are not only the material condition of the workers but the high principles of right and justice.

These principles imply the need to substitute for the present exploitative system a society in which the means of production are collectively or socially owned and everyone owns the product of his work; and the replacement of the capitalist regime's ignoble egoism by a scientific organization of production and by a nobler social morality making all humanity a single family of free, honest, dignified, and intelligent workers.

We must repeat that socialism isn't a question of hunger but of putting the brain to work.

Wanting to fight, knowing how to fight—accidents born of will and understanding, channeling our ideals into the human finality of struggle—lead us to clear identification of the enemy to be fought.

And who is the enemy?

The crass ignorance of the workers themselves.

The worst enemy of the poor man is the other poor man.

The worker's worst enemy is his own comrade.

The proletariat is divided by patriotic questions which are irrelevant when capitalism is becoming more and more international.

Divided by religious passions, offspring of hypocrisy and fraud in their highest form.

Divided by political questions which directly favor the exploiting class.

Divided within the labor organizations themselves by the vanities of some who want higher managerial positions than others, ignoring the fact that our best interests depend not on managers but on the instruction and training of all workers so that each may manage himself.

Divided in work by strikebreakers who unscrupulously take the jobs of those who are fighting.

And divided without understanding that an injury to any member of the great proletarian family sooner or later injures the whole family.

The soldiers are proletarians.
The sailors are proletarians.
The police are proletarians.
All the servants of the capitalist class are proletarians.

Yet for all its preponderance and force, despite having prisons and judges at its exclusive service, and education and science under its official seal, without which there is no power in the state; despite all this the capitalist regime sees itself threatened with death or doomed to inevitable disappearance.

Why?

Because it makes the great mistake of thinking it can survive in the midst of a great mass whom it leaves disinherited.

The disinherited are beginning to rebel.

Feeling the ravages of the virus of pauperism, the poet, the writer, the scientist, the manufacturer, the laborer—all the exploited people whose brains have been entered by thoughts of emancipation and equality—rise up against an exploiting system that perpetuates every kind of social immorality and injustice.

Capitalist concentration itself provokes the rebellion of the disinherited.

The great monopolization of industry, agriculture, and commerce in hands that become daily fewer and more idle condemns to artificial poverty hundreds of thousands of men who have enjoyed, if not great fortunes, at least an independent existence.

And we must agree that these dispossessed of today and tomorrow are not made for servitude like the worker, who from father to son, has acquired the habit of bowing to the master and to poverty.

And surely these people of intellect who are being dispossessed by capitalist concentration will be the yeast for the rebellion of the proletariat.

Here, then, we have posed the social question as a principle of liberty, as a question of right.

Here is socialism as an intelligent design for social transformation.

PART TWO

Chapter 1

Colonial system—The fundamental law—Political liberty —Economic independence—Capitalism is cosmopolitan— Bureaucratic representation—The capitalist game

It is vital that socialism make its ideals felt in the brains of intelligent Puerto Ricans.

It is a question of positive identification with our human condition, as exploitative capitalism develops its artificial poverty.

Where penury bespeaks slavery in its highest form, one cannot speak of liberty.

As a people, Puerto Rico takes the prize for poverty.

Poor in political rights.

Poor in social rights.

Poor in economic rights.

Yet wealth is here. It is a matter of disposing of Nature's bounty, which is always free.

As a geological entity, Puerto Rico's wealth stands unrivaled.

Rich in vegetation.

Rich in natural products.

Rich in the quality of its produce.

Here is the contradiction between man and Nature, between poverty and wealth: the contradiction created by the regime of human exploitation.

And this contradiction, which surely must awaken intelligence and the spirit of rebellion, is of course posed by the social question.

It is a human problem: the right to life, the right to liberty.

Puerto Rico has a great productive population suffering the rigors of artificial poverty imposed by capitalist concentration.

Its political problem is appalling, its economic problem inhuman.

An oppressed and exploited people.

Oppressed by the barbaric law of conquest.

Exploited by the criminal law of plunder.

Puerto Rico is part of the colonial system.

And that system is the political crime in which all so-called civilized nations are implicated, whatever their forms of government: the brutal performance of arming ships and filling them with soldiers to impose capitalist rule at gunpoint and so broaden the privileges of exploitation.

Consider, then, in what form the social question has been implanted in Puerto Rico.

What is the basis of its organic law?

The right of conquest . . .

And what is the tendency of this injustice?

Surely, to centralize local administrations in the hands of genuine representatives of capitalism.

This is evidenced in the exemption of local property while denying it to the municipalities themselves, for the direct or indirect benefit of the dominant, exploiting class.

Exemptions, concessions, privileges—everything that implies ascendancy is denied the country's collective or social interest and granted to individual, capitalist interest.

No law protects the dispossessed, who represent the many.

All is done for the interest and whim of the owners, who are the few.

This is the social organization of scorn and contempt for humanity.

Let us now analyze the situation politically.

Does liberty exist in Puerto Rico since it is under the aegis of what is considered the world's most liberal and democratic republic?

Politically, the answer is painfully in the negative.

The gift of a vote to elect "representatives" who proceed to legislate exclusively in favor of the individualist, capitalist class, is more than political immorality: it is a mockery of the collective liberty of the masses.

In the colony as in the metropolis, the significance of this is clear.

In the context of the social question we see that, under the capitalist system aiming at human exploitation, a republic is no different from an empire, a monarchy, or Caesarism.

Under the absolute control of the capitalist class a republic, however much it proclaims itself democratic and free, remains a bourgeois republic, precluding the legitimate interests and aspirations of the social republic.

The exploiting class is the dominant one under any form of government.

It dominates, because, as well as owning the means of production, it owns the brains, which constitute power.

And power creates the law.

And the law, in present society, is the right of the strongest.

On the other hand, does Puerto Rico enjoy economic independence because it belongs to the greatest commercial metropolis of the New World?

We won't mention the hunger-induced anemia which the highest commercial circles have jocularly suggested is contagious.

Only that out of a million inhabitants 980,000 are crippled by artificial poverty, compelled to buy articles of prime necessity at prices so inflated by the impositions of trade that often those who made them can't have them.

As a country wrapped in the colonial system, Puerto Rico cannot enjoy economic independence.

Colonization is a political crime committed by the capitalist class, through which it maintains the colonials in economic dependency and servitude.

Trade is imposed by the colonial system which denies the right of organization.

And this trade necessarily tends to centralize everything.

And with each step in that direction, whether moral or material, slavery and death draw nearer to us.

All this leaves us with the key fact that in the colony of the world's most liberal republic, the municipalities are blocked and impeded from mutual association.

Clearly such association between communities reduces their dependency and creates positive avenues toward political liberty and economic independence.

And it is precisely these avenues that are in the custody of exploitative capitalism, whose tentacles will only be weakened by a supreme, united effort of will and a grasp of the principles of liberty on the part of the colonized.

Thought is a function of the brain; the heart yields up its perceptions to the intellect.

Let us not be blind to the fact that the capitalists, masters of the means of production and of all effective state power to maintain their privileges, will not graciously surrender what they owe to their cohesion as an exploiting class.

Does capitalism change its nature by being republican, imperialist, monarchist or Caesarist?

The social question reveals its noxious influence in whatever form.

Certifying the political farce that puts the masses to sleep, it raises a bureaucratic class out of the sharpest elements in the political parties and assigns to them the defense of its exploiting regime.

What does capitalism care about a nation's fulfillment, the good of a people, the happiness of a country?

Nothing: capitalism is cosmopolitan, it is internationalized everywhere.

Capitalists of the whole world are represented in a nation whatever its form of government.

And it is they who constitute the power of the State.

The people are only a nerve in the body.

In the United States they have proportional representation of English, German, Austrian, Italian, French, Russian, etc., millionaires, and all these, combined with American millionaires, dictate the laws that impose the terms of trade.

And these laws dictated by millionaires of assorted nationality, congregated under one nation's aegis, comprise the political crime of colonialism.

Was it perchance to bring Puerto Rico some economic independence or political liberty that they armed ships, filled them with soldiers, and performed a bloody show of war?

Here we see the fundamental law of plunder.

Six bureaucrats, installed as sovereigns by the laws of trade, constitute the representative assembly of exploiting capitalism.

And beneath the scourge of these modern feudal princes fall all the interests of the country.

Without their approval, imposed by the masters of machinery and money, nothing is done.

So this is the plight in which we find ourselves.

Does the liberty of the Puerto Rican people interest the capitalist regime?

Was the change of sovereignty made to improve the country's political, social, and economic conditions?

Our soil's abundant production of sugar cane, coffee, tobacco, and other such lucrative crops for the market—that is what interests them.

If it were otherwise there wouldn't be those exorbitant valuations that force smallholders to get rid of their pieces of land, which then fall directly into the exploiting companies' hands.

This explains the great centralization of sugar cane and tobacco—surely, coffee is also on the agenda—with their lush profits ending up in the banks of London. Paris, the United States, Berlin, etc., where the masters distribute dividends every six or twelve months.

It explains how the "New York and Porto Rico [sic] Steamship Company" has maintained its privileges and imposed its scandalous exploitation and trade monopoly divorced from all justice, reason, and right.

And it explains how the foreigners, with money they extract from Puerto Rico's treasury by fair means or foul, steadily encroach on and monopolize our lands. A capitalist concentration which, unless rebellion intervenes, will see the day of the colony's degeneration into one enormous factory.

Chapter 2

**Let us take the road of positive liberty—The figures
don't lie—Puerto Rican intellectuals not concerned
by the social question—The three big lies—Ignorance
of cause—Artful planning—Puerto Ricans against Puerto Ricans**

We have reached a culminating point in history where we must decide either for a liberty that assures subsistence to all, or for a slavery that denies the right of life to the great proletarian family.

It is too late to dream.

We must take the side of liberty or of slavery.

Neither half tints nor chiaroscuro are admissible in the real picture of our society, basking in the sun of modern civilization and penetrated by all the bright rays of science.

The dilemma is here:

To accept the liberty of all humanity, abolishing forever the barbaric system of man's enslavement by man;

Or to admit tacitly that liberty is the exploiters' exclusive patrimony and thus the eternal luxury of that minority.

These are the great alternatives for the human problem posed by the social question.

The tendency toward liberty.

The tendency toward absolute slavery.

Either to win ground in the field of positive liberty by socializing all the means of production, humanity's only source of relative happiness and well-being;

Or to return along the road of absolute slavery by perpetuating private property in land, water, machinery—in all the means of production monopolized by a capitalist-class minority whose exploiting system is as disruptive to humanity as it is useless.

Man's intelligence has reached astonishing maturity. He has calculated time, measured space, compressed distance, perfected grandiose inventions, made marvelous discoveries.

Man's intelligence, then, must decide that liberty shall not be broken, however much it is stretched; that is, it shall redeem and emancipate all humanity from the slavery imposed by a minority monopolizing Nature's bounty.

If this were not so, man's intelligence would have to show that the objective of all the sciences he cherishes, of all the knowledge they represent, is for nothing but to lead humanity from progress to progress toward barbarism.

Liberty and slavery are two clouds charged with electricity.

Human intelligence stands between them.

The clash is inevitable.

As we have continued to repeat, socialism isn't a question of hunger but of right or, better said, of liberty.

If only the hungry were socialists, the social question—the human problem—would certainly be resolved by hushing the rumbles of the stomach, which, as we well know, can be done with bread or clubs.

But the social question is one of the intelligence, and it is intelligent men who must solve the problem.

Let us open our eyes to what our own country shows us about the present regime of exploitation.

Puerto Rico produces four times more than enough for the needs and pleasures of its million inhabitants.

Fertile of soil, prolific and wealthy in products and crops, it has an enormous peasant class in a state of illiteracy, naked, living in palm- and straw-thatch hovels, with no food but roots and ground corn, living, in short, almost as did the Indians found by Columbus; but with the notable difference that the Borinquen Indian worked for himself, while the Puerto Rican *jíbaro* works like an animal for the lords and masters of this land.

The figures don't lie. Just add up the millions of dollars extracted from sugar cane, tobacco, coffee, minor crops, cattle, everything that is exported.

All that remains here are the salaries of the plantations' and factories' few technical employees, the pittances of small farmers, and the beggarly wages of the workers.

So that artificial poverty imposed by exploiting capitalism cripples 980,000 of our million inhabitants.

And crippled too by scarcity, along with the worker and laborer, are the poet, the writer, the journalist, the scientist, the manufacturer, etc.

Meanwhile, our indifferent intellectuals pay scant attention to the social question and, contrary to their own interests, waste energy and brains in abstractions and futilities, sometimes combating the ideals they most need to defend their own cause.

Eminent poets and writers chanting hymns to the fantastic illusions of mythology and the mystical inventions of the religious lie.

Learned and obviously talented historians abandoning the glorious camp of modern sociology to wander in the social absurdity created by this decrepit and immoral society.

Intellectuals who, crippled by the artificial poverty of capitalism, lend themselves to fortifying the brain of the exploiting system.

And clearly, that brain which capitalism so badly needs to maintain its regime is supported by three big lies.

The religious lie.

The political lie.

The social lie.

Charity! cries the Pope from his splendid gold prison; and so saying, hauls off millions of dollars to the bank with evangelical zeal. Charity! cry the cardinals, archbishops, monks, etc., most of them getting their payoffs from steamship lines, railroads, factories, mines, etc.

Fatherland! cry the politician-usurpers of natural wealth; and so saying, divvy up the capitalist swag, caring little or nothing that a hundred or two hundred thousand of their fellow human beings die of hunger each day.

Equality, fraternity! cry the very people who keep humanity divided; and so saying, extract more profit from the antagonisms that capitalist power legitimizes.

And Puerto Rican intellectuals, often perhaps from ignorance of the ideas that exalt the social question, reject their own weapons to grasp those which directly or indirectly favor the exploiting system.

Journalists crippled by scarcity, fleeing from the ideals of social emancipation, give impressive headlines to the churches' sermons and hallelujahs, laud the feats of plundering patrioteers, and extol the bureaucrats, direct agents of capitalism.

Enlightened men, crippled by scarcity, blush to defend the

shirtless ones and plunge into eulogies of ostentation and frippery.

Brains detached from the noble redemptive cause of humanity, defending the idleness and parasitism of exploiting drones!

Thus capitalism steadily extends its tentacles over this earth, destroying everything, while the poor in their misery tear each other to pieces.

And there has certainly been no shortage of capitalist brains to carry out the plunder.

The capitalists have organized everything with great skill.

A civil government with no citizenry of its own.

A policy with no platform of its own.

A House of Representatives with no representation of its own.

Town councils with no authority of their own.

And a people with no say in its own despoliation.

And all this so artfully planned and coordinated that for the past five or six years—years on which one looks back with shame—it is Puerto Ricans who have been shedding Puerto Rican blood.

Puerto Ricans who, as unwitting agents of the despoilers' infamous cause, have drowned Puerto Rican homes in tears and mourning.

Puerto Ricans who have dull-wittedly degraded and discredited Puerto Rico.

Puerto Ricans who have delivered Puerto Rico in manacles to unparalleled plunder.

Puerto Rican magistrates who have given to the hangman the rights that belong to the people.

Puerto Rican judges who despicably persecute those who crave liberty for this land.

Puerto Rican police who pursue day and night the malignant mission of hounding their brothers in misfortune, always ready to gun down defenseless people who, hungry to the verge of death, cry out for bread and work.

And meanwhile, the surfeited masters of the booty make a clean sweep of everything.

> The land lacerates itself in dubious battle
> And the monster's maw yawns wider.

Memories of the Free Federation
Luisa Capetillo
(1911)

The U.S. occupation of Puerto Rico in 1898 was accompanied by a transformation of our economy. The big sugar and tobacco firms of the metropolis hastened the process of converting a semi-feudal hacienda agriculture into a capitalist agriculture. Intensification of agrarian capitalism turned *campesinos* into a new type of proletariat, a proletariat of the sugar plantations and tobacco-elaboration centers. The experiences of this proletarian situation created a base for a potentially strong class-consciousness.[1] The original nuclei of the Federación Libre de los Trabajadores (FLT—Free Workers Federation), mainly consisting of artisans in urban centers, carried this class consciousness through the plantations in what they called "The Crusade for the Ideal,"[2] and steered it into the class struggle. Thus the FLT grew by leaps and bounds, mobilizing nearly all the workers in sugar districts like Ceiba.[3] Luisa Capetillo's "Travel Impressions" describes FLT activity at the start of this process.

The essay has an additional value: Luisa Capetillo interweaves her descriptions with an exposition of her own ideas and aspirations.

She is a legend in our working-class history. Old labor leaders whom we asked about her began without exception by mentioning that she was the first Puerto Rican woman to wear trousers (or culottes) and the first to defend free love. In her writings, and in her actions as a labor and feminist leader, she combines anarchism, spiritualism, and the principles of women's liberation. We find all this in the four of her works which have been preserved: *Libertarian Essays* (1904-1907), *Humanity in the Future* (1910), *Influences of Modern Ideas* (1916) (plays and letters to anarchist friends abroad as well as essays), and *My Opinion on the Liberties, Rights and Duties of Woman as Companera, Mother and Independent Human Being* (1911). The essay we present here is from the last-noted book.

Travel Impressions, July 1909

I left for Isabela at ten in the morning As the train moved out from Arecibo, through plantations with soil prepared for seeding, I saw a child with one hand holding up her poor little skirt as a pocket for seed, scattering it with the other hand in the open furrows. A lovely and poetic figure!

A fine symbol of that constancy in work which relentless egoism, the greedy hydra of exploitation, strangles in its monstrous arms: destroying the poor child's beauty and health to jettison her for a squalid, stricken, and unsupported old age. A whole life of want and penury ending perhaps as a beggar, perhaps in the hospital, the only refuge for those who produce everything and enjoy nothing.

Ah, beautiful symbol of toil and perseverance, I salute you in the name of universal brotherhood! And you, exploiting monster, beware lest you fall into the precipice of your vanities, the abyss of your errors.

Watch your step lest the Justice of Liberty catch up with you!

Tremble! Shiver with dread at the terrible end awaiting you for your indifference toward your brothers, the human sacrifices whom you plunge into the deepest degradations of poverty! But everything has an end and yours is near. Tremble, tyrants of all the ages, at the Social Revolution that is coming to reduce you to the level you deserve!

On guard!

I stayed some hours in Isabela and left the same night for Aguadilla. In that city I had the great satisfaction of greeting some carpenters who have organized themselves. It is the only labor organization in a community where politics doesn't allow workers to think of defending their wages. Wage slavery is the slavery of today, the oppressor that has made and will make more hungry people and criminals than the slavery of race and of feudalism. It is more cruel, more unjust. The slavery of the purchase and sale of human flesh was pitiless. The feudal seigneur, lord of castle and land and all rights and privileges, didn't permit the unhappy peasant to sell a stick of wood or piece of fruit, nor even part with it without authorization, nor give his daughter in marriage without bowing to the lord's right of the first night, nor buy any necessary thing: all went to the feudal coffers and priests, leaving the wretch without even a will of his own. Slavery in that time squeezed the laborer dry; whatever he did, he was fleeced by those usurious tyrants; the dignity of the human being was trampled underfoot and he was ignominiously bound to his place. Yet how much do conditions differ now? The campesino is allowed to buy and sell. He can marry without giving up his wife on the bridal night. He can go and come freely—yes, attend meetings, everything! Ah, but he is in a subtler kind of slavery, covered with the veil of hypocrisy.

Workers!

Look at this touted freedom of yours. Feel the reality of the penury you inherit from family to family, from generation to generation: no place even to stretch out your aching bodies, not enough wages even to feed yourselves. Where is the product of your work? The princely riches from tobacco, sugar, coffee: where is it? In the coffers of him who exploits you, who has made himself a capitalist while you lack even the concept of what it is to be a human being. Doesn't your work produce? Where does your exploiter get so many thousands of dollars? What produces them? They are cynical enough to say: Nature. Your work means nothing. Nature doesn't need man's aid. Right? They would be capable of saying so.

Workers, you are in a worse state of slavery than of old. Don't you itch to get out of it? Don't forget that you hold in your hands the redemption you need.

Campesinos! You pass from generation to generation and still have no more abundance in your homes, no more education. You are still slaves. Once the master maintained you, depriving you of will; now he frees your will but deprives you of the means to use it. The same slavery with different procedures. Doesn't he oppress and humiliate you, bind you to the earth, to a machine, to toil that exhausts and brutalizes you so that you lose the concept of what it is to be free men and become obstacles to universal redemption? And at best all you think about is politics which gets you nothing, doesn't defend your rights, only uses your ignorance to bind you and make you submissive, always slamming the door to your freedom.

I left Aguadilla and reached Mayagüez between 2:00 and 3:00 P.M. I visited the *Unión Obrera* and met the distinguished journalist and writer, friend Rafael Martínez Nadal.

In this poetic and unique city I stayed several days. At the time, the Executive Council and Joint Consultative Body of the organized tobacco-workers' unions were meeting, and I attended. We had a public rally in honor of the 14th of July, organized by *Unión Obrera* editor Julio Aybar, one of our most zealous companeros.

I spent some delightful hours of pleasure and entertainment with my comrades in work, struggle, hardship, and ideals.

We went in groups for walks, meals, and sessions and, as comrades, passed very pleasant and happy hours.

I recall that in the middle of a session our comrades Alejandro Escalet, Alfonso Torres, and Antonio Clavarría left with their suitcases on the sacred mission of the "Ideal Crusade," to spread its redemptive labor ideals through towns, cities, fields, and villages. The seed they sow will bear the finest fruit in the future, creating the elements of an instructed proletariat; a great contribution by our valiant leaders with no reward but the general good of the workers.

On bad horses and under a burning sun they went from community to community bearing the good news. They continued far into the night sounding the alert to the workers from the Red platform.

Ah, you honest propagandists! You who have never studied in fine schools, never coveted titles or distinctions: you know how to speak the truth more faithfully than those who have studied lucrative professions, who have more worldly knowledge and skill to enlighten the people.

No honors or diplomas, no honorable mentions await you; no one will erect statues of you. Why should they?

You don't want them. You go to your daily work, and agitating from the platform is your leisure.

Martyrs of truth, heroic defenders of human liberty! Why don't we strew flowers in your path? Let me scatter them to ease your anguish and heartbreak. . . . The solemn hour will come for us to enjoy the gifts that Nature offers so prodigally. You have done your duty and all humanity will be thankful to you.

I left Mayagüez for San Germán. In this lovely city with its enchanting hills I stayed a night and a day. On the night of my arrival I visited the "Love and Charity" center. A meeting was in progress and I met Sr. Caledonio Carbonell; after I had spoken in praise of the equalitarian virtues of anarchism, they ended by calling me a materialist. . . . Materialist, me? Why? I don't know. I only feel I am a human, a very human being.

Materialist? Well, so what? Am I the only one? Are materialists to be despised? Perhaps because I don't talk sophistically and stupefyingly about God, as, for example: Oh God, Thou art everywhere, Sublime Creator, Thy Name is written in space with shining stars; in the uttermost depths of the sea, in the mysterious abysses, Thou art there! Oh Thou, Celestial Creator that stirrest in the calyx of flowers; the sighing breeze kisses them and pronounces Thy Name!

Thou art in the microbe that lives in a drop of water, Oh God! In the bacillus that destroys thousands of lives, there Thou art also! Thou soarest like the potent and majestic eagle; Thou art in the lion that shakes the jungle with his roar.

The turtledove hymns Thee in the thicket, the nightingale in the wood; Thou art also in the panther and the tiger that prey upon the useful sheep.

Thou art light and shadow. Thou stirrest in the heat and tremblest in the cold. In all art Thou, Oh God! . . . and not to leave anything out, in the moron who waits his chance to plunge the dagger in his brother's breast to get his watch and purse; similarly in the brainy hypocrites who for centuries have humbugged their brethren in Thy Name, there too art Thou. And the atoms and molecules proclaim Thy kingdom, Almighty Lord, and the zephyr pronounces Thy Name!

And the little birds fly joyfully entoning hymns to Thee, powerful uncreated Creator!

Well, now that I have praised and exalted and adored God, tell me, have I performed something sublime?

Ah, fools! And you call yourselves rationalists. The wretch who lacks every necessity of life, what does he get praising God? The exploited laundress who goes without food to pay the landlord, nervous from lack of nutrition, whom every trifle plunges into despair: what good can hallelujahs do her? And mine—why should God need them? One might think God feeds on eulogies and exists by prayers.

I don't accept this form of ignorance. I am a rationalist, and reason is austere: it needs no eulogies.

Truth calls for no such practices. These habits are the residue of past errors established to make the multitudes submit to the noose of tyranny and despotism.

We rationalists seek to demolish all the pernicious customs which have kept the people from thinking freely, unscared by supposed punishments in unknown regions which science has failed to discover.

All human beings are free to live in accordance with the laws of nature, not those imposed by human error. A person wanting to travel by balloon or ship doesn't need to commend himself to anyone, for all his entreaties are useless.

How many people pray to harm others, to affect the lives of their neighbors? If they were heard, what would happen to the liberty and life of each one of us? We would be at the mercy of any angry and malicious person misguided by ignorance.

Acquire habits that are good for yourself and your fellow men, and the rest will be added. The logical consequence of drinking too much is drunkenness; he who curses another curses himself. Don't be fooled: everything comes out of ourselves; we are free to the extent that justice is in us.

There is a saying, or maxim: "Your own conscience must be your judge so that for what you do now, you won't suffer later."

But you can do many things out of ignorance, and in that case you can reform yourself later.

It is well said that ignorance is the mother of the greatest crimes.

Let us enlighten ourselves well, then stop to meditate, then put our reflections into practice. It has to be better than before we meditated.

Humanity has always been precipitated into wrong ways because of excessive pride and not stopping to analyze.

Excessive pride is egoism, and he who is dazzled by it goes wrong.

Out of it come false ideas about dignity and honor, and the desire to elevate them above nature's laws, so that crimes are committed.

From the excess of pride that is egoism the jealous lover, unable to accept the fact that his beloved can leave him, falls into the crime of revenge.

Where egoism doesn't harm or thwart the will of others, it can be tolerated. Otherwise it is perverse and only brings affliction.

Excessive and idolatrous love can make a mother harm others' children for the benefit of her own. This should not and can't be condoned: "Don't wish for others what you don't wish for yourself." He who is guided by this lofty maxim has the true concept of liberty, equality and fraternity.

I have managed to dominate all in myself that tends to harm others even indirectly.

Indifference is criminal: to be indifferent is not to be human.

The true concept of the natural laws must be understood for the good of all. He who offends the natural laws harms humanity.

Concepts of honor and honesty accepted by our society are aberrations caused by human ignorance.

Nature's laws contain nothing that is dishonest or dishonorable.

That is all an invention of human egoism, a contradiction of natural law by a mistaken notion of one's own interest.

But within natural law—that is, free will in the interest of all—these errors will disappear. The whole social system of the family as now constituted, the whole commercial system, will give place to the free family and free commerce.

Established customs contrary to the spontaneity of nature will disappear.

The educational system will be replaced by one more in harmony with the common good.

The flag of this or that nation will have no part in the future system of education; absurd and idolatrous respect for governments will be abolished.

Brotherhood as the supreme law, without frontiers or divisions of race, color, or language, will be established as the religious ideal in schools.

Above all, the common interest as emblem, the truth as watchword.

The one religious ideal, "Love one another," will reign in all hearts.

From San Germán to Yauco, from Yauco to my home town, Arecibo, where I read to my children some pages to interest them in the sufferings of humanity.* And in August I left for San Juan.

I went to join my comrades and friends Eugenio Sánchez López, Rafael Alonso, and Santiago Iglesias: tireless propagandists and fighters for the proletariat, and with the most advanced ideas at present. They direct the only institution that defends the working class with energy and perseverance.

I arrived in San Juan with the intention of staying, well placed or not. I was called upon to print a new edition of my first pamphlet and see about distributing it in the factory, and to go down to Caguas and Junco where I found J.B. Delgado and José Ferrer y Ferrer carrying on the "Ideal Crusade" initiated by the FLT. I had the opportunity to attend and make my modest contribution to workers' lectures in Caguas, Junco, and Gurabo. On my return to San Juan I left for Arecibo to help with propaganda for the tobacco workers in Utuado, where we stayed for some days and had several meetings. Taking part were David Storer, a caustic and

* *Truth and Justice*, which would go into a second edition.—*Editor's note.*

blisteringly realistic orator, Nicolás María de Jesús, and myself. I stoutly attacked Catholic fanaticism, and as a result some rather discourteous and insolent (as I was told) leaflets appeared. I couldn't judge and don't censure them; I think they do well to defend themselves as long as it is on reasonable and scientific grounds. For example, since belief in the *usefulness* of baptism is widespread, they might answer me as to why in all justice they don't baptize people who, having nothing to eat, can't bring the dollar fee. And as to whether it's useful and enlightening for a lot of youths old enough to be fathers of families to have formed a green-sashed congregation named after San Luis which, instead of studying the plight of the workers, spends its time kneeling in prayer in what the priests say is God's house.

I haven't been able to return to that community. I intend to return to back up my previous propaganda with due energy. That is, to proclaim the synthesis of the one true religion: "Love one another," bless your enemies, pray for those who slander and persecute you.

Don't exploit, don't usurp the product of your brother's work, don't cheat, don't adulterate articles of prime importance for health and life.

Don't deceive any woman by pretending love for her without feeling it. Don't turn the sexual act of human procreation, the most beautiful and sacred act, into an object of impure and vicious pleasure to the damage of future generations.

Don't take woman as a mere object of pleasure; respect in her the mother of the human race.

Be useful, be just, and you will be happy. Don't lie.

Finally I ended my journeyings. I stopped off in Arecibo and returned to this San Juan of happy memories.

I became an agent for *Unión Obrera*, then founded a magazine, *La Mujer* (*Woman*).

Saturated as I was by the ills of society, I had no trouble exposing the crimes and vices that this bundle of stupidities inflicts on women.

I started dealing with the sex question from the standpoint of "Free Love," as Magdalena Vernet poses it. No matter how mystical or modest, all women reading this exposition find it reasonable and sober; but social formulas have set up a barrier that makes them keep silent.

I know of a man who thinks himself a correct gentleman, who has no woman and says he never goes with them, who ventured to criticize this approach to a young female subscriber of the magazine. The young lady no longer wished to get the magazine any more because she had been told it was immoral. And I stopped sending it to her. I didn't want to give her cause for further annoyance.

The article didn't encourage any woman to sleep with her lover or fiance; it merely explained the error and the slavery of women.

A young lady who is a doctoral graduate rejected the magazine very indirectly, but I don't accept this sort of palliative. And now I ask myself: how far can the fanaticism of this comedy of honesty go, when even with books in their hands which scientifically defend their sex, women refuse to accept this defense and become accomplices in the countless errors produced by the distortion of sex?

Please tell me: if those who should enlighten don't do so because it's dishonest or "immoral," who will be the leaders and tell the unvarnished truth? . . .

My Profession of Faith

I am a socialist because I want all the advances, discoveries and inventions to belong to everyone, and that socialization be established without privileges. Some want a state to regulate it, I want it without government. Not that I am opposed to the government regulating and controlling wealth, as it will. But I stick to my position as a decided partisan of no government: anarchist socialism.

Here I affirm and solemnly declare that to be a socialist one must have analyzed and understood psychology.

Anyone who thinks himself a socialist and accepts the dogmas, rites, and fanatical practices of religion is in error, for socialism is truth and imposed religions are errors.

Anyone thinking himself a socialist who is an atheist, a skeptic, or a materialist is in error.

Socialism is not a negation, nor a violence, nor a utopia. It is a real and tangible truth. The arts of living comfortably at the cost of someone else's work—no, they don't belong to socialism. Nor do deceit, imposition, imperialism toward the weak and ignorant. Socialism persuades with truth and does not offend. Pure reason, harmony among all, gentleness of character—these belong. It isn't a lie but the truth. It is about sincerity, not intrigue. I said gentleness of character, and some will say that is what religions preach; so let us explore further. Reason is upright, cool, and calm. Jesus was a rationalist. A person basing himself on reason doesn't violate himself; neither flees nor stays to scoff; doesn't get happiness from the misfortune of his enemy or adversary.

Thus a reasonable person has no enemies or if he has, doesn't hate them. What is the result? If he is insulted or slapped with the hand or with hurtful words, and returns it in kind, what good does it do him? (I cannot accept the slapping or mistreating of anyone for no reason.) Get even, avenge yourself, I will be told. But reason is serene, master of itself, not vengeful or injurious, and for the good and emancipation of humanity a socialist must be reasonable. He who behaves by reason is master of himself, not an instrument of vengeance and its consequences, crime, violence, and brute passions.

Socialism is in the luminous Christianity that undermined with brotherhood the foundations of the Caesars' power. And universal brotherhood will be the implantation of socialism which is abnegation, gentleness, modesty, restraint, "one for all and all for one." Solid steps that lead to human perfection, for freedom and for that spiritual progress which the multiplicity of higher inhabited worlds leaves yet undefined.

Let us instruct ourselves to purify ourselves, educate our will to do good; and let reason consume the fire of the passions—a holocaust for the freeing of mankind and the pursuit of spiritual progress.

The Tyranny
of the House of Delegates
Free Workers' Federation
(1913)

Along with the transformation of our economy early in the century from semi-feudal haciendas to capitalist plantations, the character of our political struggles was also transformed. The old struggle between *"señores,"* or between sectors of a single class, changed with the appearance of a class struggle in the political field. In addition to the changes in social relations arising from the economic transformation, trade-union action itself broke a system of relations based on deference or reverence for the lords of the hacienda. The great bourgeois sociologist, Francisco M. Zeno (also a parliamentary politician of the Partido Unión (PU—Union Party), thus bitterly noted it: "In the heat of strikes the worker undergoes a change of attitude from submissive to aggressive; he stops seeing the owner as a protector and instead sees a bourgeois who exploits him."[1] Shattering the myths of hacienda life, the workers began developing dreams of a new social order, and began fighting to realize them.

On the other hand, a colonial situation like ours presents the analyst with some complications. Supreme as the hacienda-bourgeois class was in terms of the structure of life, it cannot be called a dominant or governing class, since the ultimate reins of power were not in its hands. The hacienda lords lost political power after the North American invasion of 1898[2] (with all that it signified for the economic structure), and also gradually lost economic power to the big North American sugar and tobacco concerns. This sapped the foundations of its hegemony. With some timidity the *hacendados* put up a defense which, in the century's second decade, culminated in the independentist stance of the Partido Unión.

Thus, Puerto Rico presents a triangular political struggle—the North American metropolitan power, the internally hegemonic *hacendado* class, and the new proletariat—with two types of conflict combining in their interaction: metropolic-colony, and the class struggle. The working class sometimes resorted to the metropolitan power in its struggle with the local bourgeoisie, a tactic that left deep impressions in its ideology. This explains to a great extent the relations with the American Federation of Labor and petitions to the U.S. Congress, such as the one we offer here.

Before presenting "The Tyranny of the House of Delegates" we give two brief examples illustrating the struggle we have described, specifically in the orbit of the House of Delegates, the body to which the document refers.

Special Police for Haciendas

Mr. Ward, before his departure, left us a far from pleasant souvenir in the form of a bill. The bill authorized the Governor to make special police available to haciendas and corporations whenever they might request and need them. *Hacendados* and corporations would pay into the island treasury the wages of said policemen, who would become servants of the *hacendados* and corporations.

The bill passed the Executive Council and was remitted to the Legislative Chamber.

It was opened for discussion and de Diego[3] left the chair to defend the special-police bill. He not only defended it but introduced an amendment for the police to be supplied during the months of the hacienda *zafra* (sugar-making season), when great numbers of workers are brought in for harvesting.

Ah, one should have heard the arguments of Sr. de Diego! What concern for capital and sacred property! Poor workers! What patriotism!

Herminio Díaz also defended the bill with vociferous enthusiasm. He said he knew what happened when the workers . . . especially in the Santa Juana hacienda of which he is attorney and shareholder . . .

Poor workers! Such patriotism!

Oppenheimer likewise spoke for the bill—the "revolutionary."[4]

Finally the *simpatico* delegate Tizol spoke, calling the bill "abusive and tyrannical." He said that laws are made to trample the working class, and vehemently defended the campesinos . . .[5]

The *hacendado* Georgetti rose and declared that in the time of Spanish rule the Guardia Civil was supplied to *hacendados*.

"Yes, yes, that's true," said Tizol, "but I want to see if this House is going to approve the oppressions of those days by doing the same."

Llorens Torres,[6] the young lawyer from Ponce, gave an eloquent speech in opposition and ended:

"The special-police bill is legislation of principles in favor of the *hacendados* and bosses and against the working masses. . . ."

Speaker de Diego put it to the vote And it was approved by majority. What patriotism!

(from the newspaper Unión Obrera, *March 19, 1910)*

De Diego's Comments on Romero Rosa

The conduct of delegate Romero Rosa in the House is harmful to our party . . . we are committed to a policy and must vindicate the commitments of government, discarding all that smells of radicalism. Since the first Legislative Assembly, laws have been passed in the House that have greatly damaged us in the eyes of the people of the United States. And last year, I don't know through what channels, four bills of Romero Rosa's were sent to the Congress, which we passed in the House and which have made us look socialistic to the American government . . . this is bad for the country, and certainly for the Partido Unionista.

(from Unión Obrera, *October 5, 1906)*

THE TYRANNY OF THE HOUSE OF DELEGATES

"Our Eternal Vigilance Is the Price of Our Liberty"

We, the producing class of Puerto Rico, organized into the Free Workers' Federation (FLT) of Puerto Rico, affiliated with the American Federation of Labor, charge the House of Delegates of Puerto Rico with being a direct instrument of the Union Party of Puerto Rico, working against the rights of the people, dominated by an oligarchy, and endeavoring to raise obstacles in the way of the progress and well-being of the people at large, in the name of the independence of the country.

Statement of Corroborative Facts

The producing class of Puerto Rico represents three fourths of the population, an element to which no consideration or protection of any kind is granted, considered by the politicians and monied class to occupy the position of the pariahs and disenfranchised in Europe, and the slave in America, in spite of the fact that this condition has disappeared from the Old and New Worlds for many years.

The FLT of Puerto Rico, confronting that situation, was organized and founded on the 1st of July, 1899, upon the same fundamental principles of the universal laboring organizations, tending to remove the bad conditions of life and transform them into a life of progress and well-being. Its prime and greatest interest and mission in the bosom of the Puerto Rican producing masses has been to create respectable citizens and lovers of the soil, to destroy vices and customs that enervate the mind and ruin the organism, to give personality to workmen and elevate and dignify labor. It has been one of the most important factors in everything standing for progress and well-being for the country at large.

The House of Delegates of Puerto Rico began to act in Puerto Rico in 1900 in complete accord with the provisions established by the organic act known as the Foraker bill.

The laboring institution from 1899, has been demanding, first from the military governors during the military government, and later, on the establishment of the civil government, from the House of Delegates, reforms that for hundreds of years form part of the by-laws and constitutions of the most progressive European and American peoples, in behalf of the producing class.

These reforms, that have been qualified as socialistic and anarchistic and disruptive of public peace by the House of Delegates of Puerto Rico, are condensed under the following heads:

Creation of industrial schools and of arts and trades in all the cities of Puerto Rico for the purpose of giving instruction and efficiency to the producing hands.

To increase the appropriation for the maintenance of public schools in the island, so as to provide education to about 300,000 children that are to-day barred from the benefits of instruction.

Creation of school lunchrooms in the rural areas and some interior towns of the country where children can procure a modest lunch at midday.

Law of accidents and compensation for injuries and hurts received by the workmen in the course of their work, a law to be plain and precise in its provisions.

Establishment of asylums for helpless children throughout the island where they may secure primary industrial instruction and in arts and trades.

To grant greater attributes and authority to the Bureau of Labor created by the legislature in 1912, in order to prevent the Congress of the United States legislating upon this matter, appropriating only the sum of $9,000 for its development. We expect from Congress the creation of a Department of Labor.

Creation of housing sections for laborers, in view of the fact that in the principal industrial and manufacturing centers there exists a veritable congestion of residents, and the health of the people is constantly menaced with epidemics and illness thereby.

Grouping the country populace into villages and towns near the great industrial and manufacturing centers offering them the means of leading a social life and tending to their advancement.

Absolute abolishment of convict labor on public works, this labor being utilized in Puerto Rico in competition with free labor.

The eight-hour law reform, inasmuch as this law as interpreted in Puerto Rico is practically nil.

That there be provided by law comfortable seats in the establishments, shops, factories, and wherever possible for women and children, so that they may rest whenever it is unnecessary for them to stand.

Grant of a lot of land to the FLT for the erection of a temple of labor, which land was offered gratuitously by the municipality of San Juan, and the House of Delegates had nothing to do but authorize the conveyance of the land, such as was done by the house in the case of institutions of the rich and powerful.

Law prohibiting the employment of children under sixteen years of age in the factories and in the fields.

To levy a tax upon the capital taken out of the country without having provided in any way for schools, the embellishment and sanitation of the municipalities in which it was invested and increased.

And other measures of recognized benefit in behalf of progress and well-being of all people of Puerto Rico.

The autonomistic cabinet—created by the Spanish government in the last years of its sovereignty over the island; formed in part of the elements that now prevail in the political organism constituting the nominal political majority of the country; considering themselves supermen, with divine rights, aristocrats of the same type and characters as those that have established a sort of hierarchy or oligarchy in the majority of the Latin-American Republics—went on acting up to its ideas and sentiments, contrary to everything that stood for the rights and liberties of the producing classes of the people of Puerto Rico, taking advantage of the great ignorance that obtained in the agricultural districts, and under the specious argument that when independence was secured all that would be done.

When the island was agitated and excited under the unfortunate events that the change of sovereignty brought with it; that is to say, when the principles and foundations that upbuild American democracy collided with the effete and monarchical ideas, these men—worthy representatives of the backward ideas of the people in the way of civilization—under pretext of defending the public liberties, ruled the agricultural and producing masses of Puerto Rico chiefly in those towns and cities in which they exercised their lordly dominion, with the same measure and characteristics as the feudal patriarch the memorable French Revolution swept away; that is, a horrible and absolute vassalage; they provoked noisy and public riots and abandoned the electoral precincts so as to appear before the civilized world as martyrs to their ideas, and that a cruel tyranny existed in Puerto Rico.

As every struggle where there are sacrifices and heroism—some perhaps, born of fanaticism and error, and others out of heartfelt progressive ideas of multitude—brings with it the sympathy and admiration of the people, the laboring organizations that make up the FLT were dragged into that vortex, its men persecuted and denounced, considered by their adversaries as factors in aid of monarchical reaction that provoked them to a flaming and tumultuous struggle; and now, in that land, falling in defense of our rights and liberties as a people; those elements that constitute one of the aristocratic and bureaucratic groups, co-workers of the worst type, and of the most inhuman class universally considered, were directly benefited.

The American Federation of Labor—with more than 400 papers in circulation, with nearly 3,000,000 producing members organized throughout the whole continent of North America, with great influence in scientific and professional circles of the American Nation—placed itself beside the FLT in such wise that, counting from the arrival of Governors Winthrop and Post, the Union Party of Puerto Rico could be organized and raised, serving the federation as a pillar of strength to form majorities, to occupy magnificent positions in the administration of the country, to fill all the benches of the insular parliament in its House of Delegates, to become today a powerful obstacle for the happiness and progress of the producing masses of the country.

President Samuel Gompers, a venerated and respected figure in the American nation, nobly and disinterestedly came in 1905 to the island, visited its principal cities and towns, and helped by that great body of organized workers called the cradle of liberty, here where all the persecuted of all tyrannies and despotisms of the new as well as the old world find open arms to receive them, and where they can make a home and rear a family, kissing the generous ground where they can spread abroad their ideas and strive against human injustice, doing honor to its history, to beautiful constitutions, he rose up, active and energetic, formulated thousands of protests, the gatherings occupied the principal squares and public places, and from these places where the heralds of liberty made their sublimest and greatest harangues for the consolidation of the Republic and the liberty of the entire American continent, resounded the echo from Puerto Rico, bringing as a consequence the triumph of the Union Party of Puerto Rico. Today the labor organizations are treated by such a party with contempt, considered as exotics, the expulsion from the country of the organizations and the elements that think with them solicited, and it is declared from the very midst of the House of Delegates that the organized productive masses that appear in its ranks are too pro-American, and all those that aid them should be suppressed, as they are a menace to the independence of Puerto Rico. It wishes to override and eternally dominate all its organisms as master and lord of life and property.

What Is the Conception of the Agricultural Workers by the House of Delegates?

The rural population is composed of more than 400,000 producers, employed on the sugar, tobacco, and coffee estates, at a wage that fluctuates from thirty-five to sixty cents for twelve and fourteen hours of daily labor, having to travel long distances to arrive in time to take up the tools of labor, that commences at break of day and ends when darkness shuts down over the beautiful panorama of Puerto Rico.

These producing elements that are the sanest in the country— simple, hospitable, believing to the uttermost in the ideas that the cunning cacique and the political would-be saint gives out to them— are made use of in compact masses to deposit their ballots in favor of the dominant party in their districts, which is generally the Union Party of Puerto Rico. This name has been adopted, as well as its insignia of two clasped hands, in order to make the same impression on the ear of the countryman as the word produces in the workman's field, when it tells of his misfortunes and means of bettering his condition in accordance with the progress of the whole civilized world, while at the same time the impression is created among the American people of apparently being bulwarks of the principles maintained by the progressive institutions of America.

The cry of the country, linked with the sentimental claptrap as to the destruction of its customs, of its religion, of its social organization, by the barbarians from the North advancing step by step triumphantly over the land—these being the Americans— creates in the mind of the countryman the idea that American institutions and the affiliated trades of the American Federation of Labor work against his interests, his home, and his future. The destruction and suppression of these organizations are proclaimed, just as the Roman emperors ordered the apostles of liberty thrown into the arena of wild beasts and took pleasure in witnessing their torments under the death-dealing claws of the beasts that tore them.

Taking advantage of their confidence the countrymen are told that their wages are not raised because the Americans are carrying off their wealth, and the American Congress threatens to abolish the protective tariff on sugars in order to create or bring misfortune to the country at large. The countrymen as a body confront the political tribunes of the Union Party of Puerto Rico, the party dominating the House of Delegates, and their speakers, in the name of the country, tell them lying stories of the island, calling it irredeemable, and to hide the sophism, chant the beauties and delights of the soil, while their friends in the American organizations and institutions shudder as they look upon the haggard faces of those fellow producers, where they see depicted the indelible signs of anemia, chlorosis, and hunger, caused by exhausting work that fills to repletion the pocketbook of those who are singing the delights of the soil, and set themselves in opposition to gathering the laborers into villages near industrial and manufacturing centers, because they want to be able to exploit them more on the sly and without any unforeseen check. This is the deception, the crime of the would-be patriotic betterment.

Practically, the riches accumulated in Puerto Rico, under the protection of a legislation perfectly elaborated by the Union Party of Puerto Rico, are of no benefit to the producer. The cities and towns are destitute of embellishment and sanitation.

Bossism rules among the immense majority of the towns and cities of Puerto Rico. Slavery of mind and body exists. The modern Puerto Rican slaveholder, exploiter of popular feeling, walks tranquilly through these towns, his seignorial domain, while the freeman, the civilian, the energetic defender of the rights of his fellow citizens, has to leave the town where first his cradle was rocked, where his eyes opened to the light of day. The voice only of a clique year after year is heard among the peoples, while their social and educational development remains almost at the same stage as during the times when the conqueror, Ponce de Leon, trod the land of this island.

And while they, the countrymen, tillers of the land, those who live in the mountains and valleys, those who feel palpitating in their simple hearts the mystic sentiment of the country, those who know nothing of their despoilers, as these have at their command an infinite number of tools, constantly telling the listener that the former are good, that they love them, that at some far distant time they will make them happy, that they adore the forest life, leaping about the hill and mountains around plantations, with the peasant's hut on the side, penetrated by the rays of the sun and the torrential rains, where he dies anemic, diseased, exhausted by brutalizing work, where his best-loved one, perhaps a daughter, strong and beautiful as those who grow up in the midst of the fields and the mountains, falls a prey into wicked hands without the protection of a law that should afford complete reparation for the crime.

Perhaps the mother, the wife, or the son pursues the same road to perdition. That is of no particular consequence. But when the aspect changes when the act is consummated or accomplished on the daughter of a boss, of some of the group of privileged ones—one of the spoiled children of fortune to thom fate is more propitious than to the confiding and unfortunate countryman— then, oh, then a court of justice exists to impose the punishment deserved by the criminal. A great cry, led by the masters, goes up for reparation, and a great curse rises from every lip. This is the state of affairs. This is the patriarchal life of our fields. This is the origin of what parliament or the House of Delegates calls historic justice—that is, to condemn the poor and protect the rich. There is no justice save from heaven. Justice on earth is that of Cataline, that puts one on the scaffold or into prison—over there in that building that bears on its front the legend "Abhor crime and pity the criminal."

The struggle of the labor organizations affiliated with the American Federation of Labor must straighten out this condition of affairs, make justice shine out in sovereign absolute beauty in all the functions of the nation and be equal for all.

We do solemnly declare with all the courage of our convictions:

That every citizen has the right to appeal to and protest before the insular parliament, just as any other citizen in any country of the civilized world does it, and principally where a form of democratic government obtains, founded upon, for, and by the people.

That we do not deny that the insular legislature has made laws beneficial to be converted into a partisan instrument, or to meet in special session to inveigh against one group of citizens and agree to send a contemptuous answer to any party that appeals to it for legislation, without immediately losing its character as a popular chamber of delegated authority derived from the people and converting itself into an oligarchy.

That we do not deny that the insular legislature has made laws beneficial to the country, but we do affirm and declare at one and the same time that it has not enacted legislation essentially advantageous to the producing classes. And this affirmation carries with it the statement that in 1901 an accident labor law was passed—but an ineffective one.

That the act of March 1, 1902, legalizing the right of association and union in order to handle the question as to advancement of wages and formation of guilds, being an essential and fundamental principle in a democratic form of government, was formulated as a consequence of the struggle waged in 1900, during the great strike of constructive trades in the city of San Juan, the Spanish statute covering this subject being contrary to the American Constitution, as was proved by the special message of Governor Hunt, the opinion of Attorney General Halam, and the adverse ruling of the

Supreme Court of Puerto Rico on the finding of the District Court of San Juan, which declared illegal the formation of the Free Federation and sentenced its leaders to imprisonment.

That the act of March 12, 1903, upon the establishment of industrial schools, passed by the legislature was repealed in 1907 by Mr. de Diego, the speaker, and his legislative friends.

That the act of January 24, 1906, amending article 1486 of the civil code, declaring unlawful the lifelong service of servants and laborers, was superfluous, inasmuch as this is provided in the American Constitution, under whose protection we are, and which abolished obligatory service in 1858. And we are of the opinion that with six years of civil government to make this legislative guarantee notable by an act is to do scant honor to said speaker, inasmuch as it was thus defined by the act and mandate of the Constitution of the country.

That the first eight-hour law established in the country was by decree of the military governor, General Henry, which secured magnificent results, but after it was amended by the act of March 10, 1904, to which so many interpretations were given, that it is practically repealed.

That the acts creating emergency drug stores on the sugar plantations with a physician to treat serious cases that occur; the employment of children under fourteen years of age on work beyond their strength, and for more than six hours daily; the suppression of payment of wages by checks and tickets, etc., are drawn up in such form and in such an ambiguous manner that it has been impossible to put them into effect and compel compliance therewith. The same is the case with all others mentioned by the speaker, Mr. de Diego, and which we do not continue refuting, inasmuch as the consciousness of the sensible people in the country is awake to that fact.

That we believe the statements made in favor of independence of Puerto Rico by the speaker, Mr. de Diego, are only the aspiration and thirst for dominion over the producing masses, to secure places and to strangle in the throat of the people the blessed freedom that now exists and leads in Puerto Rico, the free institutions of the American people, the warmth of the wisest and sublimest democracy of the twentieth century, the beloved of the sciences and progress.

That the laboring classes, meaning thereby the factory hands, mechanics, and farmers, are contemptuously regarded by the House of Delegates, its speaker and committeemen, considering themselves as hierarchs or tsars of the people with the power to make them think and feel as suits them, destroying thereby the free manifestation of thought, spoken or written, and endeavoring to close the doors of that body on those not affiliated with them politically or who may have ideas of a different order to those they maintain.

That in the agricultural districts complete servitude prevails in relation to the countrymen, depriving them of the benefits of education, endeavoring to oppose a special taxation upon property for education purposes, when the first magistrate of the land, Governor Colton, proved in his message to the legislature in 1913 that an equitable sum was not contributed, as there should be, to this important branch by those who pay measly wages on their estates and proclaim in the house that the prices of coffee and sugar in spite of advancement therein do not enable them to pay more, and they take shelter under a bill pending in the Senate upon rebate of the tariff on foreign sugars imported into the United States, setting up opposition to the creation of villages near the great industrial and manufacturing centers, that would establish social intercourse among the country masses, that would change their humble position for another more in consonance with progress and civilization by means of laws and measures that are openly combated by the House of Delegates, wherein are seated twelve planters and other delegates favorable to its ideas of absolute dominion over the country people, under the argument that they are the voters of the union of Puerto Rico and they would be ruined if higher education were given them.

That in contrast to this we must express our entire sympathy with the honorable Unionist delegate for Guayama, Mr. Fernández Garcia, in his noble attitude on the case in question, maintaining with firmness that "nothing practical has been done by the insular legislature from 1900 to now in regard to labor legislation."

That the House of Delegates, composed exclusively of the Union Party of Puerto Rico, goes on record as against the free manifestations and institutions of the American people, in expressing by the mouth of the speaker and various delegates and approved by the majority, that the foreigners—that is, the natives of other countries that came to Puerto Rico and became citizens and formed a family and contributed to the progress and happiness of this island—should not take part in our political struggles or social and economic ones, and ought to leave the country, just as those chieftains in medieval times in the principal cities of the European continent persecuted the citizens or the men for maintaining religious or political principles contrary to the religion of the dominant state, confiscating all their property, and at times bringing them to the scaffold. That act is the absolute denial of the principles sanctioned by the American people, to open the doors of the country to receive all foreigners that may come to add to its riches and development. The only ones excluded are the Asiatics, because their system of living and conditions of work tend to lower and destroy the dignity of labor in America.

That the legislation upon education of the people at large, endeavoring to take out the teaching of English from the general school plan, in order to convert it into a particular branch, is only a subterfuge in order not to pass an appropriation that may tend to procure greater amounts for this important line of education and to limit even more the knowledge of the people, impeding their progress, in order to place them on a par with an educated citizen, this act representing a falling back, as it is known that in the United States, Germany, England, France, etc., there is a tendency to give wide scope to the knowledge of those languages considered commercial or utilized within the international, commerical, and diplomatic field.

That the action of the House of Delegates in opposition to the resolution covering labor legislation, demanded by the FLT is the definite expression that the labor program of the Union Party of Puerto Rico, approved in the city of Mayagüez, was only intended to create a false impression in the legislative centers of the United States of America, just at this time when the national Democratic

Party has come out triumphant throughout the whole nation with its splendid record upon labor legislation, in order by this means to try to attain its ends as to absolute dominion over the entire administration of the country, without doing anything practical in Puerto Rico to better the conditions of the Puerto Rican producing class. It is a program made up of mirages, a deception. Therefore be it

Resolved: (1) That Friday, the 7th of February, 1913, be designated as a day of protest of the producing class organized throughout the island of Puerto Rico under the auspices of the American Federation of Labor, to hold meetings, conferences, manifestations, and any other legal act, in order to protest against the House of Delegates of Puerto Rico, and to prepare and send written protests in the form of statements or telegrams to the House of Delegates, for its inexplicable attitude against the legislation demanded by the producing masses of Puerto Rico.

(2) That, rendering fervent homage to our international ideas and to our love of country, we again declare that not a single phrase, not a single conception, not a single sentence of our principles and procedures shall be changed; rather, on the contrary, in the next electoral contest, beginning from the approval of the present resolution, we shall strive for the utter rout of the so-called Union Party of Puerto Rico, which supports and defends the opinions issued by the speaker of the house, Mr. de Diego, and the majority that applauded them and with their vote approved his declarations, as well likewise as the members—Republican, Democratic, or any other group—hostile to the legislative demands of the organized laborers of Puerto Rico.

(3) That the entire debate promoted in the House of Delegates, as well as the resolution that gave rise to it, the declaration of Governor Colton in his message upon the principal problems that concern the nation in general, and the present resolution be printed in the Spanish and English languages, in pamphlet form for circulation throughout the laboring people and sympathetic press of the American Federation of Labor in the United States, copies to be provided for the office of international secretaries for distribution throughout the national centers, to the labor press of

the Latin-American Republics, so as to make known to the entire world how the directors of the followers of the independence think and feel upon the labor problem, at the same time that they are asking for more powers and for the ultimate independence of Puerto Rico.

(4) That copies of these papers be sent to the President-elect, Honorable Woodrow Wilson; to the present President of the United States, Honorable William H. Taft; to President Gompers, of the America Federation of Labor; to the insular parliament; to the governor of the island; and to each of the representatives and senators who occupy seats in the next Democratic Congress of the United States.

(5) That the representative of the FLT, Santiago Iglesias, now in the city of Washington, working for the granting of American citizenship for the Puerto Ricans, be ordered to act in accordance with the terms of this resolution in every bill introduced in Congress with the purpose of granting more political powers for the island.

And as free citizens, absolute masters of our acts and convictions, and members and defenders of the labor organizations of international principles, affiliated with the American Federation of Labor, we beg the producing people at large of Puerto Rico to be united in this righteous struggle with us, support each of their unions, and let us proclaim under the principles of the democratic epoch through which we are passing there can be no room for tyranny, even when it wears the saintly and august trappings of liberty.

And that this may be of record we sign this resolution in San Juan, P.R.,   the second day of February, 1913, in a meeting assembled exclusively for this purpose.

By the executive council of the Free Workers' Federation of Puerto Rico.

> *P. Rivera Martínez, Acting President.*
> *Rafael Alonso, Secretary General.*
> *Joaquín A. Becerrill, Treasurer.*

Vice presidents: Esteban Padilla, Manuel Alvarez, Julio Aybar, Alejandro Escalet, José Ferrer y Ferrer.

Manuel F. Rojas, representative of the Central Labor Union of San Juan.

Genaro Rivera y Bibiano Lampen, representative of the Sailors' Union, No. 300, of San Juan.

Francisco Paz Granela, Graciliano Cedeño, and Jose García, representatives of the Cigarmakers' Union, No. 460, of San Juan.

José Ma. Balzac, representative of the unions of Mayagüez.

Pedro R. de Arce and Francisco Alvarado Lugo, representatives of the unions of Utuado.

Concepción Santana, representative of the unions of Gurabo.

Juan H. Hernández, Francisco Rivera Febres, and Victor Espinosa, representatives of the Carpenters' Union, No. 1389, of Santurce.

Eleuterio Serrano and Anselmo Manzano, representatives of the Masons' Union No. 1982, of San Juan.

Manuel Ortiz, Ramón Martorell, Cesario Garrillo, Eduardo Conde, and José Ma. Torres, representatives of the Painters' Union, No. 550, of San Juan.

Antonio S. Colón, Juana Sanz, and Juan Bermúdez Sánchez, representatives of the unions of Bayamón.

Ramón Roque, Esteban Colón, and Luis F. Quinonea, representatives of the Cigarmakers' Union, No. 119, of Puerta de Tierra.

Pedro Benitez, Mateo Otero, Antonio Urquía, José Dolores Benitez, and Manuel García, representatives of the Carpenters' Union, No. 1450, of San Juan.

Lorenzo Modesto, representative of the Printers' Union, No. 478, of San Juan.

Emilio Vázquez, representative of the Uniones de Juncos.

Severo Corino Osorio, Juan Pitarzón, and Emilio Fariz, representatives of the Carpenters' Union, No. 1304, of Puerta de Tierra.

José Ventura, representative of Federated Union, No. 9625, of San Juan.

The unions of San Lorenzo, Cidra, Cabo-Rojo, and San Germán

have joined by letters and telegrams in the resolutions of the assembly, protesting against the attitude of the House of Delegates.

Vice President Ferrer represented likewise in the assembly of the unions of Caguas, and Vice President Padilla those of the district of Arecibo.

Red Pages
Juan S. Marcano
(1919)

Breaking the myths of hacienda life, the workers began shaping their dreams of a new social order and fighting to establish it. The second decade of our century saw an intensification of this fight. Those were years of great strike activity in the sugar plantations and cigar factories: of brutal outrages and massacres; years in which, with the foundation of the Partido Socialista (Socialist Party), the Federación Libre de los Trabajadores (FLT—Free Worker's Federation) threw itself into the struggle for political power.

Years, too, in which organized labor hammered out a style of procedure. A style formed to a great extent by a set of contradictions between the social order to which it aspired, and the specific action imperatives of the difficult triangular struggle of colonial politics mentioned in the previous introduction: for example, its dream of a governmentless society on the one hand and its acceptance, on the other, of parliamentary and bureaucratic participation. It was argued that a republic was needed for socialism while, at the same time, U.S. citizenship was jubilantly accepted; there was talk of revolution and at the same time a search for gradual and palliative measures.

As soon as the FLT entered the political arena by forming the Socialist Party, books and pamphlets appeared aiming for the most part to channel that struggle in terms of the ideal social order. These works sought to keep the flag aloft and bright amid all the confusion. Thus, in 1917, the Party's first electoral year, appeared Alfonso Torres'[1] *Class Spirit* and Moisés Echevarría's[2] *Virtues and Defects*; in 1918, Manuel F. Rojas'[3] *Social Studies*; in 1919, Eduardo Conde's *Accusation and Protest*, and Juan S. Marcano's "Red Pages." (This discussion culminated in debates at the Socialist Party's fourth annual convention in 1919, which we offer here after "Red Pages."

Of all these works we regard "Red Pages" as most clearly reflecting the labor *ideal* in the Socialist Party's initial years. It has the added value of having been written by a rank-and-filer, whereas prominent leaders wrote the other mentioned works. Juan S. Marcano was a shoemaker in Caguas. He participated in the Red Proletarian Theater Circle mentioned in our preface. He wrote news items and some articles in the Free Federation's official organ, *Justice.* He is not known to have occupied leadership positions even on the local level in his community. He has a place in history rather for the ardent words of his "Red Pages."

United We'll Be Strong

1.

Each human arrival in the world gives the lie to the egoist who thinks the world will be meaningless after he leaves it, and that consequently he need not worry about the welfare of others. It is axiomatic that humanity is ever new, but this needs endless repetition.

Childhood isn't the beginning of a human life but the continuation of the life of humanity. Why then do we hold life in such low esteem, making it unbearable under the weight of indifference to the common good? Experience teaches us the impossibility of guaranteeing individual life without struggling in society. And just as we are victims of the intolerance of some and avarice of others in generations preceding us, so our children will be victims of the avarice and frivolity of those living today.

We love life, yet we scorn the means to assure it. Countless people understand that the ills afflicting society are caused by its division into two distinct classes: one producing the wealth, slowly degenerating through the privations and excessive toil to which it is subjected; and the small class which, without producing anything useful, lives by squandering the products of the first. The remedy? Abolition of the parasite class, which will be done not by that class but by those whose shoulders feel the weight of the social yoke. The force subjugating us has its rationale in the disunity of those who work and suffer. Who doesn't know it? But if we give heed to the disease, we give none to the medicine which we know would cure it.

We are very aware of the contribution that the thinking habits gradually taking root in wage slaves have made to the existence of class division. But if they, albeit with weakened spirit at the outset, tried to organize the struggle for abolition of the master class, new habits would promptly take the place of the old, and there is no certainty that their effort would produce the egalitarian society. We have no need whatever for the bourgeoisie. If it disappeared, the working class would not cease to exist. On the contrary, it would find itself the absolute master of the land which is the chief factor of wealth; it would enjoy the fruits of the means of production and thus the life of each member of society would be assured.

Today, when nothing belongs to the producer, machinery and a few hands produce much more than the workers can consume, which is why many slaves become idle wanderers waiting impatiently for warehouses to empty so that industry may start up again and rehire them for a pittance.

Under the present social system machinery doesn't benefit the worker at all; rather, as his pre-eminent competitor, it is his true enemy.

Fifty years ago a worker with his hand tools produced six and a half yards of cloth in nine hours. Now he produces 445 yards in the same time.

It would be tiresome to describe the admirable change in production during recent years due to modern industrial procedures. The hopes of simple workers' organizations trying to stand up to capital by forcing employers to raise wages and shorten hours have been dashed: the worker is as poor as ever since the employer, absolute master of the means of production, laughed at these futile tactics by raising the price of his merchandise.

The world has just seen one of the greatest hecatombs in human history. A profound transformation lies ahead in the life of peoples who till yesterday remained slaves, politically speaking, under the power of an absolutist government. The rights and freedoms lost by those defenseless peoples are going to be re-won, for the effort and heroism of thousands of sons of toil are demanding it . . .

In face of this new awakening of peoples, shall we remain silent and tied to the same system of organization with which, till now, we have tried to defend ourselves from the deadly clutches of exploitative capitalism? Impossible.

A new orientation has become necessary. We must adopt new methods of struggle and resistance. With the world on the threshold of great transformation, the need is urgent for new activities, heralding true emancipation, in the struggles for proletarian redemption.

The earth with all its productive machinery must belong to those who work. Governments, whether monarchical or republican or whatever, are instituted to rule and oppress.

Let us make them disappear completely and with them the system of private property: the system that produces desolation in the homes of the poor, and which provokes wars of peoples against peoples and brothers against brothers.

Let us unite for the great battle to end all kinds of oppression and tyranny against the working classes.

United we will be strong; disunited, we will always be engulfed in sorrow, and poverty will always accompany us.

2.

As we have seen, no immediate improvements in the problem of subsistence can be won unless we fight for a relatively decent life under the banner of unity and organization of the fighters: that is, unity in aspiration, in the steadfast will of those who animate movements for proletarian demands.

Since times so remote as to have been lost to sight by most modern thinkers, the working class has been fodder for the centralizing power of international capitalism. Whenever it has tried to throw off this tremendous weight, this granite block on its shoulders, it has been crushed by the armed power of governments, of the interests that would retain slavery and tyranny as an eternal curse.

Ignorance, servility, and religious fanaticism, infused by black-cassocked men into the lowly working classes, have played a decisive role in the most radiant rebellions for freedom. In every land the peasant mass has initiated the action in revolutionary movements, but due to its ignorance and religious fanaticism the guidance has come from more intellectual persons, with the result that those movements were defeated. Its heroic and unselfish struggles would have been rewarded by universal contentment today but for the so-called "intellectuals'" intervention.

Thus humanity has continued, thus the people have lived, bearing on their backs the heavy load of exploitation, lashed to the tyrannical stake of all representative and absolute governments.

Many will say: But aren't the workers the majority? And since they are, why, for so many centuries, have they accepted the criminal imposition of tyrants, leeches upon those unhappily fated to be born under their inflexible domination? The point has, of course, some validity at first sight, but if we stop to analyze these failures carefully we find the explanation in psychology. As the most authoritative modern thinkers agree, the ignorant mass, for lack of its own initiative, has surrendered the defense of its interests to persons reputedly more versed in life's complexities, without thinking that these cannot truly interpret its aspirations to social and economic emancipation. And this results in the ignominious confusion of those who are led, who have always put trust in mediocre people lacking orientation in the interests confided to them.

A people that permits a few men to proclaim themselves true defenders of its interests, when in fact they are nothing but swindlers and insolent deceivers of the multitudes, is fated to disappear from the great plan of the universe!

That is one essential factor in the great disarray of the people, but there is another basic cause: the stagnation of those organizational forms which, ignoring the march of progress, remain in the same radius of action, showing us no glimpse of where new reforming initiatives are to come from. However much these reactionary elements may blind themselves, the reform has to come. The exigencies of our century, the awakening of the peoples—of those multitudes who begin to feel the triumph of the "Universal Liberty and Democracy" ideal—will demand the reform of their organizations for resistance to capitalism.

Everything is destined to undergo its transformation, and the next chapter will set forth our grounds for these convictions.

3.

We have said that everything in life is destined for radical transformation, and this is a fact. It is true that peoples, like individuals, remain in the same backward and servile condition. It is no less true that, with our constant hammering on the foundations of society, a movement toward a reform (although not all that it should be) exists. But we also find—and this is what we most want to demonstrate—that the institutions which inform the proletariat about world events seem little or not at all concerned to study the reforming spirit of our century. Instead of accepting and pushing those truly liberating tendencies, they continue with forms of struggle which have become obsolete through their countless failures—blind to the fact that the worker is no longer so easily fooled and is setting out toward better days, to the promise of felt happiness.

Those who confine themselves to studying society through its simple undisciplined movements cannot argue with us about these statements. Bogged down as they are in the prejudices of our present poisonous environment, which keeps humanity stagnant, they are incapable of seeing, as we do, that this is the century of the march toward total reform of society.

To be able to touch and see the advance of modern ideas one

must relate to the people, feel their misery, and suffer their pain. Then one can assert that we are moving irrevocably along the road of progress, that the potency of our generous ideals is going to bring a morning bright as the gentle, crystalline waters of a lake . . .

If humanist ideals have not yet taken hold in the civilized world it is because, as we said in our first chapter, there is no reasonable spirit of sacrifice in us. Because we are too fond of this miserable life, imagining that if we give it for a just and noble cause the world disappears for everyone, we resign ourselves to sniveling lamentations, cursing the system but aiding and abetting by our cowardice the infamous state of things that manacles us in slavery. One thing springs to every eye: that whenever a people has got set to win its true freedom, the so-called guides and mentors of the multitude have appeared like ghosts haunting the centuries with their call for compromise, telling it to be calm, that it still isn't ready, that it should study and educate itself—and that *then* it can proclaim the revolution to transform society once and for all.

This has always been precisely the reactionaries' best argument to exploit the ignorance of the people and live on its back. Organizations simply concerning themselves with momentary improvements for the working classes are out of date in this century. For every student of society's real and basic workings knows that capitalism buttresses its power more every day, due to its organization, while organizations to resist capitalist exploitation continue their same tactics without any notion of new orientations for battles of the future—battles inevitably involving greater responsibilities and higher aspirations. We are in no way against the forms adopted up till now for defending our interests. But we know and declare that to win complete economic emancipation for the people, to realize the desired reform in all social, political, economic, and moral aspects, those tactics need changing.

There can be no hope of realizing these aspirations so long as we maintain that the people aren't ready, while we keep telling them trivialities that lead nowhere . . .

Do we want the people—ready and understanding these ideas—to triumph over the exploiting bourgeoisie?

Then let us be more sincere in our explanations. Let us abandon that yearning, more appropriate to unsuccessful politicians, to make individual converts and raise up new idols for the people. Let us work harder and more tenaciously to guide the hearts of the multitude into new positions capable of throwing off our backs the bourgeoisie that has held us in black misery through the centuries.

Enough of compromises and mustard plasters. Those stick-in-the-mud procedures of our resistance organizations do not and cannot meet the needs of modern struggle. They don't respond to our century's libertarian spirit. We need unity, but unity for radical solutions—the only kind that will make us strong and invincible.

What It Is and What It Isn't

For my comrade Valentin Castrillo

5.

"The first condition for the success of socialism is to explain its goal and essence to everyone clearly, to dispel many errors created by our adversaries and sometimes by ourselves." We who take pride in being socialists must not forget our duty to expound our principles in public discussion in a simple and natural way that all can grasp, so that people understand what socialism is and what it isn't.

Our starting point must be to broaden, not to narrow down. Why?

Because our victory—that of socialism—depends on the thinking of the masses, the united force formed by peoples and nations.

And how do we win those masses who are decisive for the inculcation and triumph of socialist ideas? Here is the problem to which we must pay greatest attention and give all our mental and physical energy.

Socialist principles are clear in meaning and nobility, and try as our enemy will to belittle their essence and origin, he will get nowhere nor will he weaken our efforts, our belief in a better world, in a society with more human goals than the present ones.

But is it enough to proclaim the grandeur of socialist ideals, to affirm that they are the best and only ones which, once inculcated, will bring happiness to humanity? Would that suffice to negate the "virtuality" of "principles" and ideas that are not ours? Definitely not.

We need above all to prove with convincing facts the deficiencies of existing society, while showing the efficacy of our ideas to correct the wrongs and social injustices now committed against the nations, against humanity.

To sum up: We declare that today's society with its system of property and monopoly is wrongly organized, since it divides humanity into two classes: one that works and has and signifies nothing, the other that does no work and nothing useful, but due to this society's mechanism has and signifies everything. The working class is compelled by its backwardness to live under the yoke of the possessors of capital. To exercise or develop our faculties and energies in some way we are obliged to pay tribute to the capitalist state; but even when we do this we must still, as workers, endure heavy afflictions under the empire of tyranny.

We further declare that if land, machines, and all means of production were collectively owned, administered by the state for the common good, and were not private property as they are now, harmony would reign between people and life would be pleasanter; there would be no reason for the dissensions that characterize the present system of great social crimes.

How can we bring this state of things to an end and change all the productive and administrative forms of society?

Simply enough. As we have said, by explaining so that all may understand our true and basic democratic essence, giving our opponents every opportunity to discuss our viewpoint—the only way to win the masses.

"Socialism must have a specific plan, easy to grasp, and submit it to the representatives of the people, the representatives of the various interests.

"Social democracy is distinguished from other parties by the fact that it does not limit its activity to a few aspects of state and social life, but embraces all aspects equally and strives to reconcile the antagonisms between state and society and bring order, peace, and harmony."

The belief that socialism can only triumph through the efforts of the wage-earning proletariat is absurd. No such thing: Socialism *will* triumph, but through the strength and power of the majorities. Among these majorities we have to include that great phalanx of small landholders and manufacturers whom monopoly increasingly forces down into wage-earning ranks.

For this reason our motto must be *to broaden*, mobilizing and winning over all the conscious majorities until we can realize the socialist program in its most radical form.

The more conscientiously we expound our ideas, the better for the people who put their hopes in our shining principles.

This, then, must be our goal: to explain what is and what is not SOCIALISM.

Let Us Love Liberty

11.

Liberty is a chimera, a myth—yet we all love that myth, that chimera. It is the highest aspiration of peoples, and every individual pins his hopes of happiness and economic well-being on the word LIBERTY.

Not to love and desire it, not to fight so that the peoples may enjoy it to the full, is to negate the human personality and the right of peoples and individuals to the privileges liberty affords.

All peoples of the earth have a right to rule themselves, to decide their own destiny, and to develop their activities in accordance with their customs and aspirations. He who denies this right is a denier of liberty, a lover of slavery, ignorance, and servitude; he works toward further tightening of the chains that bind us to the stake of tyranny, exploitation, and shame, to the source of all that prostitutes and degrades. Peoples who agitate for the inculcation and integral development of modern ideas are virile peoples pursuing a sacred, sublime, and regenerative goal, heralding better days and social harmony.

And the denier of a people's capacity to rule its own destiny, to conduct its own administrative and public life, denies himself: he loses his own personality. To deny that Puerto Rico is ready to be an independent republic, with the right of full freedom to determine and administer its own interests, is to commit lese majesty against society. It is to approve of slavery and favor the absorption of our wealth and the annihilation of our people by capitalism, by foreign and native corporations which would turn us into degraded expatriates.

We who hold and propagate libertarian principles—who love liberty above all things as the symbol of well-being and happiness, and clearly understand what government of, for, and by the people is—must in no way oppose the liberty of a people that needs and has a right to it, simply because reactionary enemies of liberty are asking for it. To do this is, from our standpoint, to deny the virtues of liberty that is real and equality that is true and positive.

It is said that fatherland begins at home. The home should be free of outside influences. But the home is in the nation, and if the nation is enslaved—if it is a dependency under the power and control of another nation's constitution—the statement that the home should be free is meaningless. It is just as enslaved as the nation, since the nation cannot develop according to its desires, based on a full and true spirit of liberty.

Yet socialism, it has been said, can only come to power under a democratic republic. And it is nothing but the truth. For that is the specific prerequisite for a proletarian dictatorship, as has been shown in the French and other republics where socialism is already a power capable, when it makes its first determined thrust, of tumbling the rickety castle of the bourgeoisie . . .

We will be told that the bourgeois democratic republic doesn't fully satisfy proletarian aspirations. True, but none can deny that within its "principles," its freedom of thought and expression, we can work more decisively for the SOCIAL REPUBLIC, the only kind under which we can live in full sunshine.

In a bourgeois democratic republic we must bestir ourselves, even defend it, for it is the only regime under which we can spread our ideas on pure democracy and freedom.

For these principles we agitate publicly, for them we make great sacrifices, but we insist that every people must be free to work out its destiny within the fullest freedom which is its due.

Yes, we want more freedom, that real freedom which assures

happiness to every individual. For liberty is the precursor of great and sublime things, of generous restitutions and of all peoples' economic, political, and social emancipation.

We want that liberty for which Francisco Ferrer y Guardia, Praledes G. Guerrero, Pedro Goris, Juan Jaurés and others gave their lives. Liberty that will enable us, on a day not far distant, to proclaim the happiness of the great human family.

The Working Woman

12.

Woman has ever been the sacrificial victim of despotism, of the tyranny and authority of man and society.

As we find her in all forms of life under the existing system she exemplifies the power of capitalism, the perpetuation of religions, and the enthronement of oppression. By her religious formation society has condemned her to be *a shadow in the home.* If we look for her in the political order we conclude that she is a nullity. Politically, hers is the role of charming virgin or mobile statue, acting only under the push of empty phrases and flatteries. Her sole right is to applaud the petty itinerant patrioteer, thus helping to consolidate the prevailing social system. Neither in Puerto Rico nor anywhere has she yet occupied the position that is due to her as a human being equal to others.

Socialism is the ideal that gives this human being true liberty!

Looking for her in economic life, we find that she lives in direst poverty. Under no form of civilized life can her mockery of a wage satisfy her most indispensable needs unless she is a "heroine" in her daily labors. It is woeful to see her going to the factory, to those dens of exploitation and thievery, to leave there the most precious possession, her youth; to rot her lungs in that nicotinic hell, spewing them out on the workbench which gradually drains her life.

We can say without exaggeration that her wage for such rough toil, in relation to the cost of living, is less than that of a Chinese. This villainous exploitation makes the working woman a stranger to every comfort of life, her horizon totally bleak.

From infancy in her parents' home the working woman feels the sting of penury, without clothing or shoes to attend school regularly. Thus she is inadequately educated and overworked, and her constant chores at home, along with the lack of proper nourishment, keep her mind undeveloped. She ends by not even knowing her due place in society and her human duties and rights.

The woman who has to earn, in a factory, the means of restoring her physical strength, and of relieving the pain in her body, is victim of a double crime. Apart from the exploitation she suffers, she acquires anemia, chlorosis, or tuberculosis as inseparable companions.

These factories where our companeras have to earn a subsistence are something to see. Unfit places for such a large number of women to be penned up in for eight or nine hours a day, unhygienic, without even any ventilation. There, day by day, they deposit the sap of their existence, to be turned into dollars for the Midases' overstuffed coffers.

All is misery in the proletarian home, hovels in which it is luxury to dream of happiness and well-being. But the most pitiful aspect is that when working women, creators of luxuries and comforts for an idle class, protest against the violence of despotic, cowardly, and boorish foremen, they are put down with filthy insults and driven to despair.

But the time has come to make an end. The working woman is our companera in distress and privation and cannot continue in this shamefully exploited condition.

The Socialist Party in its civil struggles proclaims her right to participate in all social questions. Defenseless women, we rise to defend you. We will not consent to the outrages you suffer under the lash of man's despotism and the prevailing system.

Think for a moment about how little your fate matters to the bosses. It is all because you walk in disunity.

Arise, sister in misery, lift yourself from the torpor in which you are mired and prepare for the struggle—the struggle for your LIBERTY.

The March of Progress

For my esteemed friend and comrade
José Ferrer y Ferrer

15.

Through the centuries of darkness and servitude humanity marches, step by step, toward an era of light and progress.

Today, peoples who have lived since legendary times under the iron yoke of tyranny, exploitation, and obscurantism are propitiously girding themselves for the great final battle.

Progress is a force that none can check, "for it crosses oceans, pierces mountains, and the steppes cannot stop its advance." This work of transformation cannot but affect Puerto Rico; recently it has shown signs of life here, although our evolution has been held back by a forcibly imposed despotism without parallel in the history of human woes. Progress could not have bypassed us in this age when communications among all the world's peoples is so easy.

So here, too, we see the awakening of a people, a new day. Yesterday's darkness, reaction, and obscurantism is today's light, progress, liberty, justice.

A short while ago the cause of the disinherited seemed a chimera, technical transformations an impossibility. But libertarian ideas pushed forward and the progressive evolutions of socialism began.

Too late now to stop their march!

The class situation is monstrous. Merely the fact that it is so in the minds and convictions of the world proletariat isn't going to end it.

But the proletariat isn't to blame. It has been denied schooling and decent treatment and today learns in its own way what education didn't teach it.

It compares the wealth it sees from afar with its own pigsty poverty. There is no love in its heart because it has always been treated with contempt. Only its own instinct of preservation will slow its march.

Civilization says to the powerful: The proletariat is your brother: in the aggregate he contains an irresistible force; he is an ocean, you a ship, give him your hand. Ah, says the despot, but no, never, the world is mine, it belongs to me!

"Poor humanity, always condemned by its aberrations to grow old in sorrow!"

We love the ideal of liberty but how far away it is! Ideals that don't march toward practice are futile, sterile romanticism to the world's progress. Let us be active, not passive, let us instruct the people and prepare them for the future society. Special study-centers, the labor press, and organization are the best ways of propagating our beloved ideals.

Today more than ever the ideals of human emancipation need to be spread and known everywhere.

How can we put this worthy educational design into effect? Through initiative, through public meetings and sociological study-centers where the people can get to know the rights of man and how to win them. For make no mistake, most of us working-class writers know how to break down but don't know how to build up.

This, we think, is due to our preoccupation with studying political economy, law to know how to legislate, and other matters related to the country's political life.

Lift your spirit into infinite space, tune your steps to the clamor of the angry, struggling multitudes who, like a thunderous sky, scatter bolts of destructive and proliferous lightning.

All hands to the work!

Remember that rationalism will free man from the fearful shadows of prejudice.

There is the sublime march of progress

The Dreamers

*To my toiling compañeros, brothers in poverty, pain,
and despair, to all victims of this society and all who
fight for humanity's freedom and happiness, I dedicate
these modest pages inspired by the shining principles
and ideals of Equality, Liberty, and Fraternity.*
I WISH YOU HEALTH AND REVOLUTION.

*The Author
Caguas, P.R., June 1919*

16.

Dreamers, utopians—these are the kindest of the names they call
us. Such has been the cry of all reactionaries, through all the ages,
against those who try to set foot outside the wall imprisoning the
human being.

Dreamers, utopians, they cry. And when they know that our
demands for justice include giving the wealth to the people, the
cries get shriller and the insults stronger: hypocrites, traitors—the
kindest of their names for us.

But it is to the dreamers and utopians of all the ages that humanity owes its progress!

What we call civilization—what is it but the fruit of the utopians'
efforts? The dreamers, so scorned by "serious" persons, so
persecuted by the "paternalism" of governments, hung on gallows
here, shot down there, burned, tortured, jailed, carved to pieces in
all eras and all lands: Have they not been the driving force of every
movement forward? Have they not navigated the blind masses on
luminous courses leading to glorious landfalls?

The human family would have to renounce all progress, all hope
of justice and grandeur, if in the space of one century it lacked
some dreamers and utopians.

Let our "serious" friends scan the list of the dead whom they
admire. What were they but dreamers? Why are they admired,
unless it is for their dreams? What wreathed them in glory if not
their utopianism?

From this scorned human species sprang Socrates, derided by the
"serious" and "sensible" folk of his age, admired today by the

same people who would then have opened his mouth to make him drain the hemlock.

And Christ: if they had lived then, our "sensible" and "serious" gentlemen would have judged, sentenced, and even nailed to the cross that great utopian dreamer before whose image they cross themselves and genuflect today.

No revolutionary, in the social sense of the word, no reformer has ever existed whom his reactionary contemporaries didn't attack as a utopian dreamer.

Amid the trivialities of our day the utopian dreams of a humanity more just, more beautiful, more healthy and wise and happy. And as he gives voice to his dream, cheeks pale with hatred, the police spy goes to work, the jailer picks up his keys, and the tyrant signs the death warrant.

Thus humanity through the ages has mutilated its best members and obliterated the noblest humanizing initiatives.

But no matter. Forward! Insults, iron bars, and threats cannot stop the utopian from dreaming.

Fourth Annual Convention
of the Socialist Party
(1919)

In previous introductions we have traced some of the processes leading the working class to adopt its own political positions and to fight for political power. It was in Arecibo, the island's fourth city, then surrounded by big sugar plantations, that the spark emerged to give shape to these processes.

Along with the Federación Libre de los Trabajadores (FLT—Free Workers' Federation) the workers had formed a political party of labor in 1899. But it hardly existed as a party since nearly all its efforts went into developing and broadening trade-union organizations.[1] The workers of the Arecibo Free Federation were the first to break the basically economic nature of that struggle. They revitalized the party of labor on the local level and undertook strong electoral campaigns in 1910 and 1912. In the 1914 elections they startled Puerto Rico by winning in their municipality.[2] Stunned by the spectacle of tailors, barbers, tobacco workers and cane-cutters taking high municipal positions, the bourgeoisie, aided by Puerto Rico's American governor, Arthur Yager, put a ruthless brake on the development of this workers' government. Indignation at this, in the flush of victory, provided in Arecibo the final spark for formation of the Partido Socialista Puertorriqueño

(PSP—Puerto Rican Socialist Party) in 1915.[3] In the following (1917) elections the Party established itself as a weighty political force by winning control of seven municipalities, seating two representatives in legislative chambers, and getting 14 percent of the popular vote. [4]

After the 1918 elections two tendencies began to appear in the PSP. On the one hand were those who saw the Party as an instrument for transforming the social order, represented by some of the Arecibo group and the most radical sectors of labor organizations; on the other, were those who saw this transformation as more remote and limited themselves to attacking injustices or, basically, to improving the working people's conditions of life. Predominating in the latter group were those who had been closest to North American labor organizations and most directly tied to the process of resorting to the metropolitan power in their struggle with the local bourgeoisie.

These tendencies confronted each other at the Party's Fourth Annual Convention, from whose minutes we present the following excerpts. First, we have the opening speeches, each representing one of the tendencies. Then the debate set off by resolutions 1 and 18, in which the lines of the conflict are clearly seen.[5] Finally, the Party program as it finally emerged from the debates.

Economic independence cannot be obtained by fighting only in the economic field. As long as the capitalist receives the power that springs from the people and converts it into law—a law cooked up for capitalism's sole benefit—it is not possible, comrades, to think of economic independence in the absence of laws to help attain it. We must get the laws of privilege changed into laws of general protection, and to this end we must vote in our genuine representatives. Here, in the first convention of the party we represent, we must resolve to unite all the forces of the people to struggle for the social economic and political emancipation of the people.

Manuel F. Rojas, Secretario de Estado
(1st Socialist Party Convention, Cayey, March 21, 1915)

SPEECH BY THE CHAIRMAN
(SANTIAGO IGLESIAS PANTIN)

After the appointment of committees the Chairman yielded the chair to Vice-Chairman Julio Aybar and addressed the gathering as follows:

Nineteen years have passed since the first convention in this theater of workers organized in craft unions, at which no discrepancies based on political or religious belief emerged. There was nothing to separate or divide the workers at that time; the delegate at that convention was a member of the Socialist Party and of his craft union. Only when the bourgeoisie began making its influence felt among them in the direction of political partisanship did that pressure give rise to a division of forces, a division extending from economic organization to the politics of our class. But today we all aim directly at one goal, united behind a complete transformation of forms of struggle for immediate benefits and for absolute economic independence.

If we could drop the word "politics" we would do so with great pleasure, because a better title for us is the one that unites our comrades in every land—fighters against the present social system, which includes all the bourgeois phraseology we associate with "politicians." I think it's a serious error to accept this title of "politicians."

I like the way the Soviets put it. They have said, through their representatives in the United States: "We didn't come to this country to solicit political recognition, only for recognition of our right to intervene and take direct action to resolve questions affecting our people."

The Soviets have done away with the old bourgeois system and discarded the program of moderate socialists. They are following true communist practices and it is those practices that now prevail in Russia.

It has been the habit of this country's political leaders to flatter the workers by telling them they are intelligent. But only a few idiots swallow this bait. We mustn't forget that the bourgeoisie and its political parties have created the many obstacles that keep the working class from maturing their minds, and because of this our masses have endured a life bereft of well-being.

We must keep our wits about us to avoid beguilement by songs of democracy and freedom. We still don't enjoy the healthy benefits that those precepts can bring when they are more genuinely propagated and practiced. Only when they are can they have positive effects and produce the well-being that the masses of all countries yearn for.

The sacred ideas of freedom and democracy cannot be implanted by those least willing to recognize the rights of the masses, of all those citizens who seek broader horizons of life and an opportunity to develop themselves in a more spacious environment.

The ship of social justice in which the masses have embarked can be run by the masses themselves with the power of a common emancipating ideal and spirit of organization, animated by their own intelligence and united in firm solidarity.

The workers should be able to impose their ideas of emancipation and make them prevail against all others, against the despotic practices that reaction has imposed on them.

I emphatically deny that the bourgeoisie are prepared to rule and redeem our people. Only the workers are preparing to free themselves from oppression and capitalistic political tyranny. The workers must struggle openly for justice and for the rights of the people which politicians and the bourgeoisie continue to abrogate.

The incitements to murder workers are the result of a joint conspiracy by capitalism and politicism. Yet, what great strides our Socialist Party has made! But mark this well: equally great is our responsibility not to fight to sustain individual men. For our fight is against a system: it is principles that we defend and solutions that we sustain.

He who thinks and says in his community that he is the man, that the advance of his party and people is for him, deceives himself and shows himself to be a partisan of the bourgeois system.

Where have our ideas and understanding of our struggle come from? They all come from other peoples and other minds dedicated to a sacred ideal.

Don't count votes nor aspire to hierarchical rewards; count

rather on the progress of our ideas. Put your trust in what has been brought to us from afar, from environments which enable these regenerative ideas to be more intensively developed.

Don't ask applause nor run after false popularity. All that belongs in the sick and poisoned atmosphere created by the bourgeoisie.

Popularity is fickle and slips easily from the fingers of its momentary possessor. He who basks in it today soon finds himself forgotten by those who acclaim him. On the other hand, he who doesn't fear unpopularity, and continues disseminating his ideas calmly, honestly, and without mystification, slowly but surely overcomes and will see the day of complete victory.

I have aroused plenty of hatred and you have seen how it has gradually abated, to the point where the haters of the past now speak favorably of me. But I have never changed my line nor stopped speaking for the ideas I always defended.

Some deplore the aggressive tone of our speakers. I tell them, don't be surprised or resentful but rather study what causes your attitudes. When we explain to them how we propose to organize society for the potential well-being of all, their annoyance with our leaders fades and they begin to understand what motivates our hard talk. They realize that socialist hearts are lined with big and generous sentiments and that what we fight for is the liberalization of the world and regeneration of humanity.

There was a distinguished young lady who thought humanity's ills were due to lack of Christian morality and social education. We were able to convince her of her error by drawing her attention to all the evil that has come from the very people who preach the morality of Christ. It is they who are responsible for so much public misery, so many unhappy homes, so many tragedies produced by the despair of families, so many vices and injustices degrading all that is good in social morality.

A privileged class consisting of usurious Jews has appointed itself as missionary of social regeneration.

Had we the power of the Russian Soviets we would be in a position to assure the happiness of our people as those gallant fighters are doing for theirs.

You, as Puerto Ricans, should not use the phrase, "my country, my people," to deceive yourselves. But, only for your own better understanding, you should use it to ask the privileged by what right they seek to monopolize what must and should belong to the whole people.

Never forget those elements among us who use that phrase and show that they are sincerely doing something for the common good.

You see how the bourgeoisie proposes to reform the educational system. Their whole reform is part of the conspiracy against educational benefits that would be useful to the people. Theirs also is the conspiracy to spare recipients of unearned income from paying their due taxes.

As the Federal Incomes Law shows us, the realization has dawned in the United States that receivers of unearned income should pay the largest share of state expenditure. In this country, on the other hand, the Incomes Law is so benign that we can't raise three or four millions for public education, as we would have been able to do under the Federal law.

The corporations have used the Puerto Rican Incomes Law as an escape hatch from the effects of the Federal law, and to achieve this have incorporated themselves in Puerto Rico. The result is the failure of really important projects submitted to the Legislature.

Our Party must study the whole economic problem that is to come before this Convention and let the people know what action we will take on this absorbing issue.

To measure the arrogance of people who have touted democracy and liberty in France, consider this:

The assassin who tried to kill Clemenceau has been condemned to death, but the assassin of Jean Jaures has been acquitted. Now the celebration of May Day has been forbidden in France. This hasn't happened here because no general strike has been called, but here we have a deployment of police beyond anything that the circumstances can justify.

Those who abet the oppressions and crimes against workers' lives turn out to be the greatest of all assassins and most intolerable of all despots.

We can say that Russia is freer and more democratic than the French Republic.

Nor can we forget what happened to our dear comrades Ramón Barrios and Alfredo Negrín in Cuba, the island ruled by President Menocal. Those comrades were held incommunicado by the authorities of a republic where, against every liberal democratic principle, the representatives of capitalism jailed two peaceful citizens without any right of defense and deported them to Puerto Rico with no law to justify it.

There is no doubt that governments everywhere are organs formed by the capitalist social system to oppress and tyrannize over citizens and peoples.

I say that we are going to protest in the strongest terms against President Menocal's despotic assault on the freedom of two citizens of this country. We will do so because we have a few Menocalistas here who have made it clear what they would be capable of if they were presidents of the tropical republic; to make clear to *them* how we feel about and respond to their despotism, reminiscent of the famous Lili in Santo Domingo and Porfirio Díaz in Mexico.

Those who talk most in terms of Creole patriotism are in fact the most iniquitous oppressors and enslavers of their people. The only guarantee or hope for our future lies in our suffering people's preparations for a struggle independent of all political institutions, of any class that seeks to maintain the capitalist social system; a fight based on social, economic, and political organization for human liberation and dignity.

Never say, as do the reactionary caciques who cultivate idolatry, "my people." Don't talk in fatuous self-praise about the influence you have with the working class. Wait for others to acclaim your merits, but take the acclamations with due modesty.

People with less cultivated minds are not affronted or ashamed to make someone else's speech. The day comes when the lessons of others make good thinkers and speakers of them.

With the representation of fifty cities that we have here and now, we can look forward to a great victory in the 1920 electoral campaign.

It warms my heart to see, in this Socialist Party Convention, young people along with the old-timers who have given years of time and energy to the fight to advance our ideas. It is a victory for them that the youngsters have come to reinforce this glorious social movement.

Our campaign to win our rights through the Legislature gives us something to think about. We have to see that the men we send there are worthy to represent us, that they are not upstarts, intruders, or politicians. Those who have joined in our toughest battles and been on deck at the time of need are the ones we want.

To conclude, comrades, on this beautiful May Day: may the people of all nations and races unite more closely in the fraternal ideal of saving humanity from the horrors of barbarism and despotism.

REPORT BY THE SECRETARY TREASURER
(MANUEL F. ROJAS)

Comrade Delegates and Chairman of this Convention:

I welcome you all to this city where capitalism appropriates the wealth from the earth and from manual labor, where bureaucrats enjoy their comforts at the expense of the working and suffering people. We can't offer you keys to the city because they are still not in our hands; perhaps we'll soon have them and the city will then be yours. In the course of time I think this may well happen.

We may congratulate ourselves on having survived to discuss the affairs of the political collective we founded in Cayey for our class's social liberation and economic independence, and to give correct and successful leadership following, as we should, the Socialist Party program based on teachings of the master, Karl Marx.

We can derive satisfaction from being the organizers or a political party of our class—a party that fights boldly against all the causes of the poverty to which past and present leaders and representatives have submitted our people.

We have reasons for pride that we hold high the flag of peace and justice, of love and brotherhood, that enfolds the disinherited masses of this country and of the world.

Our Party's struggle has grown and surpassed all the great

struggles of former times. Our enemies prophesied our defeat but have seen the proletariat become more keenly alive under the banner of socialism.

Our opponents are nervous and worried at the spectacle of the determined masses tumbling the walls of centuries of autocratic power. Two great empires have been overthrown; the absolute masters of two powerful nations have been ousted. The red flag flies from the battlements of anachronistic castles—now but memories of the feudal system under which Tsarist terror resisted progressive ideas and the new, essentially democratic ways of liberal humanism.

Our brothers across the ocean have been the first to sound the revolutionary bugle call. The revolution is telling those who called our ideas utopian that the day of reckoning has come for the system holding the world's people in misery.

We have had to move within a narrow circle. We have fought against great obstacles to develop our methods of struggle. Nevertheless, we made enough headway to have no reason for disappointment. We have taken new ideas to the people and they have welcomed and continue welcoming them. Hence the progress we see in the masses of our country.

As the masses become more convinced of our principles, and grasp the validity of our solutions to their serflike condition and unbearable poverty, their faith in the integrity of our struggle grows and with it their hope for practical results.

Puerto Rico's economic problem affects professionals, businessmen, and small industrialists and landowners. If these elements wanted to show their altruism they could take the opportunity our Party offers them to lend a hand in freeing our people from oppression and poverty.

Our declarations, repeated countless times, have found an echo in the consciousness of the island's productive people. They are now moving eagerly and resolutely into the coming electoral battle. We are going to see great bodies of workers depositing their ballots under our Party emblem, the only possible way to heal their pain at the roots.

A great disaster would await us if we failed to join, all together, in this self-defense effort. It is the masses of the people who, by their solidarity, can stop the torture capitalism inflicts on them.

But we must never put our trust in offers of small reforms, which are nothing but sedatives, plasters on a broken chair leg, incapable of relieving the cruel pain we suffer in this society. The trouble with the main arteries of our social organism is chronic. Since the disease goes back a long time it calls for the most potent of remedies. Nothing less will cure the acute economic and political condition afflicting and destroying our hapless people.

The revolutionary glories of the French people were mocked by the bourgeoisie; let us never forget it. Revolutionary hymns turned into cries of rage from the exploited masses as the bourgeoisie proceeded to reimpose the same tyrannical practices used in feudal times. Out of the debris of the revolution arose wage slavery to take possession of the land and legalize exploitation with different procedures no less fatal to the peasant and urban worker.

It stirs our hearts to recall the days of that revolution and its conquest of the rights of man, but a little thought reminds us that those rights don't exist. The right to life isn't guaranteed for those who work and produce; natural wealth is still usurped; society is divided into possessors and dispossessed, exploited and exploiters.

We don't want to be hypocrites, and should not fool ourselves and our fellow men by talking about ephemeral salvation, about alliances with deceivers who suck our blood and devour us as ferociously as a wolf devours its prey.

We know the ways of the social vultures, how they seize from us our right to enjoy life. We know how many forces are bent on holding us back, turning us from the correct path in our daily, dangerous struggle for a new and just order. But we cannot look back nor yield a single step, for we would surely fall into the noose that the bourgeoisie holds out to strangle us. We know that the pirates of society lie in wait, that the bloodthirsty tiger watches our every move and will never graciously release what is once in his claws.

If, out of impatience for immediate gains, we allied ourselves at any stage or in any way with bourgeois elements, we would not only be infected by their ugly practices. We would spread through our own forces, now inspired by a new faith, a demoralization which we—having ourselves initiated such a move—would be powerless to control.

Never let us force upon the masses the unacceptable, which they don't want. It is better and more honorable to stay in the firing line to the last bullet than to suspend hostilities for dishonorable negotiations with the enemy. Let us give up any notion that morality will dawn in the brothel without total destruction of the gang of criminals who run it.

The proletariat cannot get justice without eliminating the causes of its imprisonment. We cannot do justice to ourselves unless we hold the means of life in our hands. Otherwise the cloud of penury and affliction will be eternally over the face of our people. Everywhere in the world the poverty of the multitudes produces the same fatal consequences, the same hateful servitude.

There is no peace because the causes of war haven't disappeared, and they won't disappear as long as capitalism and autocracy prevail—not until military and capitalist power are sent to the guillotine. This is the logical dilemma. The contrary can only be maintained with cynical deceit.

To win peace we must put justice on a pedestal beyond reach of the prevaricators and corrupters who would prostitute it.

While aristocratic, capitalist, and bureaucratic society bends the producers' famished backs under their burden, torturing millions with toil for a pittance; while industrial prisons haunted by agitation drain the lives of thousands of workers, and peasant and worker slave to provide groups of idlers with a life of ease, serenity cannot come to our homes and the cry of the exploited, tortured, and enslaved victims will grow even louder.

When the peoples stop being sheep and fit themselves to curb the wolf that decimates them, then they will be able to impose their government, establish lasting peace, and sing the praises of the faith that freed them.

The meekness of the lamb has encouraged his executioners, drinkers of his blood.

We have been tolerant with the disembowelers of children and women, the torturers of old people; we have complaisantly allowed the viper to sink his poisonous tooth into our naked flesh whenever he felt like it. The cost of this has been the slow and agonizing death of whole generations, falling one after the other into the blackness of the tomb. These sacrificed lives cry out from the depths for justice.

There can be no peace until this demonic organization of society, animated by the system of usurpation, by its lust to exploit and its extortionate egoism, is totally changed.

We do not believe in any preachment of democracy and liberty by those who restrict the free flow of thought, voting rights, freedom of association and press; by those who furiously resist the peoples' resolve to build their own social democracy, giving land to the tillers and factories to the workers, so that those who produce shall receive the full value of their work.

We will always distrust spokesmen for the autocratic murderers of defenseless peoples, the reapers of lives, the destroyers of civilized advances; for the autocracy that moves over the fertile earth leaving rivers of blood, and tears to ribbons all hopes for a new world well-being for the dispossessed masses.

An autocracy that builds up exterminating armies and gloats over the hungry multitudes awaiting at factory gates a chance for an ill-paid day's work. That accepts the degeneration of exploited men, women, and children to enrich capitalists, and by these intolerable conditions corrupts morality, spreads vice and ignorance, and secures a bunch of thugs in top administrative positions in our communities. An autocracy that fosters a vulgar commercial spirit, and lets prostitution flow tranquilly on its course without the smallest effort to control it, cannot secure peace nor regenerate the world with the true practice of democracy and freedom.

Let us keep saying to our comrades: "Proletarians, build with your own bodies a rampart against the attempts to stop the liberation of your class. Free the land from the hands that usurp it. Smash the privilege of controlling natural wealth and the products of thousands of toilers in workshop, factory, and field! Into action in the noble fight to impose the will of the majority, the natural and just precept: 'HE WHO DOES NOT WORK SHALL NOT EAT.' "

The scriptures tell us that God said to man: "In the sweat of thy brow shalt thou eat bread." Well, let the divine will be done. We are not to be made fools of and we scorn to receive gifts from filthy hands. We agree that all who populate the earth should do their daily stint and wrest their sustenance from the earth. He who does no work should be deprived of his daily bread.

DEBATE ON RESOLUTIONS 1 AND 18

RESOLUTION 1, proposed by Secretary Treasurer Manuel F. Rojas, to include in the Socialist Party program the following definition of Political Status:

RESOLVED, by this 4th Annual Convention of the Socialist Party: To advocate and defend the Declaration of Independence for the Island of Puerto Rico, with the character and principles of a democratic-industrial republic in which all active and intelligent forces of labor participate; and

RESOLVED, that the Independence of Puerto Rico be established on the following bases, assuring to all inhabitants their inalienable rights to liberty and well-being, and to achieve this goal by the following means:

a. By the consolidation of true social democracy through freeing the land from private ownership and its natural resources from industry.

b. By winning political power to dispose of, nationalize, and regularize all the resources and wealth of the soil, thus resolving the problem of the economic-slavery system which impoverishes the proletarian masses and compels them to work and produce with no hope of well-being.

c. We demand a complete change of the present regime and derogation of all laws of privilege perpetuating social inequality, which restrict the free exercise of public rights and keep the majority of the people from free development and from obtaining the necessities of life while the minority, who assume the direction of public affairs and own the means of production and consumption, exercise these rights without limitation.

d. In the democratic-industrial republic the right to life must be guaranteed by legal measures obliging every citizen over twenty-one to work and produce and thus qualify for satisfaction of his needs.

e. All citizens of Puerto Rico must be obliged to contribute to public services, including education and the provision of food and clothing to all children, who will be placed under the state's protection from age eight to age eighteen. At the latter age, after a complete educational process through primary and elementary to study of the arts and sciences, children shall be returned to their families.

f. We maintain and reaffirm all the provisions respecting political rights for all citizens, as set forth in the Socialist Party program approved by the Convention of June 21-22, 1917.

RESOLUTION 18, proposed by delegate Alfonso Torres, containing the following:

resolved, by this Fourth Convention,

First: That the Socialist Party incorporate in its program the political independence of Puerto Rico as one of its immediate goals.

Second: That simultaneously with propagation of the goal of independence, the call be sounded to use it for the benefit of the working classes.

Third: That all propaganda be suppressed which suggests cowardice and submission of Puerto Rico's working masses before the tyrannical attitude to the people of the present leaders of capitalist parties; that, on the contrary, our propaganda shall stimulate a climate of civic courage, of working-class power over the capitalist class.

Fourth: That the final goal of Puerto Rico's Political Status be that which the socialist-industrial republic of this country shall resolve upon.

The Committee report on the above resolutions contains the following declaration:

Committee Report

After studying these important drafts your Committee strongly recommends:

That this Fourth Convention declare that the Socialist Party finds no necessity at this time to write any definition of Political Status into its program, there being good reasons not to do so for the time being;

That the resolutions in question be referred to forthcoming Conventions for their adverse or favorable opinion;

That this Convention declare itself emphatically against any public declarations, on the platform or in the press, either attacking or defending the political solutions discussed; that such statements be not made until the issue is resolved by a Party convention;

That a most serious question arising from this measure is to be forearmed against any solution of the issue that might give rise to controversy among Sections that hold a different view.

Fraternally,

Sandalio E. Alonso, Secretary   *Emilio Fariza, Chairman*

Vice-Chairman Julio Aybar asked for the floor and mentioned the agreement by the Executive Committee regarding certain questions proper for discussion in special private session. He thought that what had been presented pursuant to the decision of the Territorial Executive Committee should be discussed in private.

The Chairman explained to the Convention that the Report was not in accordance with proper procedures. Delegates Jorge Rivera Gautier, Moisés Echevarria and Cristino Domenech opposed the Declaration of Independence definition of Political Status. The proposer of the first resolution, Manuel F. Rojas, defended it with arguments for the belief that a Socialist Party could never and nowhere oppose the peoples' right to rule themselves and determine their own affairs. The Party had raised its banner, he said, to fight for the peoples' inalienable right to freedom and happiness through the control of their destinies. The Socialist Party, as such, had to define its political goal clearly and decisively.

Delegate Antonio Arroyo opposed any exclusion of the political solutions as presented.

Julio Aybar said he was for independence but in a very different form from what advocates of the Tropical Republic were asking.

Eduardo Conde opposed the definition of Political Status.

Alfonso Torres moved a point of order in that the speakers were not confining themselves to whether or not the Socialist Party should define Puerto Rico's Political Status. They had gone to the fundamentals of a question that was not up for discussion. The only point to be decided was whether the party should or should not make declarations about Political Status.

The Chair declared the motion out of order: speakers should state their arguments for or against the definition of Status.

Manuel F. Rojas said:

"Comrade Chairman and delegates: I think we have to define our Political Status since we live in a country that isn't considered a nation, not even a State of the United States nor an Organized Territory. A U.S. court has held that the national Constitution doesn't apply to Puerto Rico, so that we are not really American citizens. Hence our status is simply that of colonials.

"U.S. socialists don't need to spell out a Status definition in their program because they move and agitate in a sovereign nation. The sovereignty of Puerto Rico rests in the U.S. Congress and we are barred from ruling our own destinies and resolving our problems in our way.

"Wherever the Socialist Party is organized it declares that the peoples should have freedom within such independence as will let them run their own show.

"It is most strange that we should oppose the clearest and most radical definition of Political Status just when all the peoples are demonstrating for their independence. All socialist parties aim at this goal. The British Labor Party has demanded freedom for India and for Ireland. The American Socialist Party has called for the same thing. Russia, or rather the Russian Soviets, have declared the peoples of Lithuania and the Ukraine free and independent. Why should we be against the definition of independent Status that we have proposed?

"Not that we should beg for independence. Freedom isn't begged but fought for, but we have to set forth the claim to rule our own destinies."

Alfonso Torres again moved his point of order. The Chair ruled against it and he appealed to the delegates.

The Chairman left the chair to Delegate Antonio Arroyo, and Torres then explained the basis of his appeal.

It was put to the vote and the Chair's decision was overruled.

Moisés Echevarría moved that the matter be referred back to committee for further study.

Bolívar Ochart said the discussion should continue.

Chairman Iglesias got the floor and began as follows:

"I am against everything that the Convention has resolved. This report should be defeated because it is a fallacy, contrary to definitions in the Socialist Party program: our orientation is already defined. If we accepted it we would only be showing that we have been influenced by the atmosphere breathed by the politicians.

"Those elements who use the press to talk of 'my people and my country' show that they have been perverted by radiations from the politicians who use those same phrases to deceive the ignorant."

As the speaker extended his remarks beyond the time limit, the Chair called him to order, saying his time was up.

Several delegates wanted him to continue and to be given another hour of time.

A motion by delegate Arturo de Santiago, Jr., to allow comrade Iglesias more time to finish his remarks was carried, and he resumed:

"This business of defining Status only gives perverse politicians the opportunity to say to the ignorant people, 'You see they have no clear definition, they don't know what they want'—when that isn't true since we have this definition in the program."

Julio Aybar interrupted him: "Can we resolve our economic problem in the actual setup we have under this regime?" Iglesias replied:

"Yes, when we have a majority and can pass appropriate legislation for the sovereignty of the people who support us. But the wording of the committee report is ridiculous. We must give everyone the chance to express his ideas. If their statements are harmful we will call their attention to it, and if they persist we will tell them to go with the Independentists."

Alfonso Torres: "Will the speaker yield?"

Iglesias: "With pleasure."

Torres: "Is it your view that what was read out in the program is really a definition of Political Status or simply an ideal goal?"

Iglesias: "Yes, an ideal goal."

Torres: "So properly speaking it isn't Political Status?"

Iglesias: "What is Political Status? The answer is this. According to capitalist parties it's the organization of governments, but we don't need to define any Political Status to establish our ideal system."

Torres: "If you weren't an American citizen, could you vote in Puerto Rico?"

Iglesias: "Of course not, but that is due to the system."

Torres: "Then we have to operate within the terms of the regime."

Manuel F. Rojas: "Will the speaker yield?"

Iglesias: "Yes."

Rojas: "What's your opinion of those who approve of coalition with bourgeois parties?"

Iglesias: "I am convinced that that shouldn't be done."

Rojas: "And what do you say about the approval of socialists supporting the war?"

Iglesias: "I have never approved it."

Aybar: "May I ask one question?"

Iglesias: "Yes, all you want."

Aybar: "What do you say about a socialist representative who supports compulsory military service?"

Iglesias: "You are referring to me, but what I did was to support principles. But we have no business making political definitions, we should follow the example of the Russian representative when he confronted the power of the nations. He said: 'I don't come to ask for political rights, our nation isn't organized under any Political Status, but we've organized it economically and we rely on the power of labor to maintain the new regime we've established there.'

"Understand me well: don't look so much at your own country, look at the world, look toward all the peoples and think with the mind of humanity. Forget all the feelings evoked by fatherlands, blot out the old political tendencies, move always toward the exaltation of labor."

Andres Aruz: "Delegate for section 37, Santurce. I move rejection of the resolution and the report and confirmation of what's in the program."

Alfonso Torres: "I move that the words 'Political Status' be changed to 'Ideal Goal' and that this be an amendment to delegate Aruz's motion."

The question was put to the vote and the last motion with the amendment was carried.

PROGRAM OF THE SOCIALIST PARTY

(The Socialist Party assembled in Convention on May 1, 2, 3, and 4 of 1919 made the following declarations—and agreed to implement them if the people decided to grant it the public power necessary for so doing)

Basic Principles of Doctrine

We declare:

If we consider that the wealth of nature is monopolized by capitalist individuals and corporations, so that most citizens enjoy it in infinitely smaller proportion than the lower animals and we find the so-called king of creation—especially the worker in field, factory, and workshop—eating poorly, lacking air and light, the slave of a fellow man who exploits and oppresses him;

If we find furthermore that the products of human thought and genius are equally shackled so that the march of science—so dazzling when studied in books and reviews, so useful and magnificent on paper—is useless for thousands of unfortunates in the very communities where human power astonishes us with its marvels, not to mention the countryside where men are reduced to semi-savage ignorance;

If we find that the great inventions, far from alleviating the worker, produce the double evil of ruining the small industrialist and plunging the worker in poverty;

And if, finally, we take into account that social wealth, the product of generations of study and application, is controlled under capitalism and its government by groups privileged to monopolize all sources and activities of human life; and that it only feeds the corruption and arrogance of powerful domestic and foreign idlers, so that instead of spreading fruitfully over the land for the happiness of those who ennoble themselves by work, it is scandalously robbed from them;

If to our misfortune and humanity's shame all this is so, the Socialist Party declares to its members that, as directed and controlled by the blind and fatal forces of capitalism, human society cannot attain its goal of civilization and justice now and in the future.

This monstrous absurdity and injustice can be explained, on analysis, by the fact that our existing society had to be a fact before we could apprehend it. Contrary to the process with the individual who thinks first and then acts, this human collective embracing all of our species and in which all participate—some commanding and enjoying, others producing and obeying—was formed by the necessities of individual impotence before reason could be brought to bear. And when the peoples felt the effects of the error, and critics pointed out the absurdities to which it led, the evil was already rooted and privilege established beyond the reformers' weak power to resist.

This is where we are; such are the causes and effects; and this state of things must not and cannot continue. The considerations we have reviewed impel socialists to defend their ideal, the most humane ideal so far known. It is not new but the same ideal, more precisely defined, that inspired the oppressed of all the ages and that we hold to be the inevitable substitute for the morality and doctrines of capitalism.

"The Ideal Goal"

The Socialist Party declares that the Political Status of Puerto Rico will be fully defined when legislation approved by the country establishes the social democracy of labor.

We denounce as a big lie of conventional politics the statement of Puerto Rican capitalist parties that the country will get full freedom in the remote future by working for years to obtain what they call autonomy, or the declaration of Statehood, or Independence.

The Socialist Party declares that the full freedom, happiness, and well-being of the Puerto Rican people now depend exclusively on their own organized productive forces. United under the banner of the socialist ideal, these can destroy the visible and invisible power of the plutocracy that burdens and enslaves us, establishing social democracy to free our people from the economic crime of today.

United Action

Throughout our island we see a spontaneous, growing, inevitable social movement. It is the very spirit of our age of industrial, economic, and mercantile transformation.

The Socialist Party calls on all the nuclei of struggle for economic change and well-being to study our united principles and doctrine and to close ranks with the active forces of social life, giving them vigor, potency, and solidarity. To coordinate the forces of labor's economic struggles in a high-principled campaign to enlighten public consciousness about socialist and labor solutions, with discipline to make the action prompt, direct, and effective.

The Socialist Party concept would be incomplete if it did not, above all else, undertake the principled education of the workers and of all whom we know as intellectuals.

The Socialist Party will fight for speedy restoration to all the people, without distinction of origin or race, of the Puerto Rican land which has been captured by private, speculative, foreign-organized monopolies, thanks to the prevailing legalized system of expropriation of human labor by capital.

We accuse the agents of capitalist parties and corporations of responsibility for the usurpation of our lands, illegally accomplished through use of the Legislature and governmental power.

We propose to rid Puerto Rico in an immediate and practical way of the legal economic system under which all our lands pass with alarming speed into the hands of big, anonymous, foreign and domestic business interests.

We will introduce equitable measures of taxation to keep capital, as far as possible, from periodically emigrating in the form of interest and rent to absentees.

By means of *legislative petitions* and effective representation of our country we will make known to the U.S. Congress that the demand for a few concessions of a political character, under the pretext of autonomy, statehood, or independence, promises nothing more than ephemeral power in the hands of a privileged class of politicians and monopolists in our country protected by the plutocracy.

We will inform the U.S. Congress that the greatest of tyrannies and foulest of crimes will be committed against the people of Puerto Rico if our masses are not freed from their present economic, industrial, and commercial bondage.

Puerto Rico has been turned into a factory worked by serfs, and sixty percent of the products of its wealth leaves the country; the interest on investment is three times greater than in any other country, producing such a monstrous imbalance that the whole island shows its results in poverty and hunger.

We will tell the people that the government, while annually announcing a growth of wealth in its "official reports" to the U.S. Congress, conceals the monopolization of that wealth—the product of human toil—by the internal and external power of the plutocracy.

We accuse the capitalist parties and their leaders of being the chief accomplices in this crime.

The Socialist Party will put into effect the simplest and most effective procedure for regulating the country's production in accordance with its interests, and thus put a stop to the economic disorder that results in ever greater production of wealth for internal and absentee monopolists.

We declare that the only practical way to lower the cost of living is the suppression of middlemen. We will therefore adopt the most effective means to develop a system of genuinely native agricultural and manufacturing industries, to provide all the people with their basic consumption needs in greatest abundance and quality and at lowest cost. Thus, we will retrieve our own domestic market and give our country the utmost possible freedom from agricultural, manufacturing, and mercantile monopolies, with a wholesale-and-retail marketing system to supply needs at reduced cost.

Another cause of our worsening condition is the wicked inequality, as between classes, of a tax system bearing more heavily on the majority of small taxpayers—a bonanza for the owners of most of the wealth the productive class produces, such as the rich native and foreign corporations, big owners of sugar mills, land, and industries, and corporate monopolists of all kinds.

By turning the industrial and transport companies into public-service institutions of the island government, we will take due steps to reclaim the wealth they have taken from the Puerto Rican people. Thus, the railroads, streetcars, navigation and its component activities, telephone and telegraph communications, and electrical installations will be declared the property of the Puerto Rican people by appropriate legislation.

In response to the trade unions' and the people's minimal demands for labor legislation, the Socialist Party will exert all efforts through its popularly elected representatives to legislate and implement the following measures:

1. Direction and control by workers' organizations of the Departments of Agriculture and Labor of Puerto Rico, to develop all means for putting legislation into effect and improving agriculture.

2. Immediate creation of a People's Bank with branches in every municipality, mainly concerned to eliminate rampant speculation by rich interests and facilitate low-interest, long-term credits for all citizens without distinction.

3. The People of Puerto Rico own 250,000 *cuerdas* of arable land and pasture; we will place them by law in the workers' hands and the Treasury will cooperate, with adequate loans, to establish numerous farms throughout the country.

4. All franchised waterfalls, rivers, and irrigation and the use of lands and streets will be declared public services, and corporations using them legally will be indemnified.

5. 355,000 children are still without schools in the island. The Socialist Party declares that its first measure will be to give education and books, gratis, to all Puerto Rican school-age children, as well as food and clothing to children of needy families.

The Department of Education and others used by the administration will be controlled by those who serve in them in accordance with community goals.

School authorities will provide adequate medical and dental care for the pupils.

Schools and other public buildings that can be used for organizational or union meetings, for lectures or other affairs of a popular character will be put at the organizers' disposal without excuses.

The Socialist Party will work actively for a radical change in methods of self-improvement hitherto available to the people, as also in the Sunday-observance laws, to the end that new methods and customs may extend sources of honest pleasure and prevent the channeling of public distractions into vice and immoral acts.

In appropriate areas near the ocean new laws will establish parks, dance halls, gymnasia, concert halls, etc., for the enjoyment of the public.

6. Sanitation will be organized independently of all political or capitalist influence, and all officials will be required to comply strictly with the law, providing whatever is necessary for viable sanitation in communities and needy homes and constructing aqueducts, drains, and electrical wiring throughout the country.

7. We support the elimination of middlemen in public-works contracts by granting concessions for cooperative works to labor organizations by law.

8. The compensation-and-responsibility law for employers will be reformed so as to effectively protect and assure workers' lives.

9. The maximum work day will be eight hours, and wages adequate for the cost of living will be paid equally to men and women where they perform equal work. The problem of workers without work will be resolved.

10. Absolute abolition of labor by children under sixteen, of night work in industry by women, and of work for pregnant and nursing women.

11. Immediate construction of workers' housing developments in cities and of workers' villages in the country. These will be built on land belonging to the people of Puerto Rico, or by expropriation through low-interest, long-term government credits to the workers.

12. Pensions for old people of both sexes worn out by toil. Establishment of the weekday half-holiday, in addition to Sunday. Effective inspection of workshops, factories, and housing. Regulation of the rent system now monopolized by landlords, by obliging them to pay interest on the security payment they demand.

13. The penal system should be transformed by removing inmates from the present jails and establishing a large farm where they will work the land and grow their own food, and by establishing workshops for them. The state will pay these confined workers the exact value of what they produce in accordance with the market price, so that they may have the wherewithal to support their families. We are against the use of prisoners for public works. We denounce the capitalist parties for the filthy condition and brutal regime of existing municipal jails.

14. Abolition of the *casas de misericordia* and other charitable institutions, and the substitution of a direct protective system for widowed mothers and their children and for old people. These will be put in the care of relatives or persons volunteering as an act of solidarity. Similarly, orphans will be given up by the state to families who will feed, care for, and educate them under protection of the public Treasury.

15. Any industry or personal property not providing more than the basic needs of the citizen who keeps it in good order, and whose value does not exceed $500,000, shall be tax-exempt.

16. A tax of fifty percent shall be levied on all incomes derived from profits of any corporation, company, inheritance, rents, or other institution of the capitalist system, pending total abolition of the rent and inheritance system.

17. Absolute freedom of press, association, speech, and assembly; all misdemeanors committed in the exercise of these rights to be judged by a grand jury of citizen peers.

18. Inviolability of the home guaranteed to every citizen.

19. Universal and secret suffrage for men and women. Adoption of the popular initiative, referendum, and recall, and proportional representation in the National Congress of the island. Abolition of the Senate and the gubernatorial veto.

20. Expulsion from the island police of all cruel and vicious officers and men. Reduction of the number of police chiefs.

Transformation of the corps into a civil organization paying
adequate wages for a decent life and for the independence required
by this public service.

21. The powers of Courts of Justice must be regulated, and their
decisions subject to popular referendum both in civil and criminal
cases. Judges will be removable by popular vote.

22. Abolition of the death penalty.

23. Our country's cemeteries to become true monuments of art,
beauty, and public consecration. The state will require municipalities to effect all necessary reforms that sentiment and gratitude and
the imperishable memory of our ancestors can inspire in the minds
of legislators, to show we are a people that goes beyond individual
egoism in enjoyment of this life's satisfactions, a people
unforgetful of beloved parents and children who disappear for all
eternity. If the municipalities fail in this, the state will do it. Our
cemeteries, then, must be the expression of our altruistic
sentiments, of our unbounded love for those who live and those
who have passed on. We denounce the state of the island's
cemeteries under the capitalist system as a demonstration of the
crude egoism which our ruling classes conceal behind a curtain of
pseudo-civilization.

All these demands, and others that may be adopted in the future
for protection and betterment of the people's condition, are put
forward by the Socialist Party. The Party pledges itself to
implement them if the people give it their votes in the next or in
future elections, empowering the people's representatives to
crystallize in practice this monument to the principles, lofty ideas,
and proposals which we set forth frankly and simply before the
Puerto Rican people's conscience.

The Puerto Rican nation will decide in the electoral contest
which of the parties deserves election by the suffering masses.

Workers make up more than ninety percent of the Puerto Rican
population. They are the ones who suffer most, and the middle
classes, who also suffer, constitute an important minority. If both
are ready to make a great and deep transformation of the nation's
life, they should vote as one man for the Socialist Party.

Remember always that capitalism has retained power for years
and for centuries, and that our present evils are due to it. If you

want to change radically the desperate situation of the Puerto Rican people, elect our candidates.

If you don't, capitalist tyranny will continue its work of human iniquity.

The FLT Begins to Break Up
(1934, 1945)

The Federación Libre de los Trabajadores (FLT—Free Workers' Federation) and Partido Socialista Puertorriqueño (PSP—Puerto Rican Socialist Party) were genuine offspring of the working class and for a time *the* instruments of that class. But the thrust of their political and trade-union actions led to a contradiction between them and the cultural forms from which they arose—the forms and processes characterizing the working class. Almost exclusively stressing immediate gains in the workers' condition of life, the measures adopted slowly submerged these institutions' vision and the hope of a new social order.[1]

The vision had not yet been lost to sight by the working class but the Socialist Party's coalition with one of the bourgeois parties,[2] followed by its sharing of positions in the government permitted to the colony, clouded the perspective of the struggle as one of classes. Yet in daily life the workers remained the exploited, with exploiters those to be fought. To maintain the coalition (which meant the possibility of some immediate improvements through governmental participation) and their presence within it to legislate such reforms, the *tajureos* changed the FLT and Party struggle from one of cane-field burning, strikes, torchlight marches, the

Marseillaise, and hunger demonstrations into meetings behind closed doors in the halls of the Legislature and the Labor Department. The working class, however, didn't see these as the right battlefields.

The contradiction exploded in the sugar workers' strike of 1934. The top FLT leaders (who were at the same time the Party's top leaders) met in San Juan with the sugar lords and signed a collective agreement for the whole country. In many sectors—mainly the island's Eastern sugar zone, which was just where the Socialist Party had always had greatest strength—the workers rejected it as far below what they wanted and thought they could get. Thus began Puerto Rico's first strike not directly aimed against employers, but against the workers' own leadership, whom they considered traitors for signing the agreement.

The strike was basically spontaneous, but three participating groups call for mention. First, Afirmación Socialista (Socialist Affirmation)—undoubtedly the most important group involved. It was formed by Socialist Party and FLT members constituting the left wing of those organizations, who ended by being expelled from the Party for their part in the strike. Second, Partido Nacionalista (Nationalist Party), used in effect by the workers for what it symbolized in total, frontal opposition to the regime. Last, members of some Marxist circles which formed the Partido Comunista (Communist Party) later that year.

The strike was brief and brought few immediate results. In the situation of fighting against its own instruments of struggle the working class found itself momentarily impotent. But this strike marked the beginning of processes that would culminate in creation of a new instrument, a new labor council.[3] The Confederación General de Trabajadores (CGT—General Workers' Confederation) was founded in March 1940, and until 1945 spread like fire through a cane field. With it arose a new militancy, enthusiasm, and configuration of goals.

In this section we present three documents through which the processes outlined above can be seen. First, a selection of news items about the strike published in the newspaper *El Imparcial* in 1934; second, documents concerning the expulsion of Social Affirmation members (taken from books by that group's outstanding leader, Tadeo Rodríguez García); third, the Secretary General's Report at the third CGT Congress, excellently illustrating what the new working-class instrument signified.

ORIENTE SUGAR WORKERS' STRIKE:
NEWS ITEMS FROM *EL IMPARCIAL* (1934)

Albizu Campos Active in Sugar Strike

The strike of field workers in the sugar industry, all along the South coast and in the Northeast from Carolina to Fajardo, took an unexpected turn Saturday when the workers called on the top leader of Puerto Rican Nationalism, Don Pedro Albizu Campos, who promptly left for Guayama and was expected late yesterday at a mass meeting in the Oriente area.

Albizu Campos's entry into the proletarian struggle marks a radical change in the strikers' mood and seriously threatens the existence of the local branch of the American Federation of Labor. This branch has until now been linked under the leadership of Santiago Iglesias to the Socialist Party or functioned as an *outrance* political organ. With the Nationalist leader's arrival on the scene a consolidation is beginning between left Socialist elements and those groups that, without being radical, favor nationalizing the Puerto Rican labor movement with a view to an intensified struggle against the domination of North American corporations in the country.

Most of the Free Federation leaders, according to reports from the strike area, have lost all their moral force to talk to rural workers. Although some field leaders are beginning to yield to the pressure of their superiors in San Juan, the masses remain militant and determined to maintain the strike. Since Friday the Federation has been making desperate efforts to recover control of the movement, and has sent numerous emissaries and agitators to the points toughest to control.

It is generally believed that if Albizu takes charge of reorganizing the strike and puts Nationalist propagandists at its head, along with leaders still remaining firm, the strike will continue and will assume the proportions of a real conflict.

Oriente Strikers Demoralized
by Free Federation Leaders

The striking sugar workers in Eastern centers suffered a setback Saturday when this reporter, on a visit to the affected area, confirmed that the Free Federation and Socialist Party machine, seeking to enforce acceptance of the Alonso agreement, is stirring rebellion among local leaders who have been told to instruct their respective worker contingents to resume work in the fields immediately.

At this writing we have no word of the outcome but can report that the climate for this new line doesn't seem sunny from the workers' standpoint. Most of the strikers we met in the villages seemed determined not to come to terms with their local representatives except on the basis of their own proposals. Many carried black flags and vowed to "bring down" leaders now wavering on plans to which they originally committed themselves. Any other course, said these workers, would imply victory for "the San Juan crowd," in whom they have lost all confidence.

According to information later confirmed in Carolina, the Oriente strike is not aimed against the employers, whose property has so far been respected, but against the top Federation leadership, by whom the strikers feel they have been sold out: it approved an agreement which they say doesn't satisfy them, despite its attempt to make them "understand" by every means—from sending Federation legislators into the field to using police to break up groups and keep anti-agreement leaders out of places where it is discussed.

The complete absence of protection by the Federation (according to the strikers) forced many of them on Saturday to invite by telegraph the Nationalist leader Albizu Campos to head the strike movement in Guayama and Fajardo. We understand that Don Pedro answered the first call—in Guayama—and was to speak last night in Fajardo.

One of the most dramatic episodes in this movement against the purported designs of the Federation leadership was a spectacular race on Friday night, when a car driven by "rebel" leaders Paniagua, Flores, Pino, and Betancourt took the Carolina-Fajardo road in pursuit of a car containing the Federation representatives, Colón Gordiany, Méndez Pérez Peña, and Alamo.

The chase continued to Fajardo with the following result, according to Carolina "rebel" leader Lucas Betancourt:

"In Cánovanas the workers' leader Juan Esquilín told us the commission had passed through there but the strikers wouldn't listen to them. We reached Río Grande just when the commissioners were meeting with strikers in the Pimentel school, trying to convince them to return to work. There, the police, claiming to carry out the orders of the people inside, barred our access to the building, but we were informed that the meeting was divided, some for going back to work and some not. In Luquillo the commissioners couldn't get a hearing either, so they proceeded to Fajardo where they failed again that night, according to our informants, and then decided to call a meeting."

During this chase, we were told, whatever one lot of leaders did in a place was undone later by the other lot, causing the greatest confusion between groups of strikers since some told them to work and others said the opposite.

The race starting from Carolina originated at a workers' meeting there, where "rebels confronted loyalists" in a discussion of the Alonso agreement. The commissioners told the workers they should accept it and get back on the job, then "rebel" leader Tadeo Rodriguez persuaded them to stand against it. An incident was set off among the "loyalists" by an interruption by the "rebel" Pino, who proposed that all should proceed together to test opinion in the communities en route. When this was rejected by one of the commissioners the proposer replied that the others should then follow behind since it was well known that no one could accompany the "loyalists" anywhere. These remarks, according to Betancourt, were followed by overwhelming rejection of the agreement.

Like the French Revolution, the strike has its own music. We heard it in Ceiba where the strikers are pleased with themselves for, apart from a Mayor, Don Lauro Piñeiro, who goes through the fields stirring ardor for the strike, they also have a musical number and provide entertainment with this *ritornelos*:

"Lads, lads, now's the time to strike; we'll see if the moneybags have signed on the dotted line for the [extra] peso and the eight-hour day. Kiss the wife good-by, if you have to leave her alone to go out and defend the peso and eight hours. The bosses say they won't sign now because a peso and eight hours are too much. Let Mr. Macoine [top employee of the Fajardo estate] come, let him come to Ceiba now, we'll see why he doesn't sign up for the peso and eight hours.''

Albizu Campos Charges Government
with Trying to Break Strike

The agricultural strike is alive and kicking throughout Oriente, and in the south as far as Ponce. If Mayagüez rises today, as is to be expected, this national movement will cover all the sugar plantations and paralyze their activities.

The workers have organized corporatively to acquire legal identity and so prevent anyone from purporting to speak in their name. They have their headquarters in Guayama because there, more than six thousand working men, in the most impressive gathering that one could imagine, spoke and acted for the toiling masses who constitute some ninety percent of the country's population. This is the real Puerto Rican people making itself seen and heard with serenity and courage.

At the end of last Sunday's activities the workers had organized four sections of the Asociacion de Trabajadores de Puerto Rico (Puerto Rican Workers' Association): Guayama, Fajardo, Luquillo, and Canóvanas. On Monday the noble work of organizing the whole nation will continue ardently. The assemblages in these cities were acts of pure patriotism and culture, confirming the learned Humboldt's observation on his visit here a century ago, that the Puerto Rican nation is the most intelligent society in the New World.

Our people have shown that they can get together in public, right in the plaza, and resolve any problem affecting their lives with good sense, composure, and guts.

It is extraordinary that the workers haven't organized themselves till now. Lawyers, doctors, schoolteachers, businessmen, sailors, professionals, sugar growers, trade employees, and island-government employees, chemists, pharmacists, manufacturers, tenants—in short, all professions and social activities are organized corporatively with juridical rights and responsibilities.

The workers now form the strongest corporation it is possible to organize, for they are the real power and the real source of our country's wealth.

Each section of the Workers' Association has its chairman and secretary and a representative for each branch of agricultural labor, who must be a bona fide worker absolutely trusted by his companeros—that is, a natural leader in the particular branch of work. As there are some twelve of these in sugar cultivation, the section leadership consists of up to fifteen men.

Only the specialist in each branch can understand the hardships of that particular kind of work and determine what the men engaged in it need. Thus carpenters, masons, mechanics, cane-cutters, excavators, etc., will each have a man from their own midst representing their specialty in the appropriate section of the Puerto Rican Workers' Association. The curses visited upon the workers are largely due to mass disorganization. But these will be cut off at the roots, thus eliminating the apocryphal leadership which till now has exploited the toiling masses. The barbarous exploitation to which the big, cold-blooded, employer interests have submitted the worker will also come to an end.

The workers have rejected the sugar corporations' proposals for serious reasons which are of concern to the nation. These are some of them:

"1. Because wages are being set lower than those already existing.

"2. Because the work day is maintained at twelve hours, an inhuman position.

"3. Because the purported workers' participation in sugar profits, in the event of a rise in the price of sugar, is a myth. The price is already stabilized.

"4. Because the growers make fabulous profits out of the workers' low wages and also enjoy the two-dollar-per-quintal [one hundred pounds] customs concession in the North American market. If growers with interests in Cuba make money selling their sugar in the North American market without this concession, the people can see what Puerto Rican growers are making. It is also to be noted that higher wages are paid in Cuba than in Puerto Rico.

"To illustrate, on the basis of current New York market quotations: Cuban sugar interests have to sell their sugar at $2.25 per quintal while Puerto Rican interests sell theirs at $3.25 per quintal.

"5. Everyone knows the enormous influence that the sugar industry, enjoying all kinds of privileges to the injury of the Puerto Rican people, has on the island government. And that this same official influence also privileges it in the matter of tax exemptions.

"6. The country takes note, as do we, that profits from the industry are spent abroad, in the United States, because more than sixty percent of the value of these sugar interests belongs to North American interests and the rest if mortgaged in U.S. banks.

"7. The only income Puerto Rico has is the wages we receive as workers, because with the exception of sugar, which North America wholly controls, all Puerto Rican products have to be sold in the United States at prices imposed by North American buyers. At the same time they sell their products to us at whatever price suits them.

"8. We further reject this proposal because it retains the same system of payment in script which enslaves us completely to the employers' will. That system has ruined the whole of Puerto Rican trade and industry because the sugar plantations have a system of company stores which import everything directly and avoid the taxes by all regular trade.

"The dollar paid to us goes right back to the plantation with interest.

"The people can judge this situation from the example of the Aguirre plantation. It has a complete system of company stores selling every kind of merchandise—food, cloth, hardware, etc.—plus dairies, drug stores, ice plants, and even a theater, gasoline stations, a street market, and hotels.

"9. Prices of essential consumer products have risen by forty percent. For these basic reasons we reject the proposals made by the sugar growers through official channels.

"It is in the interest of all Puerto Rico to support this strike because it is for the principle of abolishing sugar slavery."

The principle that regulates wage scales is based on the unquestionable fact that living costs have risen by forty percent. The workers' modest demand is for a raise of only forty percent to meet these costs. Their poverty will be as great as ever, but there is still too much resignation in our people.

The average wage they ask is no more than 1.25 pesos a day. Given the depreciation of the dollar, this is a mere 85 centavos.

Eighty-five centavos for a man and his family, cutting cane under rain and sun, exposed to all possible diseases and accidents. But these are the demands of the people concerned. We have done no more than organize them, leaving them to decide what is good for them.

Of course, official power wants to break the strike. This is a strikebreaking government. It exists to defend its big interests here. To do this it uses its executive-and legislative-patronage system. It seeks to take advantage of a defunct labor leadership that only knows the sweetness of inertia.

Puerto Rico has stood on its feet. The people rise to impose their right to life.

All good Puerto Ricans will see to it that the rights of the workers of Puerto Rico are respected.

P. Albizu Campos

Strike Continues in the East

At 6:00 P.M. on Saturday I arrived in Fajardo to help the strikers. All of them who were around the recreation plaza told me personally that the Federation leaders wanted to make them accept the Alonso agreement, saying that it was the law and had to be obeyed on pain of losing jobs. This fraud made me indignant and I organized a meeting which began at 8:00 P.M. For more than three hours I talked to over two thousand strikers and during the meeting the workers themselves said, "We've been sold out."

As soon as the meeting ended at 11:30, I organized a demonstration, and despite the Chief of Police's protests against the "abuse" of such a demonstration at such an hour, demonstrators marched through the main streets of the city and broke up in the Plaza.

The people cheered the strike and cried, "Death to Alonso! Down with the traitors!"

I again spoke and asked if they trusted the local Federation committee: the unanimous shout was , "No!" It was agreed that a new strike committee independent of the Federation would be formed next day.

The meeting called for the next day was postponed till Sunday evening so that Albizu Campos, who was coming to Fajardo to cooperate with the strikers, could also be heard. I visited various rural *barrios* and, with the exception of plantation officials, it can be said that there are no strikebreakers. On the night when I left for San Juan, Albizu Campos was speaking in the Fajardo Plaza to more than four thousand angry strikers who came in from all around.

Licenciado Vergne Ortiz, Communist Party

Cadets of the Republic Invade Oriente

Apart from the picturesque spectacle of Federation leaders— ranging from the intelligent Commissioner of Labor to the "radical" Licenciado Méndez—moving around with police escorts, and of district attorneys immediately "discovering" the author of a "slander" against Méndez Peña while Peña himself couldn't identify who tried to blow up the Roig plantation's locomotive number 1, it is interesting to observe the birth, flowering and activity of 1,001 ready-to-wear leaders whom the Humacao and Yabucoa strikers now have to cope with. Respectable persons tell us that even the shanty hero, Lolo Caballero, donned a leader's mantle in Yabucoa, and was seen hand in hand with District Attorney García González waving the agreement olive-branch among unconverted elements; while Corporal Burgos, not to be outdone, sounded his high threatening notes wherever he went, forgetting that this was precisely what set off the tragedy in Humacao's militia hall on the night when District Attorney Perquera lost his life. Fortunately, as we are informed, the public has shown that unerring intuition that God granted it by turning a deaf ear to the corporal's old-soldierly outbursts and shouting at him from doorways:

"Burgos, we want Méndez Bas!"

The police agent, they say, has been gnashing his teeth, but he has taken it—which is the important thing.

The "tactics" of the contending groups in Yabucoa and Humacao have been characterized by a diverting *"modus operandi."* No sooner do the government forces put out a leaflet for a meeting than the others put one out against it. When the former's meeting has started, the others sound a bugle "convoking the people" and immediately get another meeting going outside. A shouting contest. On Saturday the Federation "plenipotentiaries" in Humacao put out this leaflet:

TO THE PEOPLE IN GENERAL
OF HUMACAO
But Especially to the Agricultural Workers
of the City and Its Barrios

Compañeros:

We hereby invite all agricultural workers of Humacao and its *barrios* and the people in general to a great meeting which will take place today Saturday at 6:00 P.M. in the Plaza Principal of this city.

Speakers at this meeting will be compañeros José Ferrer y Ferrer, Luis Pérez Peña, Eduardo Méndez, Jorge Gautier, and Bolívar Ochart.

We urge agricultural workers and the people in general to attend this meeting to hear the authentic representatives of the workers of Puerto Rico. There should be no fear of listening to the compañeros who will participate in tonight's meeting, because those who have their own ideas on the viewpoints to be expressed about the AGREEMENT should not fear the arguments of others.

The workers of Humacao will show once again, by attending tonight's meeting, that they are not a flock of sheep to serve as prey for Nationalist wolves and political mercenaries.

What were the Nationalists doing in the terrible years of proletarian struggles, of the great agricultural strikes, when the right to speak was a myth, workers' demonstrations were broken up by police, and workers and their authentic leaders were imprisoned?

NOTHING! Because Puerto Rican Nationalist students never felt the sufferings of the people nor the privations of the workers, because they did not belong to the people in the past and do not belong to the people now.

WORKERS, TO THE MEETING TONIGHT!

FOR THE UNION AGRICOLA
Ramón Gerena, Félix Medina, Valentín Ortiz,
Félix Negrón, Susano Berrios, Julio Díaz.
Humacao, Jan. 20, 1934.

To this call the opposing forces replied, describing its sponsors as strikebreakers in this leaflet:

WORKER, STAY AWAY FROM THE STRIKEBREAKERS' MEETING

Tonight the strikebreakers of the government will hold a meeting in Humacao. Speakers at said meeting will be the leaders paid by the government to perpetuate exploitation of the workers.

Worker, the government wants to impose on you conditions that are unjust and unreasonable, and is using for that purpose it agents who yesterday were your leaders!

Don't go to the meeting because you would find there your hangmen of today!

The story spread by the pro-agreement leaders, that strikers who follow the movement of Albizu Campos are all nationalists, was exposed to a practical test on Saturday when we were in Yabucoa. On that occasion the Chairman of the Strike Committee, Joaquín Cintrón, a mason by trade, called a group of strikers who happened then to be in the club and checked the political affiliation of each one with this result. The group consisted of thirty strikers, residents of various *barrios* in the municipality. Ten said they were socialists, six liberals, six nationalists, and there were no republicans. The eight others said they were also socialists but belonged to a dissident local group of that party who in the last elections went to vote for a special candidates' list which apparently was defeated.

Letter Without an Envelope

January 21, 1934

Esteemed comrades:

The newspaper *El Día* de Ponce, January 19, page 5, columns 7 and 8, publishes a report on the needleworkers' strike in which appears the following, stated, according to the paper, by Don Cayetano Coll y Cuchi in the presence of Senator Moisés Echevarría:

"That he had just come from Yabucoa where the strike is tremendous, and at the head of said workers in said place is Mr. Albizu Campos, whom the police don't dare to arrest, for which reason complaints about the police there have been made to Governor Horton. That he, Cayetano Coll y Cuchi, had told the striking workers that if they didn't return to work according to the signed agreement, the Free Federation had a large number of workers, mechanics, excavators, cane-cutters, etc., ready to REPLACE all striking workers who won't work . . ."

So much for what we have copied from the newspaper *El Día* of Ponce. As a Free Federation member I wish to state my most energetic protest since it is, and has been since I joined the organized labor movement, my understanding that the Free Federation would never lend itself to strikebreaking, this being the most defamatory label that any institution or individual can wear in his life.

I am sure, esteemed comrades, that no worker would allow to cross his tongue this outburst which has emerged like toads and snakes from the lips of said gentleman; for the Free Federation will never harbor anyone who breaks a strike nor, I believe, authorize such a thing in the future. If it ever did I would be first to come out against such a colossal crime, for the strike in Puerto Rico has been, is, and will be the powerful beam lighting the path that the Puerto Rican working class must travel in its progressive mission.

Esteemed comrades, in these decisive hours in Puerto Rican labor history it is the part of free men, with common aspirations as such for the general good, to unite against the reactionary offensive that desperately seeks to revive slavery and violence with the cult of force as its only currency.

Doesn't it seem to you, companeros, that Cayetano Coll y Cuchi and others are invading our district on orders from hidden powers to weaken our stand? I think it does, and that this understanding springs from what we have seen and felt in these parts for some time.

It is up to all you honest and altruistic companeros to put a stop to this abomination which, like a ravaging horde, threatens to destroy the noble edifice of our organization.

I am not a writer nor a journalist, esteemed comrades. But just as in our remote countryside there are times when the illness is grave, the doctor doesn't show up, and some campesino comes forward as a "herbal" physician; so a man like myself, seeing the life of the Free Federation and Socialist Party in danger, scrawls these lines to put on guard the true defenders of our lofty ideals to liberate the workers.

In the name of the toiling people who are being vilified today, I ask you to act in accordance with the principles we have proclaimed, which have cost the people so dearly in lives and sacrifices.

Florencio Cabello
Member of Local 460
Tobacco Workers of San Juan
(Member of Socialist Affirmation)

EXPULSION OF SOCIALIST
AFFIRMATION MEMBERS
(1934)

*Let us stop submitting to any power, be it what it may;
the Socialist Party was born and grew in bright and luxuriant fields of battle where inch by inch it won positions that it can't simply yield up, for they cost it rivers
of blood and tears, prodigal energy, bitter anguish, a
purgatory of grief.*

MANIFESTO OF SOCIALIST AFFIRMATION

We are under an obligation to explain publicly the reasons for
our existence, the actions and propaganda we are carrying out
throughout the country, and the goal we aim at in our advance
along the true road, free from unconditional collaborationism with
the system but steadfast in affirmation of socialism.

We campaigners for Socialist Affirmation, conscious of our duty
and of our history as workers and socialists, have never harbored
either treason or idols to darken our consciences or govern our
words when we accuse and condemn.

Socialism is action. It cannot compromise before the suffering of
the people, and the moment has come to write a clean chapter of
history for the generation that will soon replace us; to give it an
inheritance free from the present confusion in which the
organizational profile can hardly be distinguished from other
political organizations of capitalist origin.

We want to be heard.

We don't want to fall into the ridiculous and barren pit of obsti-
nacy. But neither do we believe there are persons so stupid as to
believe they have a divine warrant to think for others, when nature
has endowed all human beings with comprehension and discern-
ment—precious faculties which, placed rationally at the service of
men and peoples, will save the world from the menace of privilege.

Such, in short, is the road we have taken toward our goal.

Our Origin

It is contiguous with the legitimate class struggle and the beginning of the social question.

The fierce campaigns against industrial tyranny and all its dire consequences; the unification of labor on the basis of craft and professional unions, to lend personality to work and prestige to the worker; the raising of unmistakable leaders for the producing masses; these were and are the lath and plaster of our origin.

Our existence is not the product of a mad adventure; it is in harmony with the need of these forward-marching times for a new society, whose arrival a small privileged group wants to delay, to the detriment of the manifest majority.

The best justification of our existence would be violation of the people's aspirations, in shameful complicity with the mystifiers of socialist ideals which are the foundation stone of labor's cause.

What would become of the peoples without such sparks of rebellion against those who would take advantage of the powers confided to them?

Isn't centralization of power, enforced and vulgar unity, a form of despotism and the basis of all tyranny?

If free inquiry destroyed monopoly of human knowledge by breaking with all conventions, free expression of thought complete its work, to condemn poisoners of the public consciousness, open the door for a sense of responsibility and a democracy and freedom that are more than symbols, and apply honest standards to all men and peoples.

Action

We began this Socialist Affirmation struggle at the moment when stupidity and usurious ambitions tried to destroy our organized life.

We are not speaking of ambitions for jobs. None would deny the right to such ambitions and *como han dicho los ayunos de prestigios y fenicios del ideal,* no. Merely by indulging in adulation we could get the best positions, but we would be making our children eat the bread of shame.

We can't conceive of any convinced socialist who would want the disorder and confusion recently reigning in our party to continue.

Our action is directed against the leaders of the Socialist Party who are running the party's collective interests as if they were private and personal interests.

It is time to ask an accounting from those responsible for our losing 57,000 votes in the recent elections, so that we lost out status as a main party and fell back into third position. To find our why the so-called Free Electoral Pact hasn't been implemented and who—and in exchange for what—assumed the privilege of breaking our Constitution and humiliating our members.

We won't enumerate other flagrant irregularities and abuses of power, nor the unconditional submissions, for all will be exposed in due time to socialist opinion in our country.

Our action was born to head off the catastrophe that has begun taking shape in our collective, stimulated by adulation and licentious passions. This calls for radical remedies since hatred and corruption always begin together.

Only by this cleansing operation can the cry of troubled consciences today be answered as in all justice it deserves.

We affirm this popular demand so that tomorrow we may not be burdened with the consequences of the grave errors we endure today, due to the overbearing absolutism of men who, for one reason or another, have had their heads turned by representative rank or by force. Let us bring back into our collective the free reign of the force of reason and justice, for that is what the interests of the people—and why not say it, our nation—demand.

Colonialism is something that socialism rejects: people in any kind of servitude aspire to complete freedom.

We must aspire to be independent if we want to defend our honor, and make it clear that our dislike of the North Americans isn't a matter of hypocrisy, nor of fear, nor of business.

Only those who have lost all sense of dignity have found something to worry them in our concern about this. They are *franestánicos* whose irresponsibility is to be pitied.

Our position is honorable, and because it is we don't want the least-qualified elements to wreck the ship of our collective which, without the obstacles and deficiencies we have pointed out, was capable of assuring the well-being of our people.

We want to change the direction of our collective because power in the hands of ignorance leads inevitably to the abyss, and the abyss is the negation of every effort for lasting construction.

Conscious perversity yields; ignorance in power resists. That is why we move against pretentious and harmful ignorance.

Clarity in all things is our desire.

Socialism is not an item of merchandise, it is dignity in ascending evolution. That is why our Socialist Affirmation is clarity—so that there may be no doubts or deceptions. And that is our only intention.

For the Island Committee of Socialist Affirmation (members):

Tadeo Rodríguez García: Founding member of Free Federation and Socialist Party; three times Senatorial candidate; an official in many periods of the organization and Party; Delegate to most of the assemblies, conventions and congresses; speaker in all the civic crusades; publicist, writer and propagandist in all the industrial movements and struggles of the country; Chairman of Socialist Affirmation.

Aguedo F. Vargas: Socialist speaker and writer; Secretary of Socialist Section 4 of San Juan; Delegate to the Central Committee of the sections of San Juan and its *barrios*; former Treasurer of Unión Obrera Federada 17983 of San Juan and Delegate to the Party's General Convention, Mayagüez, 1932; Recording Secretary of Socialist Affirmation.

Florencio Cabello: Chairman of Socialist Section 2, Puerta de Tierra; Secretary of Section 74, Barrio Obrero, Secretary and Central Committee member of same; founder and Treasurer of Union 190, Gurabo, and Secretary of Record of 400, San Juan; Delegate to Socialist and FLT conventions since 1900 and founding member of Socialist Party; Vice-Chairman of Socialist Affirmation.

Ramón de Jesús DuPont: Member of Island labor party; editor of *La Vanguardia*; founder of Union 940 waterfront workers; founder of Typographical Union and Secretary of same; Delegate to Second Convention of Typographical Union; Secretary of waterfront-strikers' committee, 1933.

Luis V. Pino: Labor representative and editor of *El Socialista*.

José Soto Rivera: Initiator of workers' and socialist movement in Puerto Rico, especially in Oriente district, having certified the Socialist Party in more than two thirds of the island's communities; Party representative in Supreme Court case against the Executive Secretary of Puerto Rico, Mr. Ramón Siaca Pacheco, to oblige him to accept various community certifications which had been impugned by Union Party of Puerto Rico; founder of Bank of San Juan and of Justicia publishing company; defender of over one thousand lawsuits in strike and electoral cases, all without remuneration; first socialist head of Labor Negotiations; defender of maestro Santiago Iglesias in libel suit brought by José Lora; defender of Bank of San Juan in the famous Sabalier case in which his pleading resulted in the Puerto Rico Supreme Court's reversal of judgment against Iglesias and Bank of San Juan; now Special Investigator for Industrial Commission in Puerto Rico.

Bartolomé Paniagua: Regent and Works Manager of weekly, *Justicia*; founding member of Section 4, San Juan, and Secretary of same; member of board of Directors of Bank of San Juan, later Manager and Chairman of same; Delegate to various labor congresses; Chairman of Typographers' Union; member of Local Elections Board.

Julio Enrique Pantoja: Delegate to Central Committee and active propagandist of FLT and Party.

Nicolas Rodríguez García: Founding Member of FLT and Socialist Party; member of Local Elections Board in all electoral periods; active propagandist of FLT and Party for more than thirty years.

Miguel Bernard Silva: House of Representatives candidate for District 1, San Juan; editor-in-chief of newspaper, *Justicia*; first Chairman of Local Joint Committee, San Juan; Vice-Chairman, Socialist Party; Secretary of Municipal Court, Guayama; member of Local Board, Guayama; Chairman of Socialist Section 4, San Juan.

TERRITORIAL SOCIALIST EXECUTIVE:
DEPOSITION OF FACTS AND OPINION

On January 28, 1934, a large number of bona fide socialists presented before this Territorial Executive Committee a resolution entitled, "Resolution to ask the Territorial Socialist Executive Committee of Puerto Rico that as the supreme authority it proceed to apply the political sanctions prescribed by Section 12 of the Constitution to those elements who are showing disloyalty and treason to our principles, doctrines, and tactics, and joining the enemy in a campaign of defamation, thus cleansing our glorious institution's ranks of undesirable and intractable elements who seek to create internal disturbance and divide us into factions, to the injury and annoyance of those who by our will stand at the head of the party."

Said resolution which forms a part of this document sets forth full and detailed charges of grave political actions committed against the Socialist Party leadership and its most prominent members. As morally and materially responsible authors of such acts the resolution names Tadeo Rodríguez García and Nicolás Rodríguez García, members of Socialist Section 16, Caguas; Luis V. Pino, member of Socialist Section 37, Santurce; Florencio Cabello, member of Socialist Section 74, Barrio Obrero, Santurce; Aguedo F. Vargas, Bartolomé Paniagua, Miguel Bernard Silva and Ramón de Jesús Dupont of the San Juan Socialist Section; José Soto Rivera of the Río Piedras Socialist Section; Julio Enrique Pantoja of Socialist Section 2, Puerta de Tierra. It is requested that the political sanctions prescribed in Section 12 of the Party Constitution be applied to these members.

The proofs are as follows:

In *La Correspondencia de Puerto Rico*, Tadeo Rodríguez García made the following statements:

"We have been informed by a Chamber of Delegates Representative who attended the Socialist Party's Territorial Executive Committee meeting Sunday before last that the Acting Chairman of the political body, Rafael Alonso Torres, attributed the activities throughout the Oriente sugar district against the agreement the Employer-Worker Committee is trying to impose—

to which activities we have given our best cooperation and help—to insidious and perverse origins, lacking the respect and consideration a gentleman should show toward an absent opponent or rival.

"Mr. Alonso's not very scrupulous attitude doesn't surprise us, for apart from the temperamental habits with which his friends and admirers justify his coarse and ill-advised actions, we are aware that Mr. Alonso Torres has suffered one of those tragic and highly dangerous afflictions that occur daily in men with softened brains unable to resist the effects of flattery or accept intelligent, well-aimed criticism.

"Our efforts and position have the backing of that multitude of workers and sincere friends of the people who show their feelings in telegrams and press communications of strong protest. In the face of the weakness and submission of a few government characters tied to the tyrannical capitalist bosses, absentee and resident, who rob and destroy the lives and happiness of Puerto Rico's working people, the hosts of labor stand proudly and valiantly ready for battle, to consummate the work of social, economic and political liberation that their 'leaders' and representatives in government feel too sluggish and unmanned to carry out.

"Labor and Socialist representatives committed in thought and deed to politico-economic ideals can be sure that, whatever our aediles may think about it, our actions will always be contrary to the new bureaucratic enslavement which they would impose on a hapless, trusting, and good people. Our pen and our words will be in the lists against it, revolutionizing consciences and preparing honest workers for rebellion, for the decisive struggle against all aristocracies, including that of labor. We are on a war footing. Our heads are high defending the ideal and the principles that we embraced in youth and swore to defend, if need be, with our lives. There will be no truce or rest. We have a commitment with our conscience, the only altar at which we preside and on which we have placed all the faith of the truly convinced.

"With these declarations we unfurl our fighting flag to all the winds."

In another article Tadeo Rodriguez wrote the following:

"Thirty years ago, at the time of the Puerto Rican proletariat's rebellious explosions, the wealthy and politically happy classes

condemned labor agitators, who, from platform or press denounced the selfish interest of capitalism and defended the
tyrannized working masses, to severe punishment and martyrdom
as disturbing elements, enemies of public order and of the people's
welfare.

"Thirty long years have passed, years of active and ceaseless
struggle to maintain the purity of the principles with which the
great teachers of truth—now old and tired more from the fight than
from the years—knew how to inspire us. And now we confront a
sad and bitter situation. It is not the bureaucrats and trash of
capitalism that anathematize us as enemies of order and of the
people's welfare, but the same men who, for keeping alive in our
hearts the ideals of justice and human redemption, suffered with us
the most vicious persecution.

"Thirty years of waiting! Thirty long years of pain and suffering
to confront the sad, cold spectacle of those men, the same who
agitated from press and platform like brave old soldiers of right
and liberty, cooperating in an errand of compromise and submission with the black masters of yesterday, the irreconcilable enemies
of today and the hangmen of all time.

"Strangest of all, unique in our annals, is the spectacle of Licenciado Coll y Cuchi participating in the 'Committee of Agricultural
Employer-Employee Adjustment'—the workers' most cruel and
inhuman enemy, now the inspirer of machinations being worked
out in the shadow of the people's ignorance and humility in criminal oblivion of their genuine defenders.

"In this evil exercise against workers and campesinos of the
sugar industry, one sees clearly the instinctive propensity of a man
who in his obsession for glory and power has lost awareness of his
identity, wildly assailing all those who keep faith with their ideals
and rebel with dignity for a just cause.

"We would do well to look into the prerogatives and concessions
extended by the federal GOOD GOVERNMENT laws, and above
all to identify, in our next article, who collected the money, who are
the job-hunters, who it is that serve as docile instruments of
vaulting ambitions, who are paid by the enemies of social and
human welfare, and what kind of vacuous pussyfooting has turned
bad people into good and good into bad."

Florencio Cabello made the following statements:

"How is this to be explained? For years companeros have been demanding a shorter work day at all regional and international labor congresses. They were demanding it when industry still wasn't really mechanized, when labor organizations didn't dream of such parliamentary representation as we have today, capable if it likes of imposing real labor legislation. And they demand it now, when federal laws such as the Industrial Recovery Act set a thirty-six-hour work week or six hours a day in the continental United States, with the object of reducing unemployment and gearing wages to higher living costs. How then explain that with the Industrial Recovery Act in their hands those same companeros make and sign, in the name of the organized labor movement, an employer-worker agreement setting a TWELVE-HOUR WORK DAY for sugar workers, with such an illogical wage clause that we know in advance the bosses will laugh at it? And even if it were to work, is the businessman going to wait for sugar to rise or fall to raise his prices as he sees fit?

"Isn't this in itself a crime of high treason? It is. And I am quite certain that seek as they may for a justification they won't find it, unless they resort to sophisms or to the kind of driveling literary extravagances that were put out years ago."

Luis V. Pino said in an "interview":

"So do you think that the leaders of socialism in Puerto Rico have evolved backward and lost the workers' support?"

"This is a strike by agricultural workers who for thirty years have been getting guidance from socialist leaders. When our island's expectations were raised by the auguries of President Roosevelt's clear and deep humanity, those same leaders applauded and told our campesinos that now President Roosevelt and his Congress were giving legal and compulsory form, through the NRA, to the aspirations that the Federación Libre de los Trabajadores (FLT—Free Workers' Federation) of Puerto Rico sowed, watered with tears and fertilized with blood for thirty years.

"Those same leaders told the workers that the hour had at last come to get the eight-hour day, to raise wages to a level of humane remuneration for their work. And they themselves put in writing, in a contract approved at an FLT meeting on December 15, 1933, that no campesino should earn less than two dollars for a six-hour work day.

"And this contract has been repudiated and belied by those same leaders in the agreement they just signed, an agreement for the employers' benefit, not the workers'. In repudiating that, the workers repudiate the leaders and sound the alert for a movement to reorganize the workers' instruments of defense."

Bartolomé Paniagua wrote in part the following:

"This time companero Alonso's performance is so dishonest that the people have most spontaneously rejected him.

Together with companero Prudencio Rivera Martínez he advised the police, in his humaneness, to use tear gas instead of guns against the striking workers. Likewise, these leaders of the island labor movement have recently declared that Mr. Maxwell, general manager of the Guanica plantation, the corporation that most exploits its workers, is an accessible man and a fine gentleman to deal with his workers' affairs."

Ramón de Jesús Dupont published the following article:

"Drop by drop a rain of disgrace has fallen on the shoulders of the pseudomasters of the Puerto Rican labor and socialist movement: the needleworkers' strike in Mayagüez and elsewhere, the Barrio Obrero rent strike, the strike of women workers in the Puerta de Tierra collective, the printers' demand for a raise, the vigorous waterfront workers' strike, other movements crushed at birth, and finally the agricultural strike in which these paladins of treason beat all their own records and were unmasked as false prophets—the strike they tried to break by a trick agreement that will go down in history as an outrage upon the working people after thirty years of struggle for social and economic improvement.

"We therefore advise the working and socialist people that if today we go into battle against the bourgeois system of our chief leaders, we must not lose faith. On the contrary, we must affirm it more than ever, thus showing we are a conscious and prepared body ready at any time for revolutions for justice. We must throw out the false prophets as a healthy example of civic preparation to open the eyes of those who think a people can be betrayed with impunity.

"The spurt of energy of Puerto Rican workers was inevitable. All healthy socialist and proletarian elements are on our side. Let us work to change the prevailing system in our ranks so that we can with full authority change the whole social system of repression."

Río Piedras meeting: The announced meeting of Socialist Affirmation was held last night with a big attendance in that city's public plaza and with these speakers: Florencio Cabello, J. Soto Rivera, Félix Rivera, Licenciado José Segarra, Julio Enrique Pantoja, M. Bernard Silva and Tadeo Rodríguez García.

Florencio Cabello spoke for about an hour on the abnormalities that in his view had to be fought, to save the Socialist Party from the discredit and confusion its Territorial Committee had brought upon it. He said that the FLT and the Socialist Party should be completely separated to stop those whom socialists have put in official positions from sometimes calling themselves representatives of one, sometimes of the other according to personal interests. For example, the Labor Department head, Prudencio Rivera Martínez, says, when it suits him, that he owes his position to the FLT and it has nothing to do with the Party, and at other times that he represents the Party and not the FLT. The speaker ascribed the present situation of general protest, which he said was destroying the collective, to this concentration of powers in the hands of Party leaders. He said he was one of the Party's founders and was not in agreement with it since the coalition with the Republican Party in 1920, an association with a bourgeois reactionary party to which he objected.

Aguedo F. Varga made these comments on the position of the Chairman: That when the pact was made with the Republican Party he had opposed it, and that socialists with advanced ideas were now paying the disastrous price of such practices. He emphatically opposed all Americanization ideas in Puerto Rico and said that they, the socialists, had all along been committing the error of believing in them, but after thirty four years of Yanqui government they had lost faith in that system and now openly favored sovereign and independent government for their country, this being the only form that could make a Puerto Rican Socialist Republic possible later. He condemned the colonial system that turned workers into serfs and slaves of capitalism and said that they would from now on support the constitution of a free and independent Puerto Rican republic.

Soto Rivera spoke and argued for the urgent need of defining Puerto Rico's political status, and said they would oppose their old leader Santiago Iglesias for having presented a petition for Puerto Rican statehood to the U.S. Congress. Explaining the motives of the protest they were drawing up, he said they disagreed with the present Socialist Party leadership mainly for having signed a sugar agreement that was shameful for the workers of Puerto Rico.

He condemned as unjust the demand by his companero Alonso Torres that they (the Socialist Affirmation leaders) should be immediately expelled from the party with no opportunity to defend themselves against the charges, contrary to the democratic practices that should prevail in all socialist labor movements. He asked the immediate removal of Alonso Torres to save Puerto Rican socialism, and said they would fight tirelessly with protest meetings throughout the island to oblige the socialist leadership to hold an assembly, at which they would nominate someone more competent and capable to lead the Socialist Party.

Another meeting, in Río Piedras, called by Socialist Affirmation leaders:

Julio Enrique Pantoja: To his compañeros' applause he analyzed the Socialist Party's present political situation with respect to the understanding with the Republicans. The wedding celebrated between them in Mayagüez had made a complete mockery of the Socialist Party; far from protesting and demanding the Party's rights, the leaders of the collective had joined the enemy, electricity monopolists like Mr. Valdés, turning against the recent popular movements to follow the bourgeois line that these people wanted to impose on the Party. He said it was shameful that socialist legislators were now too busy fawning on the bourgeoisie to be able to pass a workers' compensation law.

Tadeo Rodríguez García: He outlined the present Socialist Party situation in a moderate speech, pointing out errors that FLT and Party leaders were making; he said the rebel movement would have repercussions throughout the country and that its leaders were not motivated by personal feelings against anyone . . .

Additional excerpts from the periodical press also form part of the proof of charges against the accused in this case, as follows:

a. Article in *El Imparcial* headlined: "Will Set Up on Monday Socialist Left Wing Opposing Party Chairman and Calling for New Political Body."

b. A "Manifesto for Socialist Affirmation" published in *Unión Obrera* for January 1934, containing a general criticism of Socialist Party procedures and urging independence for Puerto Rico and a change of Party leadership.

Thus far do we have the proof of charges of press propaganda, in some cases under the signatures, authority, and responsibility of all and each of the accused, in others merely editorial reports putting in their mouths declarations, detractions, criticisms, and attacks against the Socialist Party, the Territorial Executive Committee and more especially its Acting Chairman. We must accept these as authentic and that their authors take responsibility for their words, since they have not been denied or refuted nor has any proof to such effect been presented.

In connection with all this, written proof, has been submitted tending to show that in the recent agricultural strike, a labor activity quite apart from politics, the elements comprising the Socialist Affirmation group made their hostile propaganda against the person of Rafael Alonso Torres, General Secretary of the FLT of Puerto Rico, who is also Acting Chairman of the Socialist Party, and against other officials, as the following telegram shows:

"Canóvanas, January 12, 1934: Hon. Rafael Alonso Torres, Free Federation. San Juan.—Meeting held agricultural workers Carolina theater. Luis V. Pino requested guarantee from local Police Chief to enter meeting hall, accusing Luis Pérez Peña, Colón Gordiany, and Eduardo Méndez as dangerous elements carrying revolvers to use against him. Luis V. Pino and Florencio Cabello advised workers walk out meeting hall and not consider agreement selling out and manacling agricultural workers. Tadeo Rodriguez Garcia spoke workers characterizing agreement as indecent and servile because sells out agricultural workers to voracity of capitalist wolves and associated politicians. Félix Rivera didn't cooperate with commission of which he formed part advising workers ignore our explanations. Pérez Peña, Colón Gordiany, and Mendez fully explained significance and scope of agreement. Workers by majority agreed maintain strike. Commission informed them Free Federation declined responsibility for future developments since its local leaders don't legitimately represent it.—José A. Salva, Representative.''

All the above clear and trustworthy proofs, conceived, written, and propagated in newspapers and on platforms in plain, harsh, and biting language, deliberately and maliciously designed to create discredit, dishonor, and distaste for the highest organ of the Socialist Party collectively and personally, leaves no doubt, when dispassionately considered, that the accused in the present political case, who make up the guiding group of Socialist Affirmation, stand convicted and guilty, beyond all reasonable doubt, of flagrant violation of the principles, doctrines, tactics, and procedures established by our Constitution for the observance, guidance, and government of all socialists whatever their position and hierarchy in the Party.

Sentence

For the reasons and causes set forth in ''Deposition of Facts and Opinion in the Case,'' which forms an integral part of this sentence, the Territorial Executive Committee of the Socialist Party of Puerto Rico, assembled in extraordinary session on this night of February 8, and having a quorum, agreed by the unanimous vote of all present to declare the members of Socialist Affirmation guilty of the charges of ''Disloyalty and High Treason to the Socialist Party of Puerto Rico'' and to expel the said accused from the Party.

Given in San Juan, P.R., under the Party seal, on the 8th day of the month of February of 1934.

THIRD CGT CONGRESS
REPORT BY SECRETARY GENERAL
JUAN SAEZ CORALES (EXCERPTS)

San Juan, March 1945

Five years have passed since we Puerto Rican workers opened a new chapter in the history of our people's social struggles. Five years since the Confederación General de Trabajadores (CGT— General Confederation of Workers) emerged as the outstanding fighter for the liberation of Puerto Rican workers. Five years since CGT brought new methods and tactics of struggle into the organized labor movement. The failures of the old labor movement showed us the need for new standards of organization. The Statement of Causes for Creating a Single Workers' Trade Union Council, which was the ideological basis for CGT, made a clear and specific analysis of all the faults leading to the collapse of the old Free Federation. One of its paragraphs said:

"The relationship between the Socialist Party and the FLT was of great importance in the past, and in studying it we can find the explanation of the FLT's present condition. Labor Department agents became workers' representatives who abrogated the functions of the Union, weakening it as a workers' organization. Its locals have been transformed into organs extraneous to the struggle, workers' organized into officials of the Department of Labor. Attempts were made to resolve labor conflicts not through the struggle of workers and their unions but through the Department's bureaucratic machinery. Thus unions have not been able to advance their cause because the bureaucratic machinery prevented it, and it can only be done when a union operates on the principles of worker democracy."

The successes of CGT have been largely due to the introduction of democratic practices. These have been made evident in the practice of membership discussion of their problems so that leaders may put the majority view into effect. And to arouse and maintain workers' confidence in the new organization it was resolved at the foundation of CGT that no local or insular leader could discuss with employers any matter concerning the workers unless accompanied by a committee of workers affected by the problem. By such practices, breaking with old and bad ones and introducing new and good ones, CGT has gained the workers* confidence.

Labor Unity

The CGT of Puerto Rico is the base and center for unity of the Puerto Rican working class. We, its responsible leaders, have always been conscious that the working class should be united under one banner and one organization, with one program aimed at one goal. Working-class unity is the prime objective of a movement oriented by genuine labor practices. Thus, CGT has always been and is now concerned that Puerto Rican workers should achieve unity. Today, most of the workers are united under the CGT banner, but that isn't enough. It is necessary and indispensable that all Puerto Rican workers should form one labor organization as the best guarantee for our class. Division in the workers' ranks only benefits their exploiters. Until now the efforts made to unite Puerto Rican workers have failed due to the unfortunate intrusion of politicking. But these unsuccessful efforts should be our guide in developing better plans for unifying the Puerto Rican working class.

But in doing this CGT must bear in mind and measure correctly its real worth and significance, lest we fall victim to badly oriented elements who know how to use great slogans for small ends. We must insist on our aim of unity, but must be ever more vigilant to prevent anyone from spoiling the ideal of one powerful Puerto Rican labor organization. The employers and their agents are enemies of working-class unity. We must not be trapped by the maneuvers of employers and their agents to destroy the possibility of unity under one fighting banner. Let us go forward uniting the workers until the glorious day when the workers, instead of fighting among themselves, fight as one against the enemies of our class. (Applause.)

The Labor Movement and Politics

It is more than ever necessary today that we speak clearly about the labor movement and politics. CGT has from the outset taken a correct position on this important issue.

The declaration of principles that gave birth to CGT stated clearly and specifically that although labor organizations are highly political bodies, they should at the same time be organizations with no party banner. It is timely to quote an eloquent paragraph from the Statement of Causes written by the Chauffeurs' Association in its call for a new Unión Central in Puerto Rico. Referring to the tough question of the labor movement and politics, the call made in 1940 poses the following basic principles:

"One of the greatest weaknesses in recent years of the FLT vis-a-vis the employer class has been the indifference to the class struggle and to a formal program for the solution of labor problems. Not denying the significance of political actions undertaken with great difficulties—for reasons obvious to the workers—through the Socialist Party, the character of unions as nonparty-banner organizations needs clarifying. Unions are organizations of all workers without distinction of political belief. They participate in all struggles on the working class's and people's behalf. They fight every political measure that hurts their interests. But they are not partisans, that is, they carry no political party's flag nor embrace any political-party struggle that might break or weaken their unity. The strength of unions is their members, and they should think as members of the exploited class, as workers and as an integral unit."

We quote this correct orientation from the chauffeurs' call for creation of a General Confederation of Workers of Puerto Rico, because there is now more need than ever to avoid the disorientations and false trails in the labor movement.

We have always sought in our struggle to concentrate on the basic principle that labor organizations are and should be essentially political. This is one of the positions responsible for the rapid and strong growth of CGT. Thus CGT holds that there is no problem in Puerto Rico that doesn't concern it. But this is just why it has kept its independence of action as an organized workers' movement. Puerto Rico has no problems that don't concern the workers;

the world has no problems that don't concern the workers; we workers are interested in all of Puerto Rico's problems and all of the world's problems. Thus we fulfill an essentially political role and it is for this reason that we don't want to and shouldn't be the tail of any political party. (Prolonged applause.)

Tendencies in the Puerto Rican Labor Movement

In our organized labor movement two wrong tendencies have always existed. The first is the attempt to make it a dependency of specific parties; the second is the cry of alarm because labor organizations have nothing to do with politics. Both are wrong, the first, because the movement should be no political party's tail or passive instrument if it is to do its job of organizing workers. The second, because while it is true that the movement shouldn't be the tail of a party, it is no less true that the workers and our organizations have to be essentially political—ready and able to defend any political measure of benefit to them and to condemn any that harms them. Consequently the movement needs to be on guard against politicking and politicos who try to speculate with the workers' power for ends that are not ours. (Applause.)

As we said in introducing these remarks about the labor movement and politics, this is the position that CGT has maintained ever since it was founded to follow a genuine labor line in the sense of not being like party organizations. This is the line with respect to politics which is followed by all labor organizations throughout the world.

CGT and Puerto Rican Political Status

As we are talking about the political role of workers' organizations, we can't omit the most serious of the political problems confronted by our people. Now more than ever this basic problem is being debated both in the island and in the United States. I refer to the political "status" of Puerto Rico, a problem that our working class cannot and should not ignore. It needs discussion by workers and their organizations without evasions of any kind. The Puerto Rican labor movement has, till now, taken an attitude of indifference toward solution of the "status" problem. It has limited itself to occasional stammerings in resolutions to the effect that the problem should be resolved.

But Puerto Rican labor organizations still haven't faced up to the fact that the fight against colonialism and for national liberation is the fundamental duty of the movement

While the labor movement throughout America discusses the colonial problem of Puerto Rico, and some of the biggest CIO unions have passed resolutions demanding Puerto Rican independence at their conventions, the Puerto Rican movement remains silent.

The Puerto Rican movement has the responsibility to probe deeply into the "status" question, because it is we workers who most directly suffer the consequences of colonial exploitation. As a colony we bear the brunt of all the adverse ups and downs of U.S. intervention policies, and have been submitted to the economic convenience of American monopolies which have blocked every effort to industrialize Puerto Rico. Our people will never be able to move toward reaping the benefit of its own wealth as long as it wears the colonial chain. Tied to the compulsory market of the United States, we will have no chance of molding our economic, political, and social life. For that reason the working class cannot remain indifferent to this vital problem of our people. Puerto Ricans cannot talk of economic freedom without at the same time setting out to win our political freedom. While the laws approved by our Legislature remain subject to approval by a Governor not elected by our people, appointed by the U.S. President with the American Senate's consent, we will lack stable guarantees to continue the advance of the economic-justice program that is now being put into effect in Puerto Rico.

Fortunately, Governor Tugwell has been a friend of the Puerto Ricans and friendly to the Partido Democrático Popular's (PDP— Popular Democratic Party's) economic program. But if a reactionary Governor were in his place, an enemy of our people, we would risk destruction of the gains won in recent years. While Puerto Rico has no opportunity to enter world markets freely, and while the

U.S. Congress has power to annul our laws, our fate will be subject to changes in American politics and we will live under conditions imposed on our country by exploiting interests. To keep this insecure situation from continuing and our fate from being controlled by forces alien to our interests, we Puerto Ricans have a moral obligation to fight for Puerto Rico's independence. To fight for the establishment of our own sovereignty. To defend our own culture. We want to continue speaking Spanish and living under the sun of our land, in peace and friendship with the people of the United States. We don't want to continue as an enslaved nation amid the free nations of the world. The Puerto Rican labor movement must orient itself better and fight more determinedly for national liberation. (Applause.)

The workers cannot view the struggle for freedom as someone else's business. In the struggle for Puerto Rico's freedom the labor movement should march in the vanguard of our people until colonial exploitation is swept away and Puerto Rican sovereignty established with economic guarantees for the whole population.

In the very moment when this Congress meets, Senator Tyding's independence project is being discussed in the American Congress, and Representative Vito Marcantonio is preparing to present a Puerto Rican independence bill in the U.S. House of Representatives. CGT should not be indifferent to these projects, for our future is bound up in them. We must get to know, study, and discuss them, suggest amendments, and help make the law recognizing our freedom worthy of future generations.

Humanity is living through an age of world revolution and the people of Puerto Rico should act on the high level that these decisive times demand.

I therefore propose that the program of CGT include a clause declaring the struggle for Puerto Rico's independence to be among the basic aims of CGT. (Applause.)

For Working-Class Consciousness

To conclude this report I want to mention something we have all seen in this Third CGT Congress. The fact has been palpably demonstrated here that we leaders of the Puerto Rican labor movement haven't paid enough attention to the development of a firm worker consciousness. Our shortcomings in this have exposed our unions and our leaders to confusion by divisive elements who seek a foothold in the labor movements.

This Third CGT Congress should be especially concerned to develop a worker consciousness immune to the confusion of opportunist politicians and conscienceless employers. We must create a consciousness that enables every organized worker to distinguish between labor interests and nonlabor interests.

To make possible the development of a worker ideology we must expand and improve our newspaper.

We also need to set up as soon as possible a genuine workers' school, extending from end to end of the island.

To cooperate more effectively in national liberation, and to win the total emancipation of the workers of Puerto Rico, we must shoulder the duty that cannot be postponed—to guide, direct, and educate the Puerto Rican working class. (Prolonged applause.)

Twenty-Five Years of Struggle
My Reply to Persecution
Juan Sáez Corales
(1955)

The decade of the 1930s in Puerto Rico was a time of uncertainty and despair. The three main political groups had lost their significance in terms of the kind of life they had represented. The hacienda social structure represented by the Partido Union (Union Party) was totally bankrupt. The hope of a new modern order, which the Americans were to introduce according to the early Republican Party, was trodden under the foot of U.S. colonial policy.[1] Finally the Partido Socialista Puertorriqueño (PSP— Puerto Rican Socialist Party), the party of the workers, had fallen into a simple economism, burying the hope of a radically different social order.

The life of Juan Sáez Corales in those years is a life of struggle to keep the masses struggling, fighting together to break the spell of despair. Thus the unemployed marches and the buttonmakers', longshoremen's and salt miners' strikes, in which Sáez played an outstanding part, sowed seeds and spirit for creation in March 1940 of the new, hopeful, labor organization, CGT.

The 1940s present another kind of struggle. At the end of the 1930s a second generation of *hacendado* bourgeoisie—born when the hacienda social structure was crumbling and their class had lost its political and economic hegemony—had begun to evolve a more radical ideology. (Many of them were in the liberal professions, mostly teaching). With strong roots in hacienda traditions and culture this group retained the political support of hacienda workers and small farmers and campesinos, but is new ideology and new secondary social position made possible an alliance with the important proletarian sector which, tired of the decadent and hollow[2] political organ of its own class began mustering around CGT.[3] This alliance was the Partido Popular Democrático (PPD—Popular Democratic Party), which won the November 1940 elections [4] with a program of opposition to the evils and injustices of economic and political colonialism, represented in Puerto Rico by the power of the big U.S. sugar concerns.

The 1940s are years of struggle between these two allies of the decade's early years. Years in which this second *hacendado*-bourgeoisie generation finds, in a kind of industrialization, a new base for social hegemony[5] (and in the process opens the way to a new commercial and manufacturing colonialism). Years too, in which the working class, weathered in plantation battles, weakens before a new structural situation.

In those hard years, Juan Sáez Corales's life stands out as one of militant proletarian struggle, of which his imprisonment in 1954 marks the end. The end for a time, for a few years . . . for the Puerto Rican working class is regaining its strength and beginning to demonstrate in its struggles the desire for a Puerto Rico of true social democracy.

My name is Juan Sáez Corales. I am the second of five children. I was born on December 8, 1915. I came into the world in the rural *barrio,* Sabana Grande Abajo, in the city of San Germán. My father is Francisco Sáez Báez. My mother is Lucia Corales Báez. Both my father and my mother are poor campesinos. Neither knows how to read or write.

I Was One of the Sad Children

When I was born my parents lived as tenants of a rich landlord of my pueblo. My father worked as an agricultural laborer, especially in cane field jobs. My mother did domestic work. She has done it all her life.

My parents moved to Retiro, another village near San Germán, when I was still very small. They went there to "seek their fortune," but the family's precarious economy didn't change; they went on being tenants. The only difference was that they had a new "master." My father continued as a field worker, my mother looking after the kids in the house. "Stuck for life to the stove," as she says. But on many days the stove she stuck to was cold. Meanwhile she prayed to God to let her get some food for her children.

During the First World War food was dear and scanty. Money was scantier. In those days of my childhood there was a lot of poverty. Hunger and tapeworms make kids sad and taciturn. I was one of the sad kids.

After the privations of the war came the ordeal of the earthquakes. When they happened I was three. The picture of my mother kneeling in the plantation yard stays engraved in my mind. I am in the middle of the room. The floor and ceiling were of palm fronds and bark. The hut sways like a hammock. The shaking of the house and my mother's supplications daze me. Everyone is in despair.

After the quakes came the flu. The epidemic killed many people. All the calamities had fallen on the poor. I recall the lines of a *jíbaro* song of that time which summed things up like this.

First the war,
Then the quakes,
Then the flu,
Don't talk about loving . . .

Such was the setting of my first years. There was no peace or happiness in them. I didn't have proper food. I had no toys. The fun and spirit of childhood were strangers to me.

All My Dreams of Studying Were Dashed

When I was seven my family moved to the town. We went to live in my maternal grandfather's house. My father got an ox cart. It held the family and all our household goods. I remember my sensation of seeing a march-past of trees from the cart as it rolled along. We reached the town at night. For the first time I saw electric lighting. I was astounded. I thought I was dreaming.

My parents made this move because they wanted their kids to go to school. And we went. Meanwhile my father went on working in the cane fields during the harvest. In winter he worked on construction jobs. He did all kinds of odd jobs to get our daily bread, and managed to keep us in school till I got to sixth grade. I was thirteen. The family was in such a bad way that I had no clothes or shoes. Often I went to school without any breakfast. Other times we ate once a day. Our poverty got so bad that when I finished sixth grade I had to leave school. All my dreams of studying were dashed. I wanted to be a doctor, but at thirteen I had to go with my father to work from sunup to sundown in the cane fields. To spread fertilizer and seed and cut cane.

Cutting Cane I Found the Labor Movement

My parents are devout Catholics. They engraved their religious feelings on me. At that time I went often to church. I prayed a lot. I asked God to do something about our poverty, but my prayers got no results. Things just got worse all the time. This made me think that there are so many of us poor people, and we have so many problems, that God can't solve them all by himself. I thought seriously about the precept, "God helps those who help themselves." I began to see that religious fervor wasn't enough. It seemed to me that the poor had to get together and ask the employers and government for a better life.

So it was that I got interested in the Socialist Party's talk about social justice, and enthusiastic about organizing into unions. I didn't hesitate to join a group of sugar workers who were forming a union. Working as a cane cutter I made my first contact with the labor movement. I was fourteen then.

We Didn't Earn Enough to Eat

Between 1928 and 1932 the economic crisis bore down on us. There was little work to be had. No place to earn a peseta. In my town all the workers were in bad shape. Most of the families took to needlework to stay alive. Needlework in the home was the thing then. My family also took it up.

My mother and father, all my brothers and I, spent the whole day and part of the night embroidering handkerchiefs and blouses. Then I really saw how the poor are exploited. Working day and night my family didn't earn enough for three meals a day. We could hardly manage rice and beans once a day. Sometimes we couldn't even afford that luxury and had to make do with black coffee and stale bread. In that situation disease naturally fed on poverty. The thousand ailments produced by hunger and poverty fell upon the door. My family was a disaster area. They all fell sick. My youngest sister, aged three, died. I have always believed that physical enfeeblement caused by hunger was responsible.

I was also very sick. I got typhus and hovered between life and death. My lank hair fell out. I was bald as a billiard ball. After a while my head began to sprout the curly and rebellious hair I've had ever since. After the typhus I got malaria, cold and hot fevers every day. I had frequent pains in the stomach. As if that wasn't enough I had a cataleptic attack that made me like dead for some hours. They began getting ready to bury me but luckily I revived in time . . . Those impressions are never forgotten.

At Fifteen I Felt Old and Exhausted

Such were the conditions in which I entered puberty. Thus passed my youth, leaving me no happy memory. When I look back I see nothing but melancholy and desolation.

At fifteen I felt old and exhausted. It seems paradoxical but now, at thirty nine, I am younger and feel happier than when I was fifteen. At that time I had lost the ability to laugh. Solemn and sad, I dragged along. It was around then that I started working with my father on occasional construction jobs. Meanwhile I was looking for steady work but couldn't find it. Finally I got a job as messenger and servant in the home of a rich family. They fed me and paid me four dollars a month.   My yearning to study, to know, never left me. I wanted to go back to school. One day I decided to say so to my employer. I will never forget how she reacted. She said: "What do you want to study for? You'll never be any more than you are now." In spite of my disappointment I persevered. I finally persuaded her to let me go to school while I continued working for her. While I went to school I worked. I had the good luck to finish seventh and eighth grades in one year. I couldn't go any further. There my school studies ended. My secondary school and university have been life itself.

I Finally Found a Logical Explanation of the World

While I was in eighth grade I got acquainted with some tobacco workers. One of them received labor publications. He also received Marxist books. Thus awareness dawned in me that we live in a society divided into two basic classes, workers and capitalists. I began to understand social and economic phenomena. I acquired a clear explanation of what caused the workers' poverty.

I achieved a grasp of why a minority in society is enormously rich while the overwhelming majority, we the workers, are poor. I realize that the society we live in is founded on the exploitation of man by man. Finally, I had a logical explanation of our world. Now I no longer felt helpless as before. I learned to know that the economic and social ills of the working class are not beyond remedy.

And it was then that I saw light about the colonial problem of Puerto Rico. I could explain the relationship between Puerto Rico and the United States. I saw how colonial exploitation doubles the people's poverty and how the imperialist corporations exploit Puerto Rico. I became convinced than an independent Puerto Rico would be better off.

I clearly understood that the workers are the decisive force in society. They build everything. They produce the wealth but live in penury. I learned that the working class is weak only because it is divided. I saw that if it united to demand its rights as it does to produce profits, it would never be defeated.

Then too I learned that there was a country, formerly called Russia and now the Soviet Union, where the workers ruled and man's exploitations by man didn't exist.

I noted that the Puerto Rican Socialist Party, once militant and combative, had allied itself with the Republican Party and no longer properly represented the workers' interests. The Socialist Party had taken the capitalist road.

I heard that a working-class party called the Communist Party was being organized in Puerto Rico. I joined the group in San German that was working for formation of that workers' and campesinos' party. Since then I have been a militant fighter for the progress and well-being of the working class. Since then I have fought for the independence of Puerto Rico.

Fighting in the Trenches of the Workers

In 1934 I left San Germán. My desire for broader horizons took me to San Juan. I joined the struggle to organize and reorient the labor movement.

From 1934 to 1938 I took part in various sugarworkers' button-makers', waterfront and saltmine workers' strikes, and in organizing and mobilizing the unemployed. I steered the unemployed struggle for work and social security. I was elected Island Chairman of the Unemployed Protective Union. As chairman I led, in 1939, the Hunger March on San Juan. Thousands of unemployed from all over the island joined in that great demonstration.

From 1935 to 1940 I participated in many labor and political activities. Those were years of great social and political agitation in Puerto Rico. The independence movement had a great boom. Luis Muñoz Marín was saying then that independence was just around the corner.

Events occurred, like the Ponce massacre, that stirred the whole world. The Winship governorship kindled popular anger. Winship was blatantly imposing on Puerto Rico the colonial schemes of Yanqui imperialism. For the first time the Partido Nacionalista (Nationalist Party) leadership was brought to trial and jailed. The jailing was ordered by the U.S. Government. The leaders were tried by the U.S. Federal Court in Puerto Rico and went to serve their terms in U.S. prisons.

The Congress for Political Prisoners was organized. I was part of it. That was when I first met Luis Muñoz Marín. He was a sponsor of the Political Prisoners' Freedom movement along with the present rector of the University of Puerto Rico, Jaime Benítez, the present Senate Chairman, Samuel R. Quiñones, and other personalities of today's government. I fought at their side for that noble cause.

Later Muñoz Marín organized Independentist Social Action. In speeches and articles the present Governor* supported the independence of Puerto Rico. Muñoz and ourselves were together then in a common struggle for independence.

The social and political struggles of that decade culminated in two events: in the political field, organization of the Popular Democratic Party; in the labor field, organization of the CGT of Puerto Rico.

The Constituent Congress of CGT took place on March 31, 1940. I was a delegate to that Congress. From 1941 to 1945 I was Secretary General of CGT.

CGT became a great organized force of industrial and agricultural workers. It led big strikes and won a notable improvement of wages and working conditions. With CGT the collective contract became general practice.

* As of 1955.—*Translator's note.*

They Offered Me the Sub-Commissionership of Labor

As Secretary of CGT I chaired the Sugar Strike during the 1942 general strike of workers in that industry. That same year I was a member, representing the workers, of the Special Committee of the Minimum Wage Board which studied the sugar industry and recommended minimum wages and conditions. Out of that came a minimum wage scale for sugar workers.

After the sugar strike of 1942 was won, I was offered the Sub-Commissionership of Labor. I didn't accept. I believed I could serve the working class better as CGT Secretary General. I interpreted the Sub-Commissionership offer as a bribe. I preferred to renounce the pleasant four hundred dollars-a-month salary which went with that post to continue earning fifteen dollars a week as CGT Secretary General. My fight has always been to help resolve the problem of the working class in general. When that is solved, my problems will be solved.

After I had turned down the Sub-Commissionership of Labor, many CGT leaders started being nominated to small government posts.

Opportunism Hoists the CGT Banner

After the 1942 sugar strike the PPD government began fighting to prevent an independent labor movement. To get control of CGT it used two methods: nominating CGT leaders for public office and pushing local PPD leaders into key labor positions.

The scenario was that anyone wanting to be a mayor, representative, or senator started by waving the labor banner. The CGT banner was raised by many opportunists to achieve public office. At the same time, arguments were raised within CGT against political participation by the labor movement. Thus CGT fell into a purely and simply economistic position.

We have to recognize that we lacked vision then to measure in time the size of the problem. When we began realizing the damage that economism did to CGT, it was too late.

Licenciado Ernesto Ramos Antonini, who is now Chairman of

the House of Representatives, had also erected himself as a labor leader. He headed the gang of opportunists who had invaded CGT in quest of governmental promotions and public office. While preaching against politics in the labor movement he used the trade-union organization for opportunist politicking. Ernesto Ramos Antonini can never wipe off the stain of personal and direct responsibility for the confusion and division now rampant in the labor movement. But we have to admit that our ingenuousness and lack of political vision contributed to this.

The Government Succeeded in Dividing CGT

In March 1945, to the misfortune of the Puerto Rican working class CGT split. The division of the labor movement resulted from the government policy of heading off a united and nonparty movement that would effectively represent working-class interests.

From 1945 till now the Muñoz Marín government has continued dividing the labor movement. The government has put the brakes on workers' struggles, while at the same time favoring the transformation of labor unions into employer organizations.

I Joined the Army

Shortly after the CGT split in 1945, my compulsory military service deferral was withdrawn. I had been deferred because of my position in the labor movement. I went into the army. Two months later I was transferred out of Puerto Rico, to serve as a soldier at the Santa Lucía Military Base. It was necessary to put a healthy distance between the labor movement and one of the men who hadn't let himself be bribed so as to complete the dismemberment of CGT with the fewest possible obstacles. In this way political maneuvering put me in the U.S. Army.

Convinced of the importance of defeating fascism, I served honorably in the armed forces. On May 28, 1946, I was honorably discharged with the rank of sergeant.

The UGT Was Founded

On my return from the army CGT was completely split. There were two factions, the government one headed by Ernesto Ramos Antonini and the other—known as the Authentic CGT—headed by Francisco Colón Gordiany. Two lawyers had stayed with what remained of CGT. There were many independent unions, a new lineup that made clear the tragedy of the labor movement.

Before my army discharge I was unanimously elected Secretary General of the Authentic CGT at a congress in Mayagüez. Once discharged, I was offered the Secretary-Generalship of the Governmental CGT. I must confess that at this point I didn't know how to size up the situation correctly. I made the error of declining leadership of both organizations. I made it a condition for my acceptance that they should unite, and this they didn't accept.

I began organizing the CGT Unity Committee. I was its chairman. The efforts for unity were blocked by leaders of both groups. The Committee basically consisted of leaders of unions that had disaffiliated from CGT groups. I made the mistake of depending on the leadership and not having enough discussion with and orientation from the union rank and file.

The CGT Unity Committee finally called a Unity Congress, which met on September 28, 1947. At that Congress the Unidad General de Trabajadores (UGT—General Workers' Unity) was founded and I was elected its Secretary-General.

I think the organization of UGT was a bad mistake, for it resulted in another split in the labor movement.

When UGT was founded, the U.S. Congress had approved the disgraceful, enslaving Taft-Hartley Act. The Act applied also to Puerto Rico. All the country's labor organizations meekly accepted it. Only UGT took a militant stance against its application to Puerto Rico.

Militant Struggle Against the Fascist Taft-Hartley Act

For three years, UGT fought the application of Taft-Hartley to Puerto Rico. The fight ended with strikes in which the workers showed their militant spirit. Two of these strikes—those of the Santurce construction workers and of the Ponce candy workers—were exceptionally militant.

The Santurce construction-workers' strike lasted several weeks. The state used all its repressive force to break it. Strikers were jailed and labor leaders harassed, but the workers won.

The Ponce candy-workers' strike lasted nearly two months. Strikers were beaten up and dozens jailed. In cooperation with the employers, the police and the Board created by Taft-Hartley set up a procedure to put strikebreakers in the factory. In this strike-breaking performance the Government CGT, then led by Senator Ramón Berreto Pérez, participated. The employers formed an Employers Union with the strikebreakers. The National Labor Relations Board (NLRB) recognized the Employers Union.

The Board held elections among the strikebreakers from which striking workers were excluded, and certified the Employers Union as the negotiating body.

The Ponce candy workers who had fought heroically were defeated by the power of the Board created under the fascist Taft-Hartley law, and the power of the police.

UGT Complied with Taft-Hartley Requirements

The employers and the NLRB joined, after these strikes, in a scheme to crush UGT. They succeeded in making UGT comply with Taft-Hartley. They compelled some unions to break away from UGT. They used the argument of anti-communism to confuse and deceive the workers. They said UGT was illegal because it hadn't complied with Taft-Hartley. And at its Congress on January 28, 1951, in the Santurce Construction-Workers' Hall, UGT resolved to change its line and comply.

At that Congress I resigned as Secretary-General of UGT.

The Divided Labor Movement and the Employers' Paradise

Thus the government made hay of a situation in which the Puerto Rican organized-labor movement was divided into seven central unions and numerous independent unions. None of these organizations can put up an effective fight by itself in defense of working-class interests. None can fight effectively against the shameful enslavement of Taft-Hartley.

The leadership of the various labor organizations has taken a legalistic and complacent stance toward the requirements of the Labor Department and the National Labor Relations Board.

Thus has been created an employers' paradise in which mechanization goes freely ahead without guarantees for the workers. The sold-out labor leadership tried to crush the workers' struggle and their protests against mechanization.

Puerto Rico's so-called industrialization is built on cheap labor. The government guarantees that labor will continue cheap, deepening the splits in the labor movement.

The CIO and AF of L have been imported into Puerto Rico to colonize the labor movement. Those organizations serve the purpose of the Puerto Rican government and American employers who come to Puerto Rico to pile up more wealth. But the workers' fighting spirit has not been strangled. They maintain their militancy despite the sell-out of the labor leadership. This is shown by the recent strikes of waterfront-, transport-, sugar-, and other workers.

They Want to Drown Every Protesting Voice

Now they want to drown every voice of working-class protest. To paralyze and destroy the struggle for Puerto Rican independence. This is why the government of Puerto Rico ordered our imprisonment in October 1950 on the charge of advocating force and violence.

We spent some days in jail and were then freed. There was no possible proof of the false charges against us. We were exonerated.

A New Attempt to Slaughter Us Legally Failed

On March 7, 1954, the government of Puerto Rico ordered us jailed again. We were accused of violating Law 53, known as the "Gag Law." This is the Puerto Rican equivalent of the fascist Smith Act. They set our bail at $25,000.

For some weeks Licenciado Pablo M. García, Juan Santos Rivera, and I went around explaining to workers and people the injustice they wanted to commit against us.

We were arrested on April 18, 1954, and put in the Island Presidio. But after five days there we were exonerated of the vicious charge, and they let us go.

Public opinion and the solidarity of the world labor movement were decisive factors in getting us out. The attempt to slaughter Puerto Rico legally failed.

Fighting Against the Crime of War

I have taken an active part in struggles to preserve world peace. I have joined my efforts with those of men and women in Puerto Rico who fight to free humanity from the havoc of war.

I denounced the sending of Puerto Rican soldiers to die on Korean battlefields. The tragic balance sheet of Puerto Rican dead and wounded in that exercise in rapine by Yanqui imperialism should be an example and lesson to our people on war's criminal futility.

My struggle is to help avoid the devastation of humanity in an atomic, hydrogen, and bacteriological holocaust.

U.S. imperialism, which has turned Puerto Rico into a naval and military base, seeks to crush the struggle for peace by jailing us who condemn the crime of war.

Twenty-Five Years of Struggle for Progress of the Working Class

I was a member of the Executive Committee of the Puerto Rican Independence Congress.

I was an independent labor candidate in the elections for the so-called Constituent Assembly, where the Free Associated State of Puerto Rico was set up.

All my life has been dedicated to the struggle of the labor movement and for national liberation of Puerto Rico.

I have fought for the organization and unity of workers, to demand better wages and work conditions. These activities have involved me in dozens of strikes and the negotiation of hundreds of collective contracts.

I helped organize some of Puerto Rico's most important labor organizations.

So I have given twenty-five years of my life to the struggle for progress of the working class. Twenty-five years to the fight for Puerto Rico's independence from the colonial yoke that the United States imposed fifty-seven years ago.

I Am Accused of Conspiring to Overthrow the U.S. Government

In those twenty-five years of tough proletarian struggle I have never been convicted of any crime. My activity has got me jailed and charged several times for political reasons, but I have been convicted of no crime.

I have always condemned violence as futile and counterproductive. I have defended organized action by workers and people in their struggle for progress and well-being. I have never practiced violence nor advocated violent acts. Yet now the U.S. government charges me with conspiring to teach the overthrow of the U.S. government by force and violence.

On this vicious charge I was arrested by American FBI agents on the morning of October 20, 1954. I was jailed in the San Juan District Prison, known as La Princesa. There I was held practically incommunicado till March 9, 1955, when I was freed under bail.

The bail was set at $12,000, more than is normally set in Puerto Rico for first-degree murder cases.

Ten other labor leaders and fighters for independence were jailed with me. On some of them bail was set at $20,000 and $15,000.

They haven't yet been able to raise it and remain in the San Juan District Prison.

This charge is brought against us after the U.S. government declared before the United Nations that Puerto Rico is not a colony and our country has its own government

The U.S. government brings this charge after the Honorable Governor of Puerto Rico, Luis Muñcz Marín, announced that "Puerto Rico is self-governing."

Yanqui imperialism jails us in a move of desperation without considering its statements to the UN and ignoring Muñoz Marín's Free Associated State government.

Thus imperialism demonstrates the hoax it played on the UN. With our indictment in the U.S. Federal Court in Puerto Rico, the colonial status to which the United States submits the Puerto Rican people is again unmasked.

With our indictment for violating the Smith Act of the U.S. Congress, all can see that the Free Associated State is just a new name for the old colony of Puerto Rico.

We are tried in a U.S. Court. The whole proceedings are in English. Most members of the grand jury that indicted us are bankers, industrialists, and assorted capitalists. A large part of them are Americans. The judge and prosecuting attorneys in our case are named by the United States without our people having any part in their selection.

That is my case. Twenty-five years of struggle at the side of the working class and of my people. Twenty-five years of struggle for organization of the workers, for better wages and conditions of life. Twenty-five years of struggle for my country's independence from the North American monopolies' yoke of economic and political exploitation. Those twenty-five years can't be tossed aside.

The charge against me is an absurdity. Everyone knows it. My ideology in favor of national independence, and of a system without exploiters or exploited, when most of the people are ready for it, is in any case my only crime.

I am charged with thinking. With believing in an ideal and striving to make it known. I have never been seen in an act of violence.

My position on that is well known.

But the oppressors of my people don't deal in reason. They want to paralyze with jails and atom bombs the ideology of millions of men and women. They won't succeed. The people are going to stop them.

San Juan, P.R., April 23, 1955   *Juan Sáez Corales*

Recent Rebirth of the
Puerto Rican Labor Struggle

Solidarity is a necessity in the struggle of the workers. The struggle is based on the contradiction between a collective process of production and individual appropriation of what that collective process creates. It arises out of the consciousness of solidarity an of its power. In the 1940s and 1950s Puerto Rico underwent some social processes that broke that consciousness.

The change from an agrarian to a manufacturing economy brought a momentary improvement in wages. The dominant group in the Partido Popular Democrático (PPD—Popular Democratic Party)—the new class of "children of old hacendados"—used the industrialization drive ("Operation All Hands To The Pump") as a mystique to control the class struggle to keep the working class quiet. Luis Muñoz Marín, for example, Puerto Rico's Governor from 1948 to 1964, told a congress of labor organizations that the labor movement's function was to cooperate with "the economic development of the country." The implication of "cooperate" was not to hinder the government's work by scaring off foreign investors (on whom Puerto Rican industrialization was based) by militant struggle.[1] If higher wages were tied to the establishment of manufacturing, and manufacturing came in at the government's invitation, economic improvement depended on the government. In the sugar-plantation economy of the century's first decades, the only key to economic improvement was solidarity of the union struggle against those who appropriated the fruits of labor. In the new situation of manufacturing growth the key was submission to government programs.[2]

This submission gained roots and strength from certain social processes that broke solidarity consciousness in the culture of the proletariat. First, the emergence on a large scale of a new social type in Puerto Rico—the veterans—out of World War two and the Korean War. Many of these were from the working class, but the favors extended by the Veterans Administration (for study, loans to small businessmen, facilities for purchasing in new residential areas, etc.) separated them from it.[3] While in previous decades the proletariat could only win economic demands by active union solidarity (strikes and settlements), the Veterans Administration offered a way to individual betterment, thus opening up fissures in the culture of proletarian struggle. Of special importance was the opening in study facilities which, as an individual means of climbing higher in the social hierarchy, turned education in the 1950s into "the opium of the working people."[4]

Of equal significance were the great emigrations, encouraged by the government,[5] to New York and other parts of the United States. Again, the bait to the working class was an individual route to economic betterment without class struggle.

Application to Puerto Rico of the Taft-Hartley law also had negative effects on solidarity consciousness, especially the ban on secondary strikes (strikes in one industry in solidarity with striking workers in others). Unity in worker-employer conflicts had been one of the most potent weapons of the Puerto Rican working class, who had historically channeled their struggle through a single labor federation. The complex procedures which this law imposed for resolving conflicts gave the big, wealthy, North American unions (the ill-termed "Internationals") the advantage over local unions. Puerto Rican industrialization mainly took the form of subsidiaries of North American concerns. Union representing workers in the metropolitan plant tried to organize workers in the subsidiary plant. So began an invasion by these unions, creating a climate of inter-union rivalry and breaking the earlier tradition of unified struggle.

The first document in our final section emerges from this situation of weakened solidarity consciousness and confrontation with the powerful "International" unions. It is a call to form a Central Unica (Single Federation) of Puerto Rican workers. Twelve years after issuance of this call, the Central Unica still hasn't materialized, but efforts of this kind have been pushing down roots for greater labor unity. The call is the basic stage-setter for the present Movimiento Obrero Unido (MOU—United Labor Movement) an organization coordinating the actions of many unions. Born in 1970, MOU has kept growing in importance and strength and has established a clear and challenging presence in society.

In addition to the unification movement by a group of Puerto Rican unions,[6] the 1960s have marked the rupture or transformation of the social processes that were disintegrating solidarity consciousness in the proletariat. The institutions of higher education remain inaccessible to the great majority of workers' children.[7] Emigration to the great U.S. cities resulted in even more degrading exploitation, and Puerto Ricans in the metropolis are developing strong ties of solidarity and combativeness. Wages rose but so did social inequality; income distribution has become less equitable and hence poverty has grown in relative terms.[8] The Puerto Rican worker no longer has the alternative of working in agriculture or getting a better wage in industry, for the economy of the country is now clearly a manufacturing one. The contradictions of capitalism, clouded over in the process of transformation from agrarian to manufacturing economy—the so-called "Operation All Hands to the Pump"—now become more apparent.

In close relationship with these processes, the Puerto Rican worker is recreating his old solidarity consciousness and combativeness. Since the end of the 1960s Puerto Rican society has seen a rising number of strikes, demonstrations and other challenging actions by the workers. In July 1973 their combativeness rocked the country, and for the first time in our history, the government had to resort to using the armed forces against labor militancy. The document with which we end this anthology is excerpted from the manifesto of labor and trade union policy of the

Partido Socialista Puertorriqueño (PSP—Puerto Rican Socialist Party).⁹ It examines the significance of what has come to be called "la jornada de julio" and places it in the perspective of the march to the taking of power—on a day that has to come—by the working class.

MANIFESTO OF THE CENTRAL UNICA OF PUERTO RICAN WORKERS (1961)

To All Workers of the Country

We, a group of leaders and representatives of Puerto Rican labor organizations, have created the Central Unica of Puerto Rican Workers.

This new organization responds firstly, to the urgent, immediate and, undeferrable need to end forever the suicidal war of unions against unions of workers against workers. Secondly, to the imperative of creating a solidly based and genuinely Puerto Rican labor movement, with its own personality and complete freedom from influences foreign to our people's life.

We submit that this is the only remedy for the tragic situation of a Puerto Rican labor movement invaded and penetrated by North America's so-called "International unions."

Revealing Questions

What are these so-called International unions? What did they come to Puerto Rico to do and what are they in fact doing? What are their intentions? Have they come to redeem the "humble native workers," as they proclaim? Or to leave us dangling in between while they make shady deals with the employers? Who gives the orders in these Internationals? The Puerto Rican members by majority vote? Or doesn't each International have a North American boss here, described as a "representative" and appointed in the United States, with full powers of rule and administer Puerto

Rican workers as he pleases? Where do the dues paid to an "International" go? Could a worker (or would he dare?) protest the wrongs done by the International or its boss? Isn't it a fact that anyone protesting in a shop can lose his job with the "International approval? Is there respect for the dignity of the employee in the International unions?

Has the working class aksed itself what will happen to the Puerto Rican economy if North America's so-called "Internationals" continue shackling the workers, and fastening their claws in our country's industrial enterprises for their own interests?

Don't we understand that these foreign Internationals are turning Puerto Rico into *a trade union colony, an economic colony*, by the gradual capture of our workers and industries?

Are we too myopic to see that in a few more years, if the Internationals keep penetrating our land, the Puerto Rican working class will be a prisoner in a trade-union concentration camp, ruled with a lash by North American "International" leaders for their own benefit?

Doesn't the "Internationals" fragmentation of our great labor family into a thousand pieces wound us to our very souls?

Are we Puerto Rican workers able—do we have the right— to defend and protect the formulas, solutions, and economic standards that suit our country? Or are the International leaders in the United States to decide, in their usually manipulated congresses, what's to be done with Puerto Rico?

Are we so simple as to believe that in a conflict of interests between North American and our own workers, these so-called "Internationals" will decide in favor of the Puerto Ricans no matter how much we are in the right? Isn't it always the weakest strand of the rope that breaks?

Where are we workers of Puerto Rico being led or dragged by these North American International unions?

Prospectors for Trade-Union Gold

This committee denounces to the four winds, with energy and faith, the shameful material and moral exploitations of the Puerto

Rican working class by the leaders and the North American "International" unions. These "International" unions, with the rarest exceptions, have been drawn to our country by the trade-union gold rush of the new economic order that is in gestation here. For sixty years they paid no attention to our bleak and wretched fate. They looked at us with indifference. But now that there is grist for their mill and money to be made, they invade our soil, bringing with them the worst and most degrading tricks and practices of corruption, fraud, and deception. We advise our union companeros to investigate and learn how the so-called "Internationals" operate in Puerto Rico.

Iron Dictatorship

Beneath the shiny varnish with which the International unions glaze their facilities, and behind their mask of democracy, lies a harsh and malignant dictatorship. A sham mechanism of rules serves as a screen for their leaders to commit and justify every kind of blackguardism and abuse. In the destructive, personal, and absolutist grinder of these "Internationals" from the United States a mere member, with all the force of his dignity and reason, is worth less than a sugar-cane bagasse. And all the members together, whatever the right on their side, are a toy in the tentacles of these trade-union pirates, these "new redeemers" who came with the arrogant pretension of giving lessons in justice and heroism to our workers—our tried-and-true workers who have so often known how to die gloriously fighting for their ideals.

Voiceless, Voteless Index Cards

In the "International" unions, workers truly have neither voice nor vote. They are just cards in an index file for the collection of weekly and initiation dues. No regularly scheduled meetings are held. Financial reports are made only by mail. It isn't the workers who decide freely what their wage and work-condition demands should be.

They don't run their own strikes. The Internationals call off
strikers when it suits their maneuvers and interests. The strikers
inevitably become zeros. The "International" and its boss decide
all and reign over all. As soon as the Puerto Rican worker enters an
"International" he becomes a slave. He completely loses his
identity. Some of them have gangs of hoodlums to "beat into line"
anyone who swims against the tide. Only recently, two "Internationals" used notorious thugs—popularly known as "apes"—to
commit acts of violence during organization and strike campaigns.
Such gangster spectaculars were never before seen in Puerto Rico!

Threat to the Economy

We also denounce the so-called "Internationals" as a threat to
our country's economy and industrial development. These unions
propose to organize and dominate all of Puerto Rico's workers and
hence all of its employers and industrialists. Once dominated by
collective contracts and other links and understandings, both
workers and industrialists are to be converted into a slave people
subject to the exploitation, the combines, the deals and double-
deals and conveniences of "Internationals" with headquarters in
the United States and branches in Puerto Rico.

Let's stop hiding the truth for lack of courage and honesty! We
should frankly proclaim that most of these Internationals have
come here with the deliberate aim of *preventing further movement
of factories from the United States to the island.*

Each plant moving here from the United States creates unemployment in the United States for members of the "Internationals." This unemployment naturally means the loss of thousands of
dues payers and other income, including contributions made by
employers to "International" welfare funds in the course of their
North American business. That is why those unions don't want
plants closing there to move to Puerto Rico. And that's what brings
some of North America's so-called "Internationals" to our
country. They come to organize employees as a pretext for demanding and threatening Puerto Rican wage scales equal to those
on the mainland. The idea is to intimidate the industrialists, to

scare them with reprisals to be taken in their U.S. plants. To discourage them from continuing to open and move factories in and to Puerto Rico. The "Internationals" come to create tensions, disorder, and unrest. But they perform this so skillfully, with aims so well disguised, with such beautiful programs, that some sadly ingenuous companeros welcome them with open arms and their leaders as a new breed of saviors.

He who denies this is either a lawyer in cahoots with the "International," or a native labor leader on its payroll, or one of the "International" presidents who come here like puppets posing as redeemers, pretending that they bring millions of dollars for housing when their real object is to invest money for juicy dividends and thus fatten their treasuries.

If the unhappy day comes when the Internationals run the show, *the Puerto Rican people, its working class, and its economy will be easy prey* for the misnamed labor leaders, many of whom, to make matters worse, are speculators with extravagant ambitions and unlimited egos.

Are We or Aren't We?

We Puerto Rican workers have reached the point where we must decide *if we are or are not a social class with our own life, personality, and historical destiny.*

Either, with a cowardice to shame us before our elders and our children, we accept the role of sheep for exploitations both by bosses and by International leaders from the North, or we have the courage and self-respect to declare that the Puerto Rican working class, like the French or American or Cuban working class, has rights and prerogatives of its own and therefore doesn't need to be tied to these "International" unions' apron strings.

If we are, we must take a clear and definite position without hypocrisies, without half-tints, without fear or hate or servility. A position of active, dynamic, militant, strike-oriented struggle, without strings or compromises, geared to achieve, *without risk to the country's economy*, the highest wages and social benefits that

Puerto Rican industry and business can sustain—all this in conformity with our own intellectual and dialectical standards.

If we aren't, we must abandon ourselves to the fate of a harnessed, despoiled, and scorned class of poor native proletarians heading nowhere, without future or rights, and not deserving of any.

Our Watchwords

This Central Unica declares that the Puerto Rican working class has its own life, personality, and destiny.

It further declares that Puerto Rican workers must organize in their own trade unions, and then integrate these into free autonomous federations and councils without affiliation or servile submission to any International union of the United States. These free federations and councils should subsequently join themselves to a single central body—but solely for the purpose of coordination and mutual aid and support.

The workers of Puerto Rico should have fraternal and sincerely friendly relations with the workers of the world and of the United States, and with their representative organs such as the AFL-CIO. We repeat, friendly relations—relations that could be built on the foundation of a voluntary trade-union association, but an association with no masters or servants.

We reject any relationship that involves impositions, interference, or domination of the Puerto Rican working class by any national or international labor organization.

We firmly believe in the international confederative association of the free labor movement on the basis of respect for the autonomy and freedom of action of each country's working class.

We know and affirm that the existing affiliative relations between organized Puerto Rican workers and U.S. International unions are relations of colonial-type dependency and subjection, totally contrary to the aspirations and interests of Puerto Rico's working class and of its people in general.

We therefore condemn and reject this prevailing kind of trade-union relationship. We condemn it as utterly prejudicial to development of the country's economy and as contrary to the social progress, dignity, and moral sensibility of a class—the Puerto Rican working class—which, having its own life and history, needs no extraneous transfusions for its existence.

Call to Union Integration

Fraternally and confidently we call upon all worker comrades and their unions throughout the island, offering them the efforts already begun to integrate the Puerto Rican working class in a single monolithic organization—autonomous, independent, without servile affiliations or subjections to national or international outfits.

Such an organization, guided and directed by Puerto Rican labor leaders, is the dynamic and essential factor that can make possible the stable, permanent achievement of the Puerto Rican people's economic, social, and constitutional goals. If that is true, why have we workers lost so many years fighting fratricidally among each other, changing generals and banners but floundering impotently in the search for our bearings? What are we waiting for? Why not start now, today, to work out our own unique destiny?

This organization is already on the march. On a sure, conscious, Puerto Rican march with an unalterable course and faith in our future.

For the Central Unica of Workers of Puerto Rico
Provisional Directorate
(signed) Pedro Grant, Coordinator

List of labor organizations participating in the
organization of the Central Unica of Workers of Puerto Rico:

Union of Workers of the University of Puerto Rico
Union of Transport & Allied Workers of Puerto Rico
General Confederation of Workers of Puerto Rico
Labor Confederation of Puerto Rico

Association of Radio-TV Technicians of Puerto Rico
Brotherhood of Puerto Rican Government Hospital Employees
Union of Industrial Workers of Puerto Rico
Brotherhood of Office & Allied Employees of Puerto Rico
Electricians' Association of the Commonwealth of Puerto Rico
United Chauffeurs' Union of Puerto Rico, District of Mayagüez

RISE OF THE CLASS STRUGGLE:
THE "JORNADA DE JULIO" (1973)

The July strike movement marked an outstanding point of ascent in the class struggle in Puerto Rico. Beyond a doubt, the labor actions of those days will leave deep traces in our social and political history as we fight toward independence and socialism.

It is perhaps still too soon, only a few hours after the nine-day proletarian offensive of July 1973 (from the 4th to the 12th), to analyze in depth the significance for the future of our struggle of those intense days that shook the country. The importance of this strike movement will be visible in its true magnitude later, in the light of new experiences of higher social struggle which will let us look back on this moment and see its historical role in sharp focus.

Today we can do no more and no less than draw lessons from what took place, enabling us to overcome in the future the many errors and failures of the July days. Such a critical examination will help us socialists to mature ourselves as leaders of the Puerto Rican revolution, to perfect our means of struggle and contribute toward greater unity and a better fighting spirit in the trade-union movement.

The Polarization Process

The big forward leaps in a revolutionary process come as a result of that accumulation of small victories by which man makes his slow but sure advance. The process accentuates more and more the contradictions that place one set of interests in the extreme opposite corner from another. This polarization enables the one and the other to dig in on their respective sides and from that position get a clear view of the class enemy. The same applies equally to the bourgeoisie and to the workers.

Within each of these social groups there are also contradictions, but not irreconcilable ones. When the class struggle gathers intensity, as in the nine July days, both groups tend to discard their small contradictions and consolidate. At that point in the process both are in a position to understand their role vis-a-vis their social enemy.

The workers' small victories in the day-to-day combat with the capitalist class afford them the experiences and organization necessary for bigger battles. Step by step the working class improves its victories, enriches its experience, and perfects its weapons.

The reality itself of the struggle, dynamic and changing, makes possible a qualitative leap in the process. The time taken to win small victories down the years seems to contract into a few days. Those days into which the years contract constitute what we call historical opportunities, the promise of qualitative leaps forward in the proletarian struggle.

Need for Conscious Human Action

But conscious action by man through his fighting organizations—in this case the parties and unions—is needed to make this possible.

In this respect it must be said that neither the party of the working class nor the unions—mainly the latter—measured up to the challenge of the moment. The spontaneous struggle of the working masses was far above the capacity of the political and union leadership to guide toward the heights that they were ready to storm.

In spite of this, the long-term balance of the "Jornada de Julio," as companero and PSP Secretary Juan Mari Brás has recorded it for history, is positive. More on that later.

Strikes of the Firemen and UTIER

As we know, the two big strikes that set off the process were those of the firemen and of UTIER, the Union of Workers in the Electrical Industry and Irrigation (Workers of the River Sources Authority AFF). Both movements involved around nine thousand workers. The two strikes coincided with half a score of others, which put more than fifteen thousand workers out on the streets on a war footing.

The firemen's strike began on Wednesday morning, July 4. That of the AFF workers began in the evening of the following day.

Within hours of the start of the UTIER strike the National Guard was mobilized. A little later, troops of that body had taken the strikers' workplaces by assault. The action of the troops of this branch of the U.S. Army, coordinated with a police shock force, failed to weaken the workers' fighting spirit. On the contrary, this repressive escalation by the regime contributed toward a big leap in worker combativeness.

If we compare the workers' combativeness in these two strikes with the intensity of the struggle in past strike movements, we see that in Puerto Rico there has been a continuous and uninterrupted growth in our working-class's fighting capacity.

Once again the possibility and necessity of using various methods of struggle, legal and illegal, were brought out. With picket signs outside of work, or in the country with axes and chains, these workers knew how to defend their rights.

A Problem of Force

Despite the police shock troops and the soldiers' drawn bayonets, the strikers of both movements put a remarkable show of strength. But more strength was required than the two could generate by themselves. What was needed was the planned, but fast and audacious action of the socialist and trade-union movements.

This was so because in the whole history of Puerto Rican labor's struggle for justice the government had never deployed so much force. Its action was a big qualitative leap in the repression of workers. It had moved from the era of the club to that of the drawn bayonet and automatic rifle.

Thus it was a problem of comparative strength. Against the forces of the enemy a greater force of the proletariat had to be pitted. This was the historic responsibility not only of workers directly involved in the strikes, but of the whole labor movement and of all socialists.

The labor movement went into action too late. We won't enter into hypothetical statements about whether if X had been done at moment Y, the result would have been Z. But there was a series of steps which, had they been taken in time, would have changed the relationship of forces in the workers' favor.

Three days out of the nine were decisive for the labor movement. These were Friday the 6th, Saturday the 7th, and Sunday the 8th. Each minute of each of those days seemed like months in intensity and in the rapid succession of events.

In those critical moments of our struggle, quick action was needed from the organized labor and socialist movements. We cannot see the escalation of solidarity in mechanical terms, that is, in terms of the first small picket line, the ensuing march, and the resultant possibility of a general strike. The escalation has to be seen in a dynamic and interrelated form.

We know that by Friday and Saturday conditions didn't exist for a general strike. But there *were* conditions to paralyze a series of key industries, such as freight and passenger service, aqueducts, some areas of cable and phone communications, hotels in the capital, and important sectors of the construction industry and other industries.

At the same time there existed a series of problems of which we must take note. For example, some labor leaders were reluctant to join in, arguing that there was no request for solidarity from UTIER. The leadership of that union had in the past declined affiliation with the United Labor Movement (MOU) and more recently rejected all support from it and from the independentist movement. It was only four days after the strike started that UTIER's Executive Council decided to ask for these organizations' backing.

The situation was critical not merely for the workers directly involved in the strike, but for the whole labor movement, the whole socialist and independentist movement. The regime's repressive escalation was an aggression against all Puerto Rican workers.

The country's progressive forces had to face reality regardless of the views of some clods and traitors who happened to be leading the strikes. The exception in this respect is the leadership of the United Firemen's Union, who at all times called for quick, united, effective action by the labor and socialist movement.

In the Broad Contest of the Class Struggle

The firemen's and AFF strikes were only one factor detonating the repressive escalation. True, these strikes were of wide scope and with a paralyzing effect on the country's social and economic life. But at the historic moment the regime had no alternative to mobilizing the National Guard.

For that reason the July days can only be analyzed in the context of the class struggle that has been fought in Puerto Rico for the last four years. This class struggle, impelled by the working class, has been slowly but surely pushing the oppressive system into a corner. Not for nothing did Marx tell us a century ago that the proletarian class struggle is the motive power of revolution.

From the Palmer General Electric strike of 1970 to the July days of 1973, plenty of rain has fallen. The working class has grown in experience, in understanding of how it is exploited, in organization. That first strike in which the Movimiento Pro-Independencia (MPI—Pro-Independence Movement) openly participated, and which laid foundations for our party's labor and union policy, has great historical significance in our struggle. As time passes and the blows of the proletariat are better aimed we see more clearly the great importance of the Palmer strike.

The workers' struggle escalated on various fronts and various levels during 1971 and 1972. On the economic front, there were the important Ponce National Packing strike, which included violation of an anti-picketing order under the Taft-Hartley law, the New York Department Stores strike, the Telephone strike, the *El Mundo* strike, and others. Our party's participation in these conflicts enabled us to raise the workers' general political level, organize the keenest and most combative elements into the party, and help unify and strengthen the labor movement. These achievements, closely related to the political aspect, led to a remarkable qualitative and quantitative development in our party. This and our party's three mass proletarian celebrations of May Day led to MPI's transformation into a working-class party.

All these developments in our struggle were moved forward by the growing economic crisis, analyzed and channelized by the socialist movement in terms of the social struggle.

Hence the escalation of repression by the government. The workers' small victories become big ones through a slow but sure cumulative process. Along with the fact that the economic crisis can't be conjured away under the present system, this puts the regime in an alley from which it can only force its way out.

A Positive Balance

The experience acquired by the striking workers and the labor movement in general was very positive. The whole process helped advance their understanding of the state's repressive nature and its role as defender of capitalist interests. The soldiers' bayonets, the employers' intransigence, the action of socialists in the strikers' ranks awakened more consciousness than one hundred political courses. Now is the time to push forward the one hundred political courses among vanguard workers of both sectors.

Of all the lessons of the July days the most important is the correctness of Lenin's axiom about political organization of workers in their places of work. This is so because it is in the shop that the contradiction between capital and labor stands out most clearly.

We can organize a thousand nuclei and hundreds of party committees in the cities and communities. This will make possible giant mobilizations and it is correct that we should do it. But if in the hour of preparing the insurrection to take power we have not organized the party in places of work and in industry, above all in the strategic economic sectors; if we don't have close ties with the unions that organize the workers in those sectors; then the taking of power will remain far out of reach of the proletariat.

(From *La Política Obrera y Sindical* of
the Partido Socialista Puertorriqueño
(PSP); reproduced from *Chispa*,
PSP activists' internal-discussion organ,
3rd year, special ed., September 1973)

Appendix

Letter from an Artisan
to His Newspaper
(1874)

Editor, *El Artesano:*

You have certainly taken on a tough job with the paper you edit, and to get the desired result is tougher yet.

We realize, Mr. Editor and Mr. Isidoro Colón—who, as the "Prospectus" says, have been guided by the noble sentiments of democracy in launching the paper—that our words will be a bit depressing; but we fear for the fate of your lofty intentions. Let us explain why.

For a people living so long in benightedness, the artisan class of this Spanish province is a model of prudence and good sense, but the benightedness has left it with a disease hard to cure when so deeply rooted. We suspect that incidence of the disease is general, but we know that in certain areas it is more developed than in others.

The colonial system which ruins nations, decays and frustrates peoples, and brutalizes individuals, has left latent among us the germ of its demoralizing habits; and with sorrow we see it still producing its detestable effects.

Still alive in our artisan class is that perverse passion, based on accidents of the color of skin with which nature chose to clothe us, that inculcates contempt for our fellow men. Still flourishing in our society is that system of privilege which recognizes one race's supremacy over another. And the worst of it is that our Guild of Artisans contains numerous proselytes who, dizzied by the vanity of their theories, want to put these disgraceful customs and absurd principles into practice. Moreover, the vain pretension endures in our Guild of certain craftsmen wanting higher consideration than those engaged in other crafts.

Can one imagine greater immorality in the customs of a society? Do the partisans of this privilege system think they can't fit into any pattern of decency? These giddy worshipers of a false god should know, then, that they only deserve a smile of . . . pity, from sensible people. Everyone with common sense will see the ridiculous role of these glorifiers of ignorance, these applauders of a system which, condemned by modern civilization, inspires more and more cultivated peoples from pole to pole to outlaw ignorance forever and consign its antiquated customs to oblivion.

This is the cause of my fears, Mr. Editor. Nevertheless, may God grant comprehension to the tailor that the shoemaker's contribution is needed for the better effect of his delicate work; and the same goes for the hatter, and then each in turn for the blacksmith, the carpenter and the mason.

And once convinced of the need of each craft for the other, and wanting to take the road of Progress, may *all the Artisans of our Province* grasp hands and recognize each other for what they are, brothers. And then may they strive to create "Centers" where it will not be the pretension to shine in this or that way that brings them together—as at a ball—but the desire to learn from one another, to perfect themselves in the knowledge of our political, social, and religious duties, so that marching on the road of virtue and enlightenment we may better fulfill our earthly mission, so that we may be good citizens deserving well of society, so that, serving our Fatherland better, we may one day know the satisfaction of having lived happy lives in enjoyment of UNIVERSAL BROTHERHOOD.

Mayagüez, January 13, 1874   *An Artisan*

(From *El Artesano*, January 18, 1874)

Memorandum on the
Sugar Workers' Strike
(1905)

Extravagances and presumptions of mercenary journalists;
arrogance and insults of bourgeois politicians; taunts and
idiocies of the kept press; harassments and diatribes of
bureaucrats and jobhunters; capitalist government con-
spiracy, police barbarities, and outrages.

All against the free worker!

First Dialogue: The Journalists

—Friend Gladiatore, we must sharpen our pens against these
subversive vermin who are always attacking capital with their
stupid and wanton strikes.
—Oh yes, friend Almaviva! Vigorous action is needed to stop
these strike disorders in Ponce.
—Look at this, Gladiatore: Lieutenant Guanil and two
policemen wounded. And all because the socialist spouters have
no arguments except coarse insults and subversive propaganda.
These violent harangues to the ignorant masses can only cause
disturbances, and who is always the victim? The police whom the
people pay to protect bourgeois property and apprehend riotous

strikers. Tell me, what does the worker get out of strikes. . . ?

—Poverty and hunger, if you ask me. Others get the benefit of this state of unrest, and even more so in Puerto Rico where there's no labor organization and hence no reserve funds as in other countries.

—Not a shadow of doubt about that. But what has happened in Ponce, where the good policemen Guanil and Silén got beaten up, is the natural effect of a very serious cause, against which we've taken and will always take a strong stand.

—Yes, we always should, Gladiatore. A strong and stern hand should cut off at the roots this business of a bunch of professional agitators going into a place, holding meetings, calling workers off the job, and inciting them to violence to scare the *hacendados* into quick surrender.

—Of course that's how it ought to be, Almaviva. We've seen the incitement to disorder and anarchy, and the police having to defend themselves against this rural rabble. And you know that strikes are followed by the burning of cane fields—and if the police hasn't taken certain precautions in haciendas of the south, how many acts of violence would we be bewailing now. . . !

—Right—and all because these swindlers take advantage of the ignorance of the masses, whom they exploit more than the employers possibly could. Imagine the stupidity and ignorance of these socialists who have the gall to call it robbery that a *hacendado* should make forty or fifty thousand pesos a year. As if what's good for private capital wasn't good for the country! With this imbecile propaganda, next thing you know foreign capitalists won't come, business will fall off and the people will find themselves without jobs.

—That's the kind of folly to which such ignorance leads, all right. And they've also tried to stick their noses into the House of Representatives. Remember that labor delegate who poured out gibes against the distinguished members of the House because they wouldn't condemn a guard who knocked down an Arecibo worker at a meeting in Plaza Baldorioty? And then how Mr. Santiago Iglesias and other brilliant socialist orators used up the whole vocabulary of insults against majority delegates for passing the eviction bill—as if it wasn t the Legislature's duty to pass laws to protect property? They'd like to turn the Legislative Chamber into an Anarchist Chamber.

—Yes, that's what the socialists want—no respect for property. . . !

—Well, they aren't going to get it . . . everyone knows that the worker was born to work and it's his duty to accept with good grace what he's given for it.

—Exactly. Where would it all end if workers got to living like decent people. . . ?

—For that reason we have to attack the Labor Federation, its leaders, and Christ himself if he tells us that every worker has a right to demand what his work is worth.

—Well, Gladiatore, let's take the bourgeois side. They're the ones who fork out the bread. . . . Get me?

—Right on, Almaviva.

Second Dialogue: The Politicians

—How do you feel about this strike business, Don Unionista?

—I'll tell you very simply, Don Republicano. What colossal nerve these workers have to go on strike in this time of crisis when the ruined *hacendados* are just beginning to get back on their feet!

—Yes, sir—and the idiotic reason they give for it is that the *hacendados* are exploiters.

—But don't they know that the *hacendados* have gone through years of crisis, hardly able to cover their commitments, yet never complaining nor lowering wages although forty centavos for a twelve-hour day is more than enough? Do they imagine that the *hacendados* get the land, machinery, cane, tools, and all the rest as a gift?

—Aside from that, Don Unionista, a lot of them have been ruined and many are right now burdened with debts and commitments.

—But, Don Republicano, those dumb workers think the *hacendados* pile up money by the trowelful.

—Maybe they think so, but it's a sure thing that their leaders are a pack of ignoramuses. They just don't have the ability and knowledge to understand the agricultural crisis the country's been going through.

—That's not all of it. They're plain swindlers who want to live without working, at the expense of the country folk's ignorance.

—And the vicious way they attack the political parties. . . !

—Yes, because they have no patriotism. We defend the country with the vision of its greater glory, isn't it so, Don Republicano?

—Absolutely, Don Unionista. But these precious socialists don't want to understand that, and keep insisting that life is due only to work, that the workers should demand more money, eat as we gentlemen eat, and dress like their masters.

—What idiots they are. . . ! What they're really after is disorder and anarchy, because in disorder and anarchy lies their strength. That's why they are enemies of the political parties. The parties aspire to peace and order, the foundation of all prosperity. It's not the socialists who are going to save the country or fashion its future. They've neither the skill nor the means to do it . . .

—That's God's truth, Don Unionista. It's the political parties that influence the government, that fight for the country's social, political, and economic progress and welfare. Yes, sir, it's they that have the means and the power to bring about that transformation.

—Truth cannot spare a scintilla of what you say, Don Republicano. It's the government that must be looked to for just laws and efficient means for social progress and development. Not by strikes and disorder can such laws be achieved, but by the intelligent and constant labors of the political parties. However, we mustn't pull the house down at such a price because the socialists aren't all that important. The whole working class is with us. We control the masses, and if anyone happens to resist, we have the police, the judges, the Governor, the mayors, the jails, and the penitentiary.

—That's the way it must be. That's what we have power for . . .

—And that's what we represent capital, the bourgeoisie, and the aristocracy for. The workers should be content with their lot. They were born to work and have the duty to be slaves. We were born to lead public administrations and have the right to be masters.

—We pass the laws guaranteeing property and order . . .

—And when those laws aren't respected, we have the armed forces.

—Our duty is to crack down on every socialist-type organization. That's why we attack the Labor Federation.

—Yes, we must always attack it and give its leaders what's coming to them. We'll be able to fight among ourselves when the time comes for jobs and sinecures, but we're united to crush every movement against capitalist exploitation.

—Down with the worker. . . !

—Up the bourgeoisie. . . !

—Long live the Fatherland. . . !

—Long live power. . . ! By 1906, we'll have more than enough arguments and theses to lead the flock.

Third Dialogue: Bureaucrats, Jobhunters, the Bourgeois-Political Press

—Have you observed, Don Pitanza, the bestial behavior of the rural workers? What can that rabble be thinking of. . . ?

—Not much, Don Estomago. They've just got it all wrong. They've been hearing us talk at meetings about the Puerto Rican Fatherland, liberty, democracy, progress, welfare, etc., and now they think it's all for them.

—What dummies. . . ! When did anyone tell the *jíbaro* he should get the same rights as us?

—Nobody ever told him anything of the kind. When we talk of Fatherland, it's understood we mean of, by, and for ourselves. We have the distinction, enlightenment, and intelligence for it. The *jíbaro* was born to go barefoot and jacketless, eat *mefafos*, and sleep on a mat under palm thatch.

—It would soon be the end of us bureaucrats if the campesino who sows and cuts cane got even a tenth of what we get . . . !

—We jobhunters would sure be in bad shape . . .

—But don't be scared, Don Pitanza; the press has shouldered the job of stopping all those Labor Federation troublemakers and having the strikers held down by the police and authorities.

—You're right, Don Estómago, the press is behaving well. Look what *La Democracia* says: "True, the campesino lives without a comfortable home and with no shoes or tie. Well, that's the way our campesino has lived. If that were the reason for the strike, Puerto Rican workers would have to be striking all the time, and after getting shoes would have to get used to wearing them. . . . And going back to the social question, which these upstarts don't understand nor even know, we say that Puerto Rico has no aristocracy and no bourgeoisie. There are no class or race distinctions here, here we are all together even in social relations . . ." Could you ask for anything more eloquent?

—But these imbeciles born for the plow and the sugar mill don't understand such reasoning. It has to be explained to them with the police on hand.

—That would certainly be the way. It's a waste of time, ink, and paper to print in newspaper columns such beautiful and weighty ideas as these in the *Heraldo Español*: "Educate the worker first; bring him healthy economic propaganda, the real concept of home and family. Kindle morality in him with good doctrine, instruct him in the functions society calls on him to perform, preach to him the respect of persons, of the property and liberty of others; do all this, and then, when it is all done, tell him:

—Worker, you have reached the highest peak of your class; your new way of life imposes more necessities than yesterday, with the greater needs that your dignified position calls for; far from feeling too weak to work, you shall earn enough to eat, clothe yourself, decorously support your family, and keep . . ."

—But what's the use, Don Pitanza. . . ! Those healthy ideas are not what the Labor Federation leaders give the worker.

—Clearly, Don Estómago, all they know is to call strikes, say that the bourgeois exploit the workers, and talk of socialism.

—All right, so what do these ignoramuses understand by socialism?

—Well, according to their dumb way of thinking, they understand that private property is robbery, that work is the basis of the world and of civilization; that the hick *jíbaro* is a worker and the worker is equal to the doctor, the engineer, the teacher, the pharmacist, the musician, the poet, the writer, etc.

—Holy Mother of God! The gall of these socialist imbeciles. . . !

—Don't worry, Don Estómago! Our press is on the job, giving them a taste of the whip. For that, *La Democracia*, the *Heraldo Español*, the *Aguila*, and other good bourgeois papers have got their sociologists lined up, men who understand perfectly that it's the *hacendados* and capitalists who grease the wheels of the printing press. What do the workers contribute. . . ?

—Troubles and shocks with their accursed strikes. So you see, Don Pitanza, we have to keep a short rein on these labor propagandists and malcontents, these guys who call themselves leaders as we call our heads of parties. The very idea of these hacienda workers wanting to wear shoes like decent people. . . !

—The insolence of it. . . !

—The dumbness of it. . . !

Fourth Dialogue: The Police

—Captain, order your men to get busy on the strikers. Remember we have to protect property and not let these troublemakers get away with it.

—Very good, Colonel. That's what the people pay us for . . .

—Yes, with the money of the *hacendados* and other capitalists, whom it's our first duty to serve . . .

—But Colonel, everything is quiet so far; the strikers are still acting peacefully.

—But the strike is not good anyway. The *hacendados* are already complaining that the cut cane is going to spoil and it'll be the funeral to the tune of thousands of dollars. As you'll appreciate, that's a big loss for farm capital and the country.

—All present and correct, Colonel. We'll get on with it . . .

—Of course, Captain, the *hacendados* and their properties are worth more than the strikers' lives.

—So we'll invent something . . .

—Invent what you like as long as you stop the strike and shut those leaders' mouths.

—Shall we do what they did with that black-flag demonstration?
—How do you mean?
—Well, you get the men ready for when the strikers hold a meeting. You get hold of a couple of drunks and send them in to start a row and the fists flying, then you go in like brave Cossacks and clean it all up with shots and clubs, including the platform. That way we frighten the strikers back to work in the same conditions as before or worse. And who cares about a few wounds and bruises. . . !
—Great idea, Captain. . . ! You could get a medal for this. . . !
—Er . . . one thing bothers me, Colonel . . .
—What's that . . . ?
—How do we justify our rough stuff. . . ?
—The code, the code. Don't we have carte blanche on what d'you call it . . . "disturbing public order. . . ?" Then there's "insult to the flag"—we can use that too . . .
—Okay, Colonel. What about Article One of the Constitution— we don't have to respect that. . . ?
—Constitutions and articles don't exist when capitalist interests need defending. You and I aren't workers, and we live pretty well in our job . . .
—But the men—they're nearly all country people who've worked as peons in the haciendas, and they know . . .
—That they're just a pack of animals, most of them, and if you tell them to shoot they do it even though they kill their own families.
—You said it, Colonel! Some of them, when they hear talk of a strike, think it's the work of some devil on the prowl . . .
—So they're the fellows to send against the strikers—to scare the devil . . . The orders come from the top, and the conservative press knows its lines: for the labor leaders, charges of disturbing the peace and insulting the flag, for the strikers, the club and gun . . .
—At your orders, Colonel. I'll carry it out to the letter. But we mustn't forget that the Federation and Mr. Gompers are mixed up in this thing . . .
—And the press, whose duty it is to defend the *hacendados* for

the "subsidies" it gets from them, will do a good job with our campaign using all the arguments they have. You'll see the words "anarchist," "subversive," "enemies of order," "disturbers of the peace," "agitator," ringing out more lustily than ever. . . !
—Bravo, Colonel. . . !
—Get set, then, Captain, you have your orders. . . !
—The strikers do make one point . . .
—Based on what?
—On the rise in the price of sugar—they say they have no shoes and can't live on forty centavos a day.
—Well, let them join the police when there are vacancies. That'll give them shoes and a dollar a day.
—That's very true.
—Another thing, Captain. You might make use of fires. Light a few around the place . . .
—I understand, Colonel.
—Well, get cracking, Captain.

Fifth Dialogue: The Governor and the Labor Representatives

—Sir, we come on behalf of the workers of Ponce, Arecibo, Caguas, Guayama, Yauco, and other places to ask that justice be done . . . we are representatives of the country . . .
—What's going on in those towns?
—The police are abusing the workers and won't let us have meetings or demonstrations.
—That's all right. I don't want disorders . . .
—Mr. Governor, the police are committing acts of violence and coercion.
—That's because those anarchist speechmakers are telling people to set fire . . .
—That's a slanderous invention and you shouldn't believe it.
—I have leaflets from Guanica. Incendiaries . . .
—Where are those leaflets, Governor? May we see them?
—I have them in my confidential file . . .
—Well, the authors should have been proceeded against with all

the rigor of the law. But even if this leaflet thing is true it wouldn't justify the violence of the police. Violation of Article One of the Constitution is a crime against the state . . .

—Those speechmakers talk viciously and provoke disorder. That was the reason for what happened in Ponce when they clashed with the police.

—What is said about that isn't true, Governor. The Ponce affair was a plot, and it was the same here with the black-flag demonstration. . . . Everyone knows what set it off—two drunks getting into a fight just when Eugenio Sanchez, a most correct speaker, was addressing the meeting. All the reporters give the same or similar account, "that it was an affair between two individuals in the audience, one of whom socked the other. A row started, some shots rang out, and the police entered to clean up . . ."

—Well, so what is it you want. . . ?

—That you, as Governor, instruct the police not to stop any meeting or demonstration.

—As long as they keep order, the workers can have a meeting anywhere . . .

—But when there's no disorder the police order it broken up . . .

—That would only be when the strikers are stirred up.

—We must tell you that Puerto Rican workers are peaceful and humble men, and strikes in this country aren't riotous as they are elsewhere. Our campesino is excessively timid and never gets out of hand with acts of rebellion as do strikers in the United States, Germany, Spain, France, Italy, etc. Furthermore, calling a strike is a right of the workers to defend their interests . . .

—The workers have the right to strike, but peacefully, without committing disorders.

—Up to now it's the police who commit disorders, using force against rights granted by the U.S. Constitution and making unjust arrests.

—It seems to me you have it wrong. The police tell me the truth . . .

—And we see the truth, too, in the police reports, with their trivial denunciations, that appear in the press. Hapless peasants have been arrested just for being in sugar plantations with a matchbox in their pockets. . . !

—You mustn't believe all you read in the press.
—So what the police say is even less to be believed. . . !
—This interview must come to an end. . . . What is it you want?
—That the workers of Ponce, Guayama, Arecibo, Caguas, Yauco, and other places be allowed to hold meetings without police interference.
—I have already told you that the workers can hold meetings, but with order . . . if not, the police have the duty to stop disorders.
—That's just the snag, Governor. . . !
—There is no snag. These speechmakers advocate anarchism and talk viciously . . .
—But we don't understand why the police come in shooting and clubbing people because a speaker doesn't express himself well. . . . The proper thing is to denounce the provocateur, if there is one, and guarantee our right to the meeting.
—The workers can hold meetings anywhere . . .
—And the police prohibit them everywhere.
—Their duty . . .
—But you see . . .
—The interview is over.

Sixth Dialogue: The Labor Federation and the Free Worker

—Worker, have my arguments convinced you . . . ?
—Federation, the truth stares me in the face—the bandage has been torn from my eyes.
—You know the truth. . . ?
—You've engraved it on my mind with those eloquent words: The workers' liberation is the task of the workers themselves.
—What do you think about the Ponce affair. . . ?
—A good example and lesson.
—And what must you do now. . . ?
—Bring my companeros into the organization. Tell them the *good news*, that their well-being and liberation are in their own hands. With the Union and Federation everywhere, justice will be restored to labor.

—From today on, what new arguments do you have for the ideas I believe and teach?

—This: that no one can deny that the Union and Labor solidarity are winning the day everywhere, and that the stronger the numerical force of the organization, the greater the successes of the free worker.

—What do you base that on. . . ?

—Here it is: The price of sugar has gone up, and the wretched wage was already not a tenth part of the sugar workers' due for their exhausting work which brings millions of dollars to the bourgeoisie. That being so, the workers have concluded that only organized resistance can wrest from the masters another piece of bread: they yield only to force. No sooner was the strike called in strict observation of law and order—all the arbitration formalities were observed beforehand—than *hacendados*, government, bourgeois-political press, bureaucrats, capitalist politicians, jobseekers, and landowners joined with the police to crush it and force the workers to yield and accept greater slavery. Yet against all the employer injustices, police violence, press shamelessness, bourgeois infamies, politico-bureaucratic plots, and government contempt; against the ingratitude of a part of the people, who in total ignorance of workers' rights think striking is a crime; against all these enemies the organization is winning and agricultural workers are shaking off a small fraction of the exploitation they suffer.

—Good. And who has been and is the heart and core of all this movement. . . ?

—You, the Labor Federation. . . ! You who never stop proclaiming and working for the ideas of the Universal Worker, and who show the Puerto Rican worker the path to economic freedom.

(From a pamphlet by R. del Romeral, April 16, 1905)

The 1st of March:
Why Do We Celebrate It?
(1915)

Working-class Ponce celebrated the fourth anniversary of the historic date, March 1, 1915, when life was taken from JUAN CABALLERO. The infernal weapon that filled him with red-hot lead was in the hands of one of those armed and disciplined beasts who shamelessly guard the interests of a procession of bandits. Sheltering behind the men in power, these bandits murder the producers—toilworn and stagnating in frightful poverty—merely because they ask a little higher wage and a wisp of justice.

Back in 1915 more than eighty percent of agricultural workers in the south of the island were on strike.

The movement grew more formidable every day.

The sugar plantations couldn't function for lack of workers, the few strikebreakers weren't enough to keep them rolling. There were cases in some plantations of beatings of strikebreakers who couldn't or didn't know how to do what they were told, and who consequently fled by night and joined the strike.

The famous Captain Nater, then commanding the Ponce police, stayed put in the plantation offices where he received his masters' orders.

The striking campesinos were prohibited from walking the roads of the Puerto Rican people. If they did their duty by ignoring these dismal and stupid orders, Nater at the head of his Cossacks clubbed and jailed them.

The crimes and violence grew on a wholesale scale.

On the night of March 1 there was a protest meeting at the now historic "TRAGIC CORNER."

Speakers from the city and the island took part to help liberate the oppressed campesino.

At 8:00 P.M., to a hum of many voices, the platform, adorned with red flags, was set up. More than two thousand workers crowded in front of it, eager to listen to their undaunted defenders.

The people talked to each other about the strike situation. There were outcries of protest against the men in power who were defending the capitalists. All these men were Republicans and Unionists who had dumbly surrendered their interests to their enemies. What were the people saying? Why were they protesting? Because they couldn't go on under such a wretched system.

On the four street corners were posted some gendarmes who kept glancing at each other and mumbling. They looked at the platform and the crowd, spat with scornful and malignant expressions, and edged from one spot to another like dogs wanting to eat human meat.

The meeting began. The crowd hushed, seeming to forget for a few hours the hunger gnawing at their vitals. First speaker, stormy applause, another and another. All denounced the recent events in the island before the great tribune of public opinion. Tremendous enthusiasm gripped this human mass, beaten down by poverty and an oppressive and tyrannical system, whose slow agonies would begin to vanish when the light of socialist ideals would pierce the darkness reigning for centuries in the people's consciousness.

At 9:30 it was the turn of comrade Santiago Iglesias—today a member of the Puerto Rican Legislature—to speak. Then a hurricane of applause broke the silence of the night. Captain Nater, who was a few paces from the platform, mumbled something, and zigzagging because he was rather . . . tired, slipped through the crowd and entered a bar across the street. There he got thoroughly drunk while the meeting went on normally. The speaker was attacking the police for its inability to be impartial, since it had its headquarters in the plantations and was their loyal defender, eating and sleeping in them and using their cars, horses, etc. Through all this there was absolute quiet, finally interrupted by an alcoholic cry of, "That's enough!" The police raised their rifles, there was a loud detonation, and a hail of hot lead fell on the crowd which fled in terror. More volleys followed as the people ran in great confusion.

Some minutes after calm returned to this inferno, a man lay in a pool of blood in front of the Gandaras's hardware store. On the next street a man threw himself toward the doors of the Circaciana Inn and a mounted policeman, one of the day's valiant heroes, shot him down as he cried out, "For God's sake don't finish me off, don't you see I'm wounded?"

Many of the wounded were looked after in the first-aid station. The ground was covered with shoes, hats, and bloodstained bits of shirts and coats. A melancholy solitude reigned an hour later, the city was declared in a state of siege, the Cossacks patrolled the streets on their horses, dispersing groups with guns and clubs. The peaceful workers fled and the valiant heroes imposed a reign of terror. Labor agitators and speakers were jailed. The capitalist cause triumphed, the cry for justice was stilled, and citizens' rights ended that day on the points of bayonets and clubs. A thick black cloud covered the sky, the stars hid their faces in shame for such cowardice on both sides.

So, dear readers, ended that day that filled Ponce with mourning and sadness. And to the shame of Puerto Rican society, justice still hasn't been done.

(From the newspaper *Conciencia Popular*, March 15, 1919)

"Democracy" in Character
(1919)

The campesino workers of Fajardo and environs called a strike against the powerful Central Fajardo Sugar Co.

The police, under Chief Jaime González, fire their rifles (as usual) against the defenseless people gathered in the public plaza. Many are wounded and speakers who were attacking the plantation, sole exploiter of workers in the area, are jailed. The comedy is well performed: the aim is to smash the strike to please the plantation which pays the money.

The San Juan press reports what occurred; *La Democracia* insults the workers whom it charges with responsibility, and in its Issue 13 of this month we read the usual words (among others) about them: *subversive, vile, Bolsheviks, bandits.*

The strike is against the Fajardo Sugar Co.

Jorge Bird is administrator and co-owner of this concern. Jorge Bird is Barceló's brother-in-law.

La Democracia is owned by Antonio R. Barceló, Chairman of the Senate and the Unionist Party. Antonio Barceló was much involved in Bird's business when, before becoming an "Honorable," he was a mere employee in Fajardo; now he is Bird's brother-in-law.

The strike hurts Bird.

The strike is against Bird.

La Democracia belongs to Barceló.

Barceló is a relative of Bird.

So *La Democracia* calls the Fajardo workers and campesinos *bandits, subversive, vile* and all the rest.

It was truly said by Muñoz:

"Puerto Rican capitalism, in cooperation with the corporations and traitors to the fatherland, will kill our present political organizations."

(From the newspaper *Conciencia Popular*, March 15, 1919)

We Protest the Bloodbath
(1917)

TO THE PEOPLE: On Monday the 26th, the bourgeois press of San Juan is planning a fiesta to celebrate the passing of the Jones Bill in Puerto Rico. To make it look more impressive they are inviting the working people of both sexes to this caper, paid for with the people's money while they watch their kids die of measles for lack of resources to combat it and are gunned and clubbed down by the guardians of public order for asking more wages.

Puerta de Tierra is now in mourning for the massacre committed by those who invite them to said fiesta. For this reason no worker should budge from his house on that day unless it is to demonstrate in protest against the most brutal assaults and assassinations in the history of our people. These crimes were premeditatedly and treacherously committed the day before yesterday by the police against Puerto Rican brothers in San Juan and Puerta de Tierra, for asking more wages to feed their children who die of hunger and measles while the bandits of industry divvy up juicy dividends.

The Puerto Rican press, dried-up specter of greater days, capitalist stooge that compensates with gold for its lack of shame, must have split its sides at the knowledge that its uniformed defenders of the gold brought mourning, tears, and desolation to the hapless workers' homes, and at the thought that later, having given the police corps a contemptuous kick in the pants, it would see them mingling with the very people on whom they turned their guns.

Puerto Rican workers, today we should fill our hearts with rancor and eternal hatred, tighten still more the bonds of brotherhood, and prepare ourselves by real and effective organization. For the great day of vengeance on this accursed regime approaches with giant strides, when we will build on its ruins another society without journalists hired by bourgeois gold to applaud the crimes of the lap dogs of capital and its government.

What the people of San Juan and its *barrios* should do on that "fiesta" day is adorn their doorways with black flags and crepe, and keep their children out of school, in token of mourning and of protest against those who waste their money while they die of hunger.

From today on the people should never forget that the police are the bourgeoisie's instruments to defend its gold; that these instruments have brought tears and orphaned children to workers' homes. No honest woman or man of the working class should be friendly or have any truck with these enemies of workers' liberties.

Keep on darkening our homes, Bourgeois and Journalists
Keep on torturing and shedding blood
Without pity, for the people are girding themselves
To end forever the violence and crimes
You have committed!

> For the Cigar Finishers and Tobacco
> Strippers (women) and *Rezagadores*
> *Florencio Cabello, Gregorio Valera,*
> *Carmen Orosia Cruz, Juan Valentín Soto*

Monday at 8:00 A.M. a meeting will be held on Pelayo Street, Puerta de Tierra. All working women are invited to attend.

25-III-17
La Bomba Printing Press Pub.

Notes

Preface

1. In the Puerto Rican bourgeoisie, too, there is a forgotten "history of the historyless." There is no real history of our national bourgeoisie. What we are given is, rather, the "mythology" of this class.

2. Compañero Gervasio García in his article, "Notes, on an Interpretation of Puerto Rican Reality," *La Escalera*, vol. 4, no. 1, June 1970, gives a good critique of this kind of analysis.

3. Our formulation doesn't imply that some correlations can't be shown between psychological configurations and ideological positions at a given moment.

4. What Gervasio García, "Notes," criticizes as "seeing history as a tribunal."

5. Salvador Arana Soto uses this phrase in the title of his biography of Luis Muñoz Rivera (San Juan, 1968).

6. This phrase describing the Spanish regime in Puerto Rico is not only Eduardo Conde's but recurs in many labor writers of this century's first decades.

7. A description by his friend and fighting compañero Prudencio Rivera Martínez in a talk we had with him in January 1968.

8. Acknowledgment to the student Yvette Torres de Cabrer who researched this story in Comerio.

9. The *jíbaro* appears in some historical works, but we should note the lack

of deep analysis of this phenomenon depreciated by idealization.

10. This should not blind us to the importance of some of these manifestations—the symbolic forms, for example—for an understanding of what we have called the "marrow."

11. We are aware that some forms of relations and interactions help to develop certain personality types, which hence will be more common in some countries than in others according to the type of national culture. But it is not in these types, but in the dynamism of relations, that we find the basis of culture.

12. Other examples of this approach are two short works much used in labor-capacitation courses offered by certain institutions in our country: Juan S. Bravo's essay, *Notes on the Development of the Puerto Rican Labor Movement* (1950?), and Antonio J. González's article, "Notes for a History of the Puerto Rican Trade Union Movement, 1896-1941," 1957. González work, however, has traces of a broader interpretation.

13. We are not the first to assert this. Cesar Andreu Iglesias in his article "The Labor Movement and Puerto Rican Independence," *La Escalera*, vol. 2, nos. 8-9, February, 1968, asserts for the first time the need to see "more than the role of individuals . . . the development of the working class."

14. E.P. Thompson, *The Making of the English Working Class* (London: Penguin, 1968), pp. 9-10. Thompson also develops this view in "The Peculiarities of the English," *Socialist Register*, eds. Miliband and Saville (London: 1965), pp. 357-358.

15. Use of the term "subculture" to sum up the characteristics defining a determined social group in a complex society has created great confusion in anthropological literature. The confusions arising from it, and the criticism it calls for in the framework of this discipline, are broadly discussed in Charles Valentine's book, *Culture and Poverty* (Chicago: University of Chicago Press, 1968), especially pp. 104-140.

16. The saddest example of this in Puerto Rico, we think, is the whole polemic (and the energies it has consumed) about where on the island Columbus landed—in which of the western bays.

The Social Question and Puerto Rico

1. UPR's Puerto Rican library has two documents of these societies, one from the Taller Benéfico de Artesanos of Ponce (1888), the other from the Taller Benéfico de Obreros Fe, Esperanza y Caridad of Humacao (1893). The newspaper, *El Artesano* (1873), also mentions these groups. The labor leader Rafael Alonso Torres in his *Forty Years of Proletarian Struggle*

(1939) gives a good description of these organizations (see chapter "Modern Ideas Penetrate the Popular Conscience," pp. 91-110).

2. Labor leader Andrés Rodríguez Vera in his books *Puppets of Labor* (1915), and *Triumph of Apostasy* (1930), mentions some strikes in the nineteenth century. The Puerto Rican historian Lidio Cruz Monclova tells (in an interview with *Noticias de Trabajo*, July-August, 1967, p. 7) of having found references to more than forty strikes by "coachmen, furniture makers, bargemen, laundry workers, printers," among others.

3. Best descriptions of this *Ensayo Obrero* period are provided by people who participated in it: José Ferrer y Ferrer, *The Ideals of the Twentieth Century* (1932), pp. 36-37; Ramón Romero Rosa, *Santiago Iglesias, His Biography and the Puerto Rican Labor Movement* (1901), p. 7; Santiago Iglesias Pantín, *Struggles for Liberty*, vol. 1 (1929), p. 36.

4. He ran as a labor representative on the Unionist Party ticket.

Memories of the Free Federation

1. One of the most helpful readings for a quick view of this process is Sidney W. Mintz's article, "The Culture History of a Puerto Rican Sugar Cane Plantation, 1876-1949," in *Hispanic-American Historical Review*, 1953.

2. Juan Carreras, who was an important leader of the Socialist Party—political arm of the FLT—gives a good description of the Crusade of the Ideal in his biography of *Santiago Iglesias Pantín* (1965), pp. 117-119.

3. In Ceiba, the Socialist Party, competing for the first time in elections, won 74 percent of the vote in the 1917 elections. (Data from Island Elections Board.)

The Tyranny of the House of Delegates

1. Francisco M. Zeno, *The Agricultural or Rural Worker*, Ateneo de Puerto Rico prize-winner, (San Juan: La Correspondencia, printer, 1922), p. 87. He gives all of chapter XI to an explanation of the rise of the class struggle in Puerto Rico, under the heading, "The Big Corporative Monopolizers of Land as Motive Power for Ideological Evolution of Agricultural Proletariat Toward Socialist Doctrine—Prodromes of the Class Struggle."

2. Months before the invasion, Puerto Rico had won a Charter of Autonomy from the Spanish Cortes, virtually conceding political power to the local bourgeoisie.

3. José de Diego was one of the Unionist Party's important leaders. In the first decade of our century he distinguished himself as the Party's moderate man in government, and in the second as the great advocate of Puerto Rican independence.

4. Oppenheimer was probably called "the revolutionary" because he was also among the chief advocates of Puerto Rican independence.

5. José de Jesús Tizol had a different social origin from most of his parliamentary colleagues in the Union Party. He came from a family of musicians and artisans.

6. Luis Llorens Torres distinguished himself more as poet than as politician. Socialist ideas emerge in some of his poems.

The FLT Begins to Break Up

1. Compare for example, the works cited in the introduction to "Red Pages" with the writings of Bolívar Pagán in the 1930s. (See Bibliography.)

2. The Socialist Party grew so fast that in the 1924 elections Puerto Rico's two traditional parties, Unionist and Republican, united in an "Alliance" against it. A Republican Party group rejected the alliance with the Unionists and formed the Historical Constitutional Party. This group apparently represented the Republican Party's more popular elements. It was with this group that the Socialist Party formed the electoral "Coalition" as a reaction against the Alliance.

In 1929 the majority of Unionist leaders decided to break with the Alliance. The two Republican groups got together again and were joined by the more economically powerful and more politically conservative elements of the old Unionist Party. With these groups the Socialists formed the Coalition that won the 1932 elections. (For more details and sources see A.G. Quintero Rivera, *Local Leadership of the Parties and Study of Puerto Rican Politics* (San Juan: UPR, 1970), pp. 105-106.

The Coalition was always a controversial storm center within the Socialist Party. Every time the pact was to be renewed there were bitter discussions.

3. Juan Antonio Corretjer in *Albizu Campos and the Strikes of the 1930s* (1969), analyzes the processes in which the Nationalist Party participated. Even more important were the strikes in which Communist Party leaders were prominent, as, for example, the big waterfront strike of 1938. (See *El Imparcial*, January and February, 1938.)

Twenty-Five Years of Struggle
1. See for example B. and J. Diffie, *Porto Rico: Broken Pledge* (New York: 1931), or Luis Muñoz Marín, "Porto Rico: An American Colony," *The Nation*, April 8, 1925. Puerto Rico's U.S. governors were generally appointed in payment for political favors and the island became an attractive beach-and-sun resort where military officials and politicians could retire with an honorable position. [See Roberto H. Todd, *Parade of Governors* (San Juan: 1943)].
2. In general terms, taking the organization as a whole, this is valid. However, the fact of being the workers' party lent it enough significance to retain many labor leaders of the left. Most of these leaders quit the party in 1940, but some stayed on till the end of the parade.
3. The tacit CGT-PPD alliance appears in almost all labor documents of the period which make reference to both organizations. However, René Jiménez Malaret's book, *Labor Organization* (San Juan: 1943), is especially illuminating.
4. The PPD won control of the Senate without an absolute majority of votes.
5. Inspired by the New Deal they tried to control the economy through government planning in a kind of welfare state. See, for example, the memoirs of the U.S. New Dealer Rexford G. Tugwell, Governor of Puerto Rico when the process began, *The Stricken Land* (New York: 1947). See also Clarence Senior, "Research and Administration in Economic Reconstruction," and Felix S. Cohen, "Science and Politics in Plans for Puerto Rico," both in *Journal of Social Issues*, 1947.

Red Pages
1. Alfonso Torres, Caguas tobacco-worker, was one of the Socialist Party's outstanding leaders. He got involved in labor struggles at the beginning of the century. Before *Class Spirit* he had written *Solidarity* (1905). He was Secretary-General of the Socialist Party from the 1920s till his death toward the end of the 1930s.
2. Moisés Echevarría, Ponce musician and tobacco-worker, was also an important leader in labor politics. He represented Ponce in the legislature on the Socialist ticket for three terms (1928 to 1940). *Virtues and Defects* was his first work. Later he wrote *The Red Word* (1927); *The Catalino Figueroa Case* (1932), exposing court injustice in a strike case; *Testing Values and Combating Procedures* (1938), autocriticism of the Party; and *Twelve Years of Parliamentary Life* (1941), describing his work as a labor representative.

3. Manuel F. Rojas, Vega Baja barber, was the Socialist Party's first Secretary-General (from its foundation in 1915 till the early 1930s). He did a prodigious organizing job in those first difficult years of the Party. Before *Social Studies* he had written the extraordinary book *Four Centuries of Ignorance and Slavery in Puerto Rico* (1914), and in 1919 he wrote *Victims of Workers' Migrations to the United States Speak.*

Fourth Annual Convention of the Socialist Party
1. However, the FLT tried various forms of political participation in that first decade: labor candidates in one of the traditional parties—1904— independent candidates running under the FLT symbol—1906—etc. (Gervasio García, "The Labor Movement and Political Parties, 1898-1910," chapter of doctoral thesis in preparation.)
2. FLT groups in other municipalities (mainly the Humacao sugar district) also ran in the 1914 elections, following the example of Arecibo in 1910 and 1912. None of them won but in some places they ran close. (See Bolívar Pagán, *History of Puerto Rican Political Parties*, vol. 1.)
3. Most history books state quite irresponsibly that "in 1915 Santiago Iglesias created the Socialist Party." The assembly that created the Party in Cayey on March 21, 1915 was convoked and led by the Arecibo group, namely Esteban Padilla (its first Chairman), Manuel F. Rojas (Secretary of State), and Juan Cándido Rivera (Treasurer)—all from that part of the island. Santiago Iglesias participated as one of three delegates from San Juan, of a total of fifty-six delegates from the whole island. See Socialist Party, *Actions of the First Regular Convention* (Bayamon: 1915).
4. These are Island Elections Board figures. There is known to have been considerable fraud worked against the Socialist Party in these elections. Thus the real popular support was greater than the figures indicate.
5. A total of forty-three resolutions were discussed in this assembly. See Socialist Party, *Actions* (San Juan: 1919).

Recent Rebirth of the Labor Struggle
1. Luis Muñoz Marín, *Función del movimiento obrero en la democracia puertorriqueña* (new ed.; San Juan: 1957). Teodoro Moscoso, Economic Development administrator and a leading architect of "Operation All Hands to the Pump," argued in *Un discurso y una aclaracion* (San Juan: Gobierno de Puerto Rico, 1950), that the solution of Puerto Rico's economic problem was to industrialize with foreign capital, and "the great task of the labor movement" was to help create "favorable conditions" to

attract that capital. "Any excessive demand that forces a single industry to close down is a crime against the welfare and future of all the people of Puerto Rico."

2. Muñoz Marín in *Función del movimiento obrero en la democracia puertorriqueña* openly and barefacedly tells the workers that the government is more to be thanked for their better living standards than the efforts of their unions. Ralph Hancock in *Puerto Rico, A Success Story* (Princeton: D. Van Nostrand, 1960), chap. 5, "Manpower," explains that in this situation the labor movement's battles were more on the administrative-government level (specifically in the Minimum Wage Board) than on the industrial level.

3. John P. Augelli, "San Lorenzo: A Case Study of Recent Migrations in Interior Puerto Rico," *American Journal of Economics and Sociology*, January, 1953, describes this well with respect to one Puerto Rican town.

4. Which helps explain the passivity of students in that decade.

5. Moscoso, *Un discurso*. See also Puerto Rico Labor Department, *Trade Unions and the Puerto Rican Workers* (San Juan: 1952).

6. We should make it clear that some North American unions in Puerto Rico contributed to this process.

7. See, for example, Luis Nieves Falcón, *Recruitment to Higher Education in Puerto Rico* (San Juan: UPR, 1965), or *Programa del Partido Independentista Puertorriqueño, PIP*, section on education.

8. See Castañeda, R., and Herrero, J.A., "La distribución del ingreso en Puerto Rico," *Revista de Ciencias Sociales*, Diciembre, 1965, and Ramírez, Buitrage and Levine, eds., *Problemas de desigualdad social en Puerto Rico* (San Juan: Internacional, 1972).

9. This is certainly one of the great documents of Puerto Rican labor history. In our book we include only the third part and we also eliminated some paragraphs about what the Party learned from the July events. The document begins with a very solid theoretical position on the class struggle. Part Two is a rigorous analysis of "the structure of the working masses" in the Puerto Rican economy, and of the level of union organization. It concludes in Part Four with guidelines for action by labor militants.

Bibliography

We have limited this bibliography to works most directly concerned with the history of Puerto Rico's working class and its manifestations in society. We do not include works specifically dealing with the history of the country's social and economic structures, as this would have made the bibliography too long and complicated. We wish, however, to stress what we said in the preface: the study of the development of these structures is basic to an analysis of the history of classes.

The bibliography includes books, parts of books, pamphlets, and labor magazines and newspapers. It also lists some articles in magazines and newspapers of a more general nature, but these sources have not been exhaustively examined. The bibliography may contain serious gaps with respect to writings before 1890 and after 1950, periods on which the author has done little research.

The bibliography was compiled for the most part in the General and Periodical Library of UPR (CPR) and from the labor-press material in the General Archive of Puerto Rico (AGPR), although we have also included some works examined in private libraries (BP). The work in these two institutions was exhaustive, with the reservation mentioned above.

I. Development of working class in nineteenth century; foundations of proletarian culture

A. Artisans

Alonso Torres, Rafael. Cuarenta años de lucha proletaria. San Juan: Baldrich, printer, 1939. Chapter, "Ideas modernas penetran en la Conciencia Popular." Alonso Torres, printer, was a prominent Free Workers Federation (FLT) and Socialist Party (PSP) leader. He entered the labor struggle at the beginning of the century. His descriptions of nineteenth-century artisan groups must have appeared in accounts by companeros who entered the struggle earlier. (CPR)

Andreu Iglesias, César. "Luchas iniciales de la clase obrera," in CGT, *Album* (1941). Has a good resume of the rise and development of the first guilds but cites no original documents. (BP)

Bakunin, Mikhail. Federalismo y socialismo. Mayagüez: Unión Obrera Library, 1890. Classic work on anarchism. Very interesting that it was printed, and circulated among Puerto Rican artisans, in 1890. (CPR)

Bravo, Juan S. Apuntes sobre el desarrollo del movimiento obrero en Puerto Rico. San Juan: Labor Department, 1950(?). Mentions artisan organizations but gives no sources. (CPR volatil)

Cruz Monclova, Lidio. Interview in *Noticias del Trabajo.* (Labor Department, July-August 1967.) One of Puerto Rico's most distinguished historians interviewed about his book in preparation, *El proletariado puertorriqueño en el siglo XIX.* (CPR)

Díaz Soler, Luis M. Historia de la esclavitud negra en Puerto Rico. Madrid: 1953. Chapter 10, "Los negros libres." Explains how they were one of the main sources of artisan-group growth. (CPR)

Oliveras, Blas y Crispulo. "Sintesis historica del movimiento obrero en Yauco," in Fco. Lluch Negroni, ed., *Album histórico de Yauco.* Yauco: 1960. Mainly personal recollections. (BP)

Newspaper *El Artesano.* Ponce: 1874. News, articles of island artisan guilds. (CPR)

Newspaper *Heraldo del Trabajo.* Ponce: 1878-80. General news. (CPR)

Newspaper *El Obrero.* Ponce: 1889-90. "Voice of working class of the province." (AGPR)

Newspaper *El Eco Proletario.* San Juan: 1892. "Weekly devoted to defense of the working class." In addition to news, ideological discussions on basic concepts of the labor struggle—strikes, union, etc. (AGPR)

Newspaper *Justicia.* Guayama: 1894. Mostly general material but with some reference to instruction centers created by artisans. (AGPR)

Revista Obrera. Ponce: 1893. Covers news of guilds and mutual-aid workshops. (AGPR)

Rivera Rivera, Julio. "Orígenes de la organización obrera en Puerto Rico, 1838-98" in *Historia.* San Juan: UPR, April 1955. Based mainly on Alonso Torres, *Cuarenta años de lucha proletaria.* (CPR)

Rodríguez Vera, Andrés. Los fantochos del obrerismo. San Juan: 1915, and *El triunfo de la apostasia.* San Juan: La Democracia, 1930. Chapter 8. Anti-Santiago Iglesias labor leader describes union activity before FLT. (CPR)

Taller Benéfico de Artesanos de Ponce. Reglamento. Ponce: El Vapor, 1888. (CPR)

Taller Benéfico de Artesanos de la Villa de Humacao, Fe, Esperanza y Caridad. Reglamento. Humacao: El Criterio, 1893. (CPR)

B. Journeymen-day laborers

Asenjo Arteaga, Federico. Páginas para los jornaleros. San Juan: Lib. Las Bellas Artes, 1879. Member of bourgeoisie disturbed by subversive campaign of class struggle. Moral advice to journeymen. (CPR)

Brau, Salvador. Las clases jornaleras de Puerto Rico. San Juan: Boletín Mercantil, 1882. Sociologist-historian, member of bourgeoisie, describes development of journeyman class as distinct social group. (CPR)

Del Valle Atiles, Francisco. El campesino puertorriqueño. San Juan: González Font, 1887. Similar to above but less analytical and more moralistic. (CPR)

Geigel Polanco, Vicente. "Apuntes acerca de la legislación social en Puerto Rico" in *Legislación social en Puerto Rico.* San Juan: Labor Department, 1936. Free labor news. (CPR)

Gómez Acevedo, Labor. Organización y reglamentación del trabajo en el P.R. del siglo XIX. San Juan: 1970. Analyzes how through regulation and given the economy's need for labor the numerical growth of journeymen-day laborers was made inevitable. (CPR)

C. Slaves

Díaz Soler, Luis. Historia de la esclavitud negra en Puerto Rico. Madrid: 1953. Mainly chapters 7 and 8. See also works to which Díaz Soler refers.

II. Working class in twentieth century.
Works of general character or covering
extended period of time

Alonso Torres, Rafael. Cuarenta años de lucha proletaria. San Juan: Baldrich, 1939. Especially valuable with regard to FLT's first years.

Andreu Iglesias, César. "El movimiento obrero y la independencia de Puerto Rico." *La Escalera.* February 1968, UPR. Andreu Iglesias has been active in the labor struggle since the 1930s. (CPR)

Bravo, Juan S. Apuntes sobre el desarrollo del movimiento obrero en Puerto Rico. San Juan: Labor Department, 1950 (?).

Carreras, Juan. Santiago Iglesias Pantín. San Juan: Ed. Club de Prensa, 1967. Carreras was an important PSP leader, but the book touches little on his personal experience. Gives excerpts from important documents. (CPR)

Castrillo, Valentín. Mis experiencias a través de 50 años. Caguas: 1952. PSP militant in Caguas tells his anecdotes and impressions. (CPR)

Corretjer, Juan A. La lucha por la independencia de Puerto Rico. San Juan: 1949. Chapter 8: "Partido Unionista y Partido Socialista." Interprets PSP history in terms of its chief leader, whom he sees as a traitor falling into opportunism and reformism for lack of ideology. (CPR)

Ferrer y Ferrer, José. Los ideales del siglo XX. San Juan: La Correspondencia, 1932. Printer, founding leader of FLT, of original *Ensayo Obrero* group. (CPR)

García, Gervasio. "Reseña a Lucha Obrera en Puerto Rico." *La Escalera,* 6:2, May 1972, pp. 32-34. As well as reviewing this book adds new information on the struggles of the first decades. (CPR)

Geigel Polanco, Vicente. Legislación social en Puerto Rico. Labor Department, 1936. Compilation of labor laws, with notes. (CPR)

González, Antonio J. "Apuntes para la historia del movimiento sindical en Puerto Rico, 1896-1940." *Revista Ciencias Sociales.* San Juan: UPR, September 1957. (CPR)

Guerra, Ada Nivea. "Desenterrando la historia del sindicalismo en Puerto Rico." *Revista Bohemia de P.R.*, 28/2/72, pp. 12-14. Interview with A.G. Quintero Rivera on first publication of this book; expatiates on points mentioned in it. (CPR)

Guerra de Colón, María Luisa. Trayectoria, acción y desenvolvimiento del movimiento obrero en Puerto Rico. M.A. thesis, Public Administration School, UPR, 1963. (CPR)

Mejías, Félix. Condiciones de vida de las clases jornaleras de Puerto Rico. San Juan: UPR, 1946. In addition to description of living conditions, a good chapter (Chapter 5) on history of labor organizations. (CPR)

Monclova, Irving. Una unión obrera independiente. M.A. thesis, Public Administration School, UPR, 1960. History of the Yabucoa Unions of Industrial and Agricultural Workers. (CPR)

Movimiento Pro Independencia. *Presente y futuro en Puerto Rico.* "El movimiento obrero," pp. 38-40, San Juan: 1969. Interprets whole history of FLT and PSP as result of influence of anarchist thinking in their first leaders. (BP)

Oliveras, Blás y Críspulo. "Síntesis histórica del movimiento obrero in Yauco." Blás Oliveras was an important PSP leader in Ponce.

Pagán, Bolívar. Historia de los partidos políticos puertorriqueños. Two vols. San Juan: Lib. Campos, 1959. Bolívar Pagán was an important PSP leader, especially in its last phases. He attempts a cold chronological account based on Assembly documents, but his personal view impregnates his picture of the PSP. (CPR)

Quintero Rivera, Angel G. El liderato local de los partidos y el estudio de la política puertorriqueña. San Juan: UPR, 1970. Chapter 7 questions the "great man" and "machine" interpretations of Puerto Rican politics with examples of development of the PSP. Points to the importance of changes in intermediate leadership representing different groups in the socio-economic structure. (CPR). "El desarrollo de las clases sociales y los conflictos políticos en Puerto Rico," in Ramírez, Buitrago y Levine, eds., *Problemas de desigualdad social en P.R.* San Juan: Ed. Internacional, 1972. Brief history of Puerto Rican social classes concentrating on working class. (CPR)

Roca Rosselli, Carlos. Historia de las relaciones obrero-patronales en la industria azucarera de P.R. M.A. thesis, Public Administration School, UPR, 1967. (CPR)

Silén, Juan Angel. Hacia una visión positiva del puertorriqueño. San Juan: Ed. Edil, 1970. "Un nuevo personaje en la historia," and "Más sobre el movimiento obrero." For the first time a general book of Puerto Rican history brings out the importance of the working class, but the presentation is superficial. (CPR)

II. *Ensayo Obrero* group (1896) and foundation of PSP (1915)

A. Ideology

1. Social philosophy (Workers' writings)

Balsac, J.M. and Valle, Santiago. Revolución. Mayagüez: La Bruja, printer, 1900. (CPR)

Capetillo, Luisa. Ensayos libertarios. Arecibo: Real Hmnos., 1907. *La Humanidad en el futuro.* San Juan: Bibl. Roja, 1910. *Mi opinion sobre las libertades, derechos y deberes de la mujer, como compañera, madre y ser independiente.* San Juan: Bibl. Roja, 1911. Feminist leader, anarchist and spiritualist. (See introduction to second document in this anthology). (CPR)

Cruz, Venancio. Hacia el porvenir. San Juan: La República Española, 1906. Clearly anarchist. (CPR)

Dieppa, Angel M. El porvenir de la sociedad humana. San Juan: El Eco, 1915. Anarchist. (CPR)

Honoré, Carmelo. Prologue to the naturalist novel, *Cabezas,* by Americo Arroyo Cordero. Mayagüez: 1904. (CPR)

Iglesias Pantín, Santiago. "La cuestión social en el Mundo," in *Almanaque de Puerto Rico para 1911.* San Juan: M. Burillo & Co., 1910. (CPR)

López, Juan José. Voces libertarias. San Juan: La Bomba, 1910 (?). The essay "La anarquía" is important. (CPR)

Romeral, R. del (Ramón Romero Rosa). Catecismo Socialista. San Juan: E. Propaganda Obrera, 1905. *La cuestión social y Puerto Rico.* San Juan: 1904. *La Emancipación del obrero.* Mayagüez: La Bruja, 1903. (See introduction to first document in this anthology.) (CPR)

Torres, Alfonso. Solidaridad. San Juan: Unión Tipográfica, 1905. (See Introduction to "Red Pages" in this anthology. *El Consumo y la producción al costo.* New York: Scarlino Press, 1914. (CPR)

Vilar, Juan. Páginas Libres. San Juan: Ed. Antillana, 1914. Juan Vilar is mentioned in various documents as one of the great ideologists of the early labor movement. (CPR)

2. Perspectives of Puerto Rican society
(Workers' writings)

Arroyo Cordero, Américo. Escalinata social. Mayagüez: Aurora, 1908. Articles and stories. Author apparently a schoolteacher but identified with labor struggle. (CPR)

Capetillo, Luisa. Ensayos libertarios. Arecibo: Real Hmnos., 1907. *La humanidad en el futuro.* San Juan: Bibl. Roja, 1910. *Mi opinión sobre las libertades, derechos y deberes de la mujer, como compañera, madre y ser independiente.* San Juan: Bibl. Roja, 1911. Feminist leader, anarchist and spiritualist. (See introduction to second document in this anthology.) (CPR)

Iglesias Pantín, Santiago. Gobierno propio para quién? San Juan: FLT, 1907. Report by Santiago Iglesias as delegate to AFL convention. (CPR)

Rojas, Manuel F. Cuatro siglos de ignorancia y servidumbre en P.R. San Juan: Primavera, 1914. History of Puerto Rico from a working class viewpoint. (See introduction to "Red Pages" in this anthology) (CPR)

Romeral, R. del (Ramón Romero Rosa). La cuestión social en Puerto Rico. San Juan: 1904. *El 16 de abril de 1905: lucha entre capital y trabajo.* San Juan: Unión Tipográfica, 1905. *Entre broma y vera.* San Juan: La República Española, 1906. *Musarañas.* San Juan: del Carnaval, 1904. (See introduction to first document in this anthology.) (CPR)

3. Reaction against labor ideology

Abril, Mariano. El socialismo moderno. San Juan: La Primavera, 1911. Compilation of articles published in *La Democracia.* Mariano Abril was Muñoz Rivera's right-hand man on that newspaper and generally wrote the editorials. (CPR)

De Diego, José. "Cuestiones obreras." Speech of January 28, 1913, in *Nuevas Campañas,* San Juan, 1916. José de Diego was then Chairman of the Chamber of Delegates. (CPR)

B. Styles of struggle (Workers' writings)

Ayala Maura, Eladio. El hijo de Carmen o Aventuras de un obrero. Ponce: Pasarell, 1909. (CPR). Novel by and about tobacco workers.

Balsac, Jesús María. Unión Fuerza. Mayagüez: Gente Nueva, 1910. Balsac was Secretary General of FLT in Mayagüez. (CPR)

Escabi, Norberto. "El rebelde." in *Revista Pro Patria,* Mayagüez. February 1, 1910, p. 10.

FLT. Exposición al gobierno insular y a la asamblea Legislativa sobre los grandes problemas económicos y sociales que reclaman una enérgica acción. FLT, 1915. Specific problems and demands. Santiago Iglesias signs as chairman. (CPR)

Honoré, Carmelo. "Relaciones del capital y el trabajo, influencia social de las huelgas," in *Conferencias Dominicales.* San Juan: Insular de Puerto Rico, 1914. Author of working-class origin but a Department of Labor official and not a member of labor organizations. (CPR)

Limon de Arce, José Ramón. Redención. San Juan: El Alba, 1906. Allegorical drama of labor struggle. *¡Siempre adelante!* Arecibo: 1904. Labor poem dedicated to FLT.

Rey, Miguel (?) *Rebeldías cantadas.* Humacao: Conciencia Popular, 1910 (?) Labor poems and hymns by Spanish and Latin-American socialist authors. (CPR)

Rodríguez Bernier, Paulino. Historia del Pueblo de Patillas, 1811-1965. San Juan: Ramallo. See chapter, "La Federación Libre de Trabajadores." Author, a schoolteacher, was PSP leader in his town and relates start of FLT in Patillas. (BOP)

Sánchez López, Eugenio. "Un loco revolucionario," in *Almanaque.* One of the most important labor leaders of the time describes labor agitators early in the century. (CPR)

Unión de Tipógrafos No. 422. *Páginas del obrero, colección de artículos para conmemorar el primero de mayo.* Mayagüez: La Protesta, 1904. Includes articles by Romeral, Sánchez López, Balsac, Santiago Valle, Paca Escabí de Peña, and others. (CPR)

C. Actions & events (Labor documents)

Andreu Iglesias, César. "Luchas iniciales de la clase obrera," in CGT, *Album* (1941).

Balsac, Jesús María. Apuntes históricos. FLT de Mayagüez, 1906. Very illuminating on the origins of the FLT in Mayagüez. (CPR)

FLT. Federación Libre pro Puerto Rico. San Juan: Unión Tipográfica, 1905 (?). Santiago Iglesias reports on journey and convention of AFL. Includes legislative program of labor delegates who ran on Unionist ticket in 1904 elections. (CPR, under "Iglesias")

FLT Procedimientos del sexto congreso obrero de la FLT. San Juan: M Burillo, 1910. Very rich in documentary material. (CPR)

FLT Unión de Tabaqueros de P.R. San Juan: P.R. Publishing Company, 1914. *Balance general, 1907-1912.* Bayamón: El Progreso, 1912. Very useful for understanding of workings of early-century unions. (CPR)

Iglesias Pantín, Santiago. Luchas emancipadoras. Vol. 1, San Juan: 1929; Vol. 2, San Juan: 1962. Mainly chronicling labor struggles before founding of PSP; *Quienes somos? (Organizaciones obreras).* San Juan: Progress Publishing Company, 1914. Gives list of unions, and is also in great measure a manual of tactics and proceedings for organizing a union, calling a strike, etc. (CPR)

Padro Quiles, José. Luchas obreras y datos históricos del Pepino sesenta años atrás. San Sebastián: 1950. Padro Quiles was an outstanding PSP leader in San Sebastián. (CPR)

Rivas, Nicolás F. Política del Partido Republicano Puertorriqueño y perfiles de jóvenes obreros republicanos. San Juan: Ferreras, 1903. Labor leaders not belonging to FLT. (CPR)

Romeral, R. del (Ramón Romero Rosa). Santiago Iglesias, su biografía en el movimiento obrero de P.R. San Juan: Ferreras, 1901. See introduction to first document in this anthology. (CPR)

Rodríguez Vera, Andrés. Los fantoches del obrerismo. San Juan: 1915, and *El triunfo de la apostasia.* San Juan: La Democracia, 1930. Criticizes FLT. (CPR)

D. Labor press

El Porvenir Social. San Juan: 1898-1902. Published by same group as *Ensayo Obrero.* Puerto Rican General Archive has good collection. Published three times a week.

La Federación Obrera. San Juan: 1899. Socialist weekly. Some differences but no conflicts with *Porvenir Social.* (AGPR)

El Criterio Libre. San Juan: 1899-1900. Weekly. Workers with Republican Party sympathies. (CPR & AGPR)

La Huelga. San Juan: 1900. "Published when possible." Eduardo Conde and Santiago Iglesias among contributors. (AGPR)

El Trabuco. San Juan: 1900-1901. Weekly. Originally linked to Republican Party, later independent. (AGPR)

La Miseria. San Juan: 1901. Published several times a week. Ferrer y Ferrer, Eduardo Conde, and Romero Rosa among contributors. AGPR has good collection.

La Justicia. Ponce: 1901. Republican Party sympathies; political position, "government a friend, bourgeoisie the enemy." (AGPR)

Voz del Pueblo. San Juan: 1901. Pro-Republican. Published several times a week. (AGPR)

El Pan del Pobre. San Juan: 1901. "Published whenever circumstances permit." José Ferrer y Ferrer was editor and Romeral had regular column. (AGPR)

Los Dependientes. San Juan: 1901. Organ of employees' union. (AGPR)

Obrero Libre. Mayagüez: 1902. Affiliated with FLT. Precursor of the great daily, *Unión Obrera.* (AGPR)

Unión y Trabajo. San Juan: 1902. Organ of Puerto Rican Tobacco Twisters' Union. (CGPR)

Unión Independiente. San Juan: 1903. Bi-weekly. Attacked Republicans. (AGPR)

La Voz del Obrero. San Juan: 1903-1937. Weekly, edited by Joaquín Becerril. He was probably the outstanding labor leader in the Republican Party, though the paper was relatively independent. Odd numbers of various years have been preserved. In 1937 it became a magazine. (AGPR & CPR)

Unión Obrera. Originally a weekly in Mayagüez, later a daily in San Juan: 1904-1935. FLT's most important paper in various periods. Good collections preserved for years 1904-1907, 1910-1911, and 1915-1935. (CPR)

Campaña Obrera. San Juan: 1906. Weekly. Pro-FLT political campaign. (AGPR) *Eco del Torcedor.* Originally in San Juan, then Bayamón: 1908-1909. Weekly organ of Puerto Rican tobacco workers. Alfonso Torres, editor. (AGPR)

El Centinela. San Juan: Fortnightly organ of Agrupación Socialista. Basically ideological discussion. (AGPR)

Nuevo Horizonte. San Juan: 1909. "Weekly organ of Puerto Rican tobacco workers and defender of organizational principles." (AGPR)

El Tipógrafo. San Juan: 1910. "Independent weekly." (AGPR)

La Rama. Bayamón: 1911. Tobacco workers' magazine. (AGPR)

El Vigilante. Catano: 1911. Weekly, mainly concerned with tobacco workers' strikes. (AGPR)

Justicia. San Juan: 1914-1925. Originally weekly, then daily. Official organ of FLT. There is good collection for years 1914-17. (CPR & AGPR)

Labor Day. Bayamón: 1914. Special propaganda-and-agitation paper for celebration of Labor Day. (AGPR)

La Voz de la Unión. Arecibo: 1914. Pro-worker but also defender of Unionist Party. José Limón de Arce, editor. (AGPR)

E. Other writings

López Landrón, Rafael. *Cartas abiertas para el pueblo.* Mayagüez: Unión Obrera, 1911. López Landrón was one of the few bourgeois intellectuals to support labor organizations. He was FLT's lawyer in its first two decades and supported PSP when it was formed. While his book does not deal directly with the labor problem, his general view of Puerto Rico is important. FLT sold this book to raise funds. (CPR)

Oliveras, Blás. Veteran PSP leader has been publishing, in *El Imparcial*, articles on labor history (beginning in February 1971). Oliveras actively entered the labor struggle at the end of the century's second decade. So far his articles deal with an earlier period and, beyond their factual value, they reflect the viewpoint on the first struggles of those who entered the movement later.

Socialist Labor Party. *Principios, programas y constitución del Partido Obrero Socialista de los Estados Unidos de América.* Puerto Rico: 1899. (CPR)

IV. From foundation of PSP (1915) to victory of the coalition (1932)

A. Ideology

1. Workers' writings

Capetillo, Luisa. *Influencia de las ideas modernas.* San Juan: Negrón Flores, 1916. Plays, essays, and letters "by an anarchist friend in Panama." See introduction to second document in this anthology. (CPR)

Conde, Eduardo. *Acusación y protesta.* San Juan: Unión Obrera, 1919. See Preface to this anthology. (CPR)

Delgado, Juan B. . . . *Aquilataciones.* Humacao: Conciencia Popular, 1929. Social philosophy through stories and anecdotes. (CPR)

Echevarría Morales, Moisés. *El proceso de Catalino Figueroa.* Ponce: 1932. History of Guayama agricultural strike in 1923. (CPR)

Iglesias Pantín, Santiago. "Partido Socialista," in Fernández García, *Campbell.* Humacao: Conciencia Popular, 1922. (CPR)

Lanauze Rolón, Dr. José A. El mal de los muchos hijos. Ponce: La Tribuna, 1928. Introduction by Moisés Echeverría. Lanauze was one of the founders of the Communist Party in 1934, but then belonged to PSP. (CPR)

Marcano, Juan S. Páginas Rojas. Humacao: Conciencia Popular, 1919. Excerpts are in this anthology. (CPR)

Pagán, Bolívar. El sufragio femenino. San Juan: 1924. Report on Pagan's judicial study made for the PSP Territorial Executive in 1923. The arguments reflect an American constitutionalist view. (CPR)

Rodríguez García, Tadeo. Ideales sociales. Caguas: Morel Campos, 1924. (CPR)

Rodríguez Vera, Andrés. Agrarismo colonial. San Juan: 1929. *Federación obrera pan-americana.* San Juan: Ed. La Democracia, 1924. Author and ex-labor leader, critic of FLT and its ties to AFL, PSP militant. (CPR)

2. Reactions to labor ideology

Bruschetti, Attilio. Catecismo de la obrera. Caguas: Ed. R. Morel Campos, 1925. Defense of middle class; for worker-employer cooperation. (CPR)

Delgado, Josefina. Voz de la justicia, breve disertación acerca del Capital y el Trabajo. San Juan: S.J. Printing, 1919. Defense of capital and the *hacendado*; for a society of compassion. (CPR)

Gimenez O'Neill, Francisco. El obrero urbano o de las fábricas. Typewritten, 1922. Purely theoretical thesis from conservative standpoint. (CPR)

Lebrón Rodríguez, Ramón. El problema obrero de P.R. San Juan: 1924. Author of worker origin but not member of labor organizations. Represents view of Unionist Party workers. (CPR)

Moreno Calderón, Antonio. El obrero, el capitalista y el empresario. Madrid: 1925. Author a Puerto Rican lawyer but book is treatise on industrial production without reference to Puerto Rico. Example of the Puerto Rican bourgeoisie's alienation from the labor situation. (CPR)

Rosario, José Colombán. "The P.R. Peasant . . ." Results of interviews in 1920s with rural proletarians as to why they voted as they did.

Rodríguez González, C. Catecismo para obreros y patronos. Fajardo: El Pueblo, 1918. Author, a schoolteacher, favors harmony. Respects property and order. (CPR & AGPR)

Zeno, Francisco. El obrero agrícola o de los campos. San Juan: La Correspondencia, 1922. See introduction to third document in this anthology. (CPR)

B. Styles of struggle

1. Workers' writings (FLT group)

Alonso Torres, Rafael. Hurto Menor. San Juan: 1919. Denounces court injustices against FLT members. (CPR)

Carreras, Juan. "Bandera Roja, símbolo de martirio," in Ferrer y Ferrer, *Los Ideales del Siglo XX.* San Juan: La Correspondencia, 1932. *No haga eso, señorita.* Fajardo: Siaca-Soto, 1928. This socialist leader and school head in Fajardo criticizes those who seek teacher jobs through Party contributions. (CPR)

Echeverría Morales, Moisés. Virtudes y defectos. 1918. See introduction to "Red Pages" in this anthology. (CPR)

Puerto Rico, Legislature. *Informe sobre el desempleo en P.R.* San Juan: 1930. Compiled and written by Rafael Alonso Torres, PSP Representative in Legislature. (CPR)

Rivera Martínez, Prudencio. Conferencia en homenaje a Rafael Cordero. San Juan: Voz del Obrero, 1932. (CPR)

Rivera García, Tadeo. Ideales sociales. Top figure-to-be in dissident Afirmación Socialista group criticizes tendencies he sees developing in Party in 1924.

Torres, Alfonso. Espíritu de clase. San Juan: FLT, 1917. Thinks creation of class spirit is top priority for labor struggle, and to get it proposes development of Worker Circles on local level where worker lives. (CPR)

1a. Revolutionary labor literature

Delgado, Juan B. Oro de las ideas. Humacao: 1920 (?). "Sociological" poems against oppression and injustice by international authors. (CPR)

González, Magdaleno. Arte y rebeldia. Caguas: 1920. Poetry and plays. One of leaders of Red Proletarian Theatre Circle in Caguas. (CPR)

Guerra, José Agustín. Cantos Rojos. Humacao: Conciencia Popular, 1924. Poems. (CPR)

Muñoz Marín, Luis; Ribera Chevremont, E; Coll Vidal, Antonio. Madre haraposa, páginas rojas. San Juan: Cantero, Barros & Co., 1918. Stories by non-working-class intellectuals favoring social justice; valuable for comparison with genuine worker literature. (CPR)

Plaza, Enrique. Futuro. San Juan: El lápiz rojo, 1920(?). Plays. (CPR)

Santiago, Jesús M. Flores y dardos. Caguas(?): 1918. Poetry. (CPR)

2. Descriptive, critical and other writings.

Anonymous. *Pro bono público*. San Juan: 1923. Labor legislation. Author "a humble aficionado of the study of the Puerto Rican social question." (CPR)

Araquistain, Luis. La agonía antillana, el imperialismo yanqui en el Mar Caribe. Madrid: Espasa Calpe, 1928. Chapter 9 has interesting comments on Puerto Rican labor politics. (CPR)

De la Vega, Raúl (Pedro R. de Diego). Ajilimojili. San Juan: 1923. Satires on politics in general, including PSP. Author apparently a sympathizer with labor movement. Bolívar Pagán, PSP, writes introduction. (CPR)

Puerto Rico, Departamento de Agricultura y Trabajo. *Boletin especial de la historia del Negociado del trabajo.* San Juan: Gob. de P.R., 1923. (CPR)

Ramírez Brau, Enrique. Mancha Roja. Ponce: El Día, 1929. Criticism of PSP by Unionist Party member. (CPR)

Rodríguez Vera, Andrés. El triunfo de la apostosia. San Juan: La Democracia, 1930. Criticizes FLT. (CPR)

C. Actions and events (workers' writings)

Asociación de Choferes de P.R. *Reglamento.* San Juan: La Correspondencia, 1916. (CPR volatil)

Echeverría Morales, Moisés. El proceso de Catalino Figueroa. Ponce: 1932. History of Guayama agricultural strike in 1923. (CPR)

Iglesias Pantín, Santiago. "Partido Socialista," in Fernández García, ed., *El libro de Puerto Rico.* San Juan: 1923. (CPR)

Justicia (Compañía editora de). *Informe anual.* San Juan:1920. Santiago Iglesias signs as Chairman. As introduction to the report, there is good history of labor journalism. (CPR)

Lozano, Rafael C. Relampagueos (Historia de una huelga). Ponce: El Dia, printer, 1918. (CPR)

Ochart, Bolívar. Mis dos años de prisión. San Juan: Cantero, Fdz. & Co., 1919. Author, important PSP leader in Eastern area, was tried and convicted for his part in labor struggles. The work helps us to understand the rise of PSP in a small town of the island, Junco. (CPR)

Pagán, Bolívar. Informe del representante del PS en la Junta Insular de Elecciones ante la 7ma. Convención Regular del PS, celebrada en Arecibo, 1928. San Juan: 1928. Exposes frauds against PSP in 1924 elections. (CPR)

Partido Socialista. *Actuaciones de le primera convención regular y Constitución Nacional.* Bayamón: El Progreso, 1915. (BP)

228   Workers' Struggle in Puerto Rico

Partido Socialista. *Programa, Constitución Territorial, y Actuaciones del PS*, fourth convention, May 1919. San Juan: Justicia, 1919. (CPR)

Partido Socialista. *Informe sobre la Comisión de Indemnizaciones a Obreros* delivered at sixth regular PSP Convention, June 14, 1924, by Commissioner Prudencio Rivera Martínez. San Juan: 1924. (CPR volátil)

Partido Socialista. *Constitución.* Approved 1924 and amended 1928. San Juan: 1930.

Plaza, Enrique. Futuro. San Juan: El lápiz rojo, 1920 (?). In Introduction, history of Social Studies Group in Caguas.

Rivera Martínez, Prudencio. "Federación Libre de Trabajadores," in Fdz. García, ed., *El libro de P.R.* San Juan: 1923. *Fondo exclusivo del estado versus compañías privadas de seguros.* San Juan: Justicia, 1928. For legislative action in this matter. (CPR volatil)

Rodríguez Vera, Andrés. "La Federación Puertorriqueña del Trabajo," in FDZ. García, ed., *El libro P.R.* San Juan: 1923. Rodríguez Vera tried to create this organization as alternative to FLT but didn't succeed.

Rojas, Manuel F. Estudios sociales o Frutos del sistema. San Juan: FLT, 1918. History of a strike. *Hablan las víctimas* in worker migrations to U.S. San Juan: 1919. See introduction to "Red Pages" in this anthology. (CPR)

Vargas Rodríguez, Pedro. La esclavitud blanca o el imperio de la burocracia. Guanica: Brisas del Caribe, 1918. "Deductions about the oppression under which Cía. Azucarera Guanica Centrale workers live." (CPR)

D. Labor press

Yo acuso. Caguas: 1918. Weekly. José Ferrer y Ferrer, editor. (AGPR)

Conciencia Popular. Humacao: 1919. Socialist bi-weekly, Juan B. Delgado, editor. Mainly news of Eastern-area strikes and attacks on the government. (AGPR)

El Comunista. Bayamón: 1920. "Libertarian weekly, newspaper of theory and struggle." Published by left group in FLT. Despite name, ideology more anarchistic. AGPR has good collection for that year.

Información. Bayamón (?): 1921. Official of Tobacco Workers' Union with information on strikes. (AGPR)

El Obrero de Ponce: Ponce: 1923. "Weekly of struggle and worker education." (BP)

La Tribuna. Ponce: 1925, 1929. Published by PSP members, some of whom would form Communist Party a few years later. (AGPR)

Ambiente. 1927. Weekly organ of Amalgamated Workers Union Inc. (?) (AGPR)

El Clamor del Pueblo: Río Piedras; 1928. PSP organ in Río Piedras. (AGPR)

La Antorcha. Humacao: 1929. Published by PSP members. (AGPR)

La Campaña. San Juan: 1932. "Organ for industrialization of the country and defender of women and of PSP." (AGPR)

V. Working class in the 1930s

A. FLT and Socialist Party

1. Labor documents

Afirmación Socialista. *Prontuario del libro en preparación "Opinión y sentencia."* San Juan: 1934. Criticizes PSP; see Introduction in this anthology to "The FLT Begins to Break Up." (CPR)

Carreras, Juan. El fascismo, su origen, sus errores. (Points of controversy between fascism, socialism, and democracy.) San Juan: Progress, 1937. Conference sponsored by San Juan section of PSP. (CPR)

Echeverría Morales, Moisés. Aquilatando valores y combatiendo procedimientos. Ponce: Nadal, 1928. *Doce años de vida parlamentaria.* Ponce: 1941. See introduction to "Red Pages" in this anthology. (CPR)

Fiz Jiménez, Epifanio. El racket del Capitolio (Gobierno de la Coalición Republicano-Socialista, años 1932-1940. San Juan: Ed. Esther, 1944. Documents on the PSP split in 1939. Fiz Jiménez, PSP founding leader, was then in dissident group.

Newspaper *Gérmen*. Ponce: 1936. Organ of PSP youth. (CPR)

Newspaper *Socialismo*. San Juan: 1936. Published by PSP Central Committee, edited by Nicolás Nogueras Rivera. (CPR)

Newspaper *La Tronera*. San Juan: 1937-1942. Weekly edited by M. Bernard Silva, PSP leader since early 1920s who later joined Afirmación Socialista group but apparently rejoined PSP later. Paper is, in general, pro-PSP, but is not an organ. (AGPR & CPR)

Novas, José L. Apuntes para socialistas. San Juan: 1938. Speech before PSP section of San Juan. PSP member criticizes PSP. (CPR). "Político Puertorriqueño," in *Ambio*, Revista estudiantil UPR, September 1936. Class analysis of Puerto Rican politics. Favors multiclass, anti-imperialist united front for independence and social justice. (UPR)

Pagán, Bolívar, Discurso, Significación del Día de Trabajo. San Juan: Varona, 1937. Praises the minimum wage, gives all importance to labor legislation. *Ideales en marcha.* San Juan: BAP, 1939. Essays and talks by future Acting Chairman of PSP (1937-1940) and Chairman (1940) Illustrating ideological transformation of movement (toward the right). (CPR)

Paz Granela, Francisco. El primero de mayo. San Juan: FLT, 1938.

230 Workers' Struggle in Puerto Rico

FLT Vice-Chairman shows complacency for its achievements. (CPR volatil)

Puerto Rico, Dept. de Hacienda. *Sobre compensaciones a obreros en P.R., El Seguro Agrícola.* San Juan: 1937. Labor legislation of PSP. (CPR)

Ramos, Pimentel, Bienvenido. Vendimia Roja, social verses. Caguas: Carvajal, 1936. (BP)

Rivera, Facundo. Principios e ideales socialistas. San Juan: 1938. Speech to San Juan section of PSP, stress on ethical arguments. (CPR volatil)

Rivera de Alvarado, Carmen. La responsabilidad del Socialismo ante el problema poblacional de P.R. San Juan: 1938. Speech to San Juan section of PSP in favor of birth control. (CPR volátil)

Rivera Martínez, Prudencio. 14 de julio de 1789. San Juan: 1937. Speech sponsored by San Juan section of PSP. (CPR volátil)

Rodríguez Garcia, Tadeo. Breviario historico. San Juan: 1936. See "The FLT Begins to Break Up" in this anthology. (CPR)

Serrano, Francisco. El movimiento obrero y el Primero de mayo. San Juan: 1940. Speech to San Juan section of PSP. Complacency. (CPR volátil)

B. Communist Party (PCP)

Lanauze Rolón, José A. El fracaso del Nuevo Trato. Ponce: 1935. One of founders of PC says liberalism won't do, communism is necessary. (CPR) *Por los caminos de violencia. La idea comunista.* Ponce: Ed. América, 1932. Abstract Communist ideology, nothing about Puerto Rico. (CPR) *Por que somos comunistas.* Ponce: El Día, 1934(?). (CPR) *La Revolución Rusa.* San Juan: PCP, 1936. (CPR volátil)

PC de P.R. (Sec. of Communist International). *Acuerdos generales y estatutos.* San Juan: Ed. Borinquen, 1937. (BP)

Newspaper *Lucha Obrera.* San Juan: 1936-7). Slogan: Bread, Land and Liberty. (BP)

Sáez Corales, Juan. 25 años de lucha, mi respuesta a la persecución. San Juan: 1955. See document in this anthology. (CPR)

C. Other groups and other writings

Corretjer, Juan Antonio. Albizu Campos y las huelgas en los anos 30. San Juan: Liga Socialista, 1969. (BP)

Enamorado Cuesta, José. El imperialismo yanqui y la revolución en el Caribe. San Juan: Ed. Campos, 1936. Sees redemption of labor only through nationalism. (CPR)

Magazine *Boletín del Trabajo—Puerto Rico Labor News.* San Juan: Labor Department, 1937-1940. (CPR R etc.)
Newspaper *El Martillo.* San Juan: 1939-1941. Weekly. Attacks FLT; gradually identifies with PPD. (CPR & AGPR)
P.R., Labor Department. *Publicaciones de ilustración popular.* San Juan: February-April 1936; 13 nos., edited by Vicente Geigel Polanco. Publications mainly concerned with problems of country, different problem and author in each issue. Most authors are among those who later formed PPD. (CPR)
Union Local de Chauffeurs de S.J. *Reglamento.* San Juan: 1933. (CPR)

VI. Liquidation of plantation proletariat.
From formation of CGT (1940) to publication of
Twenty-Five Years of Struggle (1955)

A. Labor documents

1. Labor Unions

Concentración de Izquierdas Sociales. *Manifiesto a todos los hombres y mujeres de P.R. que quieren la JUSTICIA SOCIAL.* San Juan: El Imparcial, 1943. Basically a boost for PPD and Tugwell by many labor leaders previously in PSP. (BP)
CGT. *Tercer Congreso, informe del secretario general Juan Sáez Corales.* San Juan: 1945. Reproduced in part in this anthology. (CPR)
CGT Asociación de Choferes de P.R. *Album.* Mayagüez: 1941. Some important articles on history of CGT. (BP)
Federación Puertorriqueña del Trabajo. *Declaración de principios, programa y constitución.* San Juan: 1940. Organization created by Bolívar Pagán when FLT separated from PSP. It didn't do well. (CPR)
Jimenéz Malaret, René. Organización obrera. San Juan: Ed. Esther, 1943. Pro CGT and PPD. (CPR)
Kuilán Báez, Sergio. "Como se creo la CGT," in CGT, *Album.* Mayagüez: 1941.
Ledesma, Moisés. "La revolución industrial y los choferes de P.R.," in CGT, *Album.* Mayagüez: 1941. Makes analogy between early-century tobacco workers and chauffeurs of 1940.
Morales, Félix. Tres maquinarias y lucha con fantasmas. San Juan: Romero, 1945. Union Chairman in one of the government's factories refutes theory that there should be no union struggles in them. (BP)
Newspaper *Justicia Social.* San Juan: 1941. Organ of Unión Protectora de los Desempleados de P.R. Edited by Juan Sáez Corales. (AGPR)
Newspaper *Lucha Obrera.* San Juan: 1948. Fortnightly edited by

Florencio Cabello, important Afirmación Socialista leader in 1930s. (CPR)

Newspaper *Acción choferil*. San Juan: 1950. Chauffeurs' Union affiliated to authentic CGT. (CPR)

Newspaper *Orientación Obrera*. 1950. Members of Puerto Rican Transport Authority unions. Conservative. (CPR)

Newspaper *Unidad*. San Juan: 1950. Edited by Ernesto Ramos Antonini. (CPR)

Newspaper *La Voz del Trabajo*. 1951. Official publication of Puerto Rican organizations affiliated with the CIO. (CPR)

Nogueras Rivera, Nicolás. *Contratación colectiva en la Industria azucarera de P.R.* San Juan: Real Hmnos., 1955. Includes documents. Author was Chairman of FLT. (CPR)

Obreros Unidos de las Ferrovías de P.R. *Primer congreso* (held in Ponce February 22, 1942). San Juan: Baldrich, 1942. Brings out CGT-PPD-PCP alliance. (CPR)

P.R. Labor Department. *Discursos pronunciados en la celebración del Día del Trabajo*. San Juan: 1943. Brings out CGT-PPD-PCP ties. (BP)

Sáez Corales, Juan. *Informe del secretario general . . ..* San Juan: 1945. "El movimiento organizado de los desempleados y la industrialización de P.R.," in CGT, *Album*. Mayagüez: 1941. *25 años de lucha . . . .* San Juan: 1955.

Santos Rivera, Juan. *Hacia unidad fuerzas del pueblo.* San Juan: Ed. Pueblo, 1960. PCP leader analyzes deterioration of CGT, mainly attributing it to actions of PPD. (BP)

Sánchez, Alberto. "Enfoque histórico del desarrollo de la Asociación de choferes y propósitos de este congreso" in CGT *Album*. Mayagüez: 1941.

Sindicales, Revista de Trabajo. San Juan: 1949. Articles, etc., somewhat PPD-oriented. (CPR)

UTIER (Union de Trabajadores de la Industria Eléctrica y del Riego). Affiliated with FLT. *Convenio colectivo.* San Juan: 1950. (CPR)

2. Socialist Party

Carreras, Juan. *Fascismo y democracia*. San Juan: Venezuela, 1941. "U.S. is great bulwark against fascism"; cheers for U.S. presence in P.R. (CPR)

Pagán, Bolívar. *Crónicas de Washington*. San Juan: BAP, 1949. PSP Chairman, named Resident Commissioner in Washington under coalition of PSP with Republican Party, emerges from his chronicle as more of a Republican Party representative. (CPR) *Discurso.* (At an affair honoring him.) San Juan: Venezuela, printer, 1943. Importance of statehood and free enterprise. (CPR) *Discurso, El gobierno fascista que oprime a P.R., análisis de la legislación del Partido Popular.* San Juan: Venezuela, printer, 1943. (CPR volátil) *La Personalidad de Barbosa.* San Juan: 1941. Importance of statehood; criticizes PPD. (CPR)

Partido Socialista. *Programa* (Aprobado en la Convencíon General Ordinaria de 1948). San Juan: Baldrich, printer, 1948. (CPR volátil)

Paz Granela, Francisco. "La salud mental en las relaciones obreros patronales," in *Memorias de la 6ta y 7ma Convención de Trabajo Social de P.R.* San Juan: 1952. FLT gave the worker "respectability," made the boss recognize his importance. (CPR)

3. Communist Party

Andreu, Jane. Por que los comunistas luchan por la independencia. San Juan: Ed. Orientación, 1944. (BP)

Foster, William. Respaldo a P.R. San Juan: PCP, 1948. Stresses that Foster's visit is in support, not to dictate policy. (Foster was CPUS chairman.) Andreu Iglesias writes introduction. (CPR)

Jiménez Malaret, René. Translations into Spanish of Marxist works that will have repercussions in Puerto Rican thought of early 1940s. Among them, Lewis Carey. *La crisis de la clase media.* San Juan: Ed. Esther, 1945; *Puede que a usted le guste el socialismo.* Ponce: *Revista Gráfica del sur, 1943; Clifford Thomas McAvoy (CIO) Las uniones de oficios de nuestra aliada la Unión Soviética.* Gob. de P.R., 1943; and, co-translated with Rafael Torres Mazorana, Lewis Feuer, *Las teorías éticas y el materialismo histórico.* San Juan: Venezuela, printer. 1942. (All CPR)

Lanauze Rolón, José. "Higiene mental," in CGT, *Album.* Mayagüez: 1941. One of the fathers of the PCP defends voluntarist view of human actions.

Marinello, Juan. Mensaje a P.R. San Juan: PCP, 1949 (?). *Sobre la situación de P.R.* San Juan: 1949(?) By the prominent Cuban Communist intellectual. (Both CPR)

Newspaper *Verdad.* 1942, 1950. PCP organ, edited by César Andreu Iglesias. (BP & CPR)

Newspaper *Brazos.* 1945. Edited by Juan Santos Rivera. (CPR)

Partido Comunista Puertorriqueño. *El camino del pueblo, Programa del PC.* San Juan: 1952. *Como organizar las finanzas.* San Juan: 1942. (BP) *Constitución.* San Juan: Arroyo, 1950. *Independencia ahora* (political resolution of Second National Assembly of PCP). San Juan 1948. (CPR) *Oye Juancho* (dialogue between two workers on Puerto Rican political "status") San Juan: PCP, 1945 (?). (CPR) *Programa y estatutos* (aprobado en 1940 y enmendado en 1942). San Juan: Ed. Esther, 1942. (BP)

Sáez Corales, Juan. 25 años de lucha . . . . San Juan: 1955.

234 Workers' Struggle in Puerto Rico

Santos Rivera, Juan. ¡Contra Hitler en el mundo! ¡Contra el hambre en P.R.! San Juan: 1942. Political report to the PCP Second National Assembly in Caguas. Projects policy of suspending strikes and letting independence struggle rest till end of war against Hitler, supporting Tugwell and U.S. Army. Criticizes Nationalist Party. (BP) *Puerto Rico, ayer, hoy y mañana* (PCP Central Committee Chairman's report). San Juan: Ed. Moderna, 1944. Proposes to dissolve PCP, back PPD, though labor movement must stay independent. (CPR)

B. Government policies toward working class

Díaz de Vega, Elisa. La enseñanza universitaria y su accesibilidad a las familias jornaleras de P.R. M.A. thesis, Trabajo Social, UPR, 1945. (CPR)

Geigel, Polanco, Vicente. Bases, naturaleza y caracteres de la legislación social. San Juan: Venezuela, 1944. Author was probably the most important ideologist of PPD social legislation. Function of social legislation as presented here is to relive certain injustices that the economic system will inevitably produce. (CPR)

Moscoso, Teodoro: Un discurso y una aclaración. Speech at CGT-CIO Assembly. San Juan: Fomento, Gob. de P.R., 1950. "As Muñoz Marín has correctly said, the worst day's pay is no day's pay." Presents foreign-capitalized industrialization as solution of Puerto Rico's employment problem, hence "any demand that forces a single industry to close is a crime against well-being, etc." Moscoso was director of the Economic Development office in Puerto Rico. (CPR volátil)

Puerto Rico, Labor Department. *Discursos pronunciados en la celebración* . . . . San Juan: 1943. CGT-PPD-PCP ties in first years of decade. *La doctrina legal del enriquecimiento sin causa.* San Juan: Gob. de P.R., 1944. Stress on social legislation. (CPR volatil) *El Negociado de Conciliación y Arbitraje, Síntesis histórica.* San Juan: Gob. de P.R., 1957. History. (CPR volatil) *Informes anuales del Comisionado del Trabajo.* (CPR) *Noticias del Trabajo.* Fortnightly publication of Labor Department. 1944 & following years. (CPR) *A los obreros que desean ir a trabajar en fincas de los Estados Unidos.* San Juan: Gob. de P.R., 1954. *Los trabajadores y las cooperativas de crédito.* San Juan: Gob. de P.R., 1949. (Both CPR)

C. Studies offering direct or indirect interpretations of labor struggles in the period

Rivera Murillo, Cármen. Estudio sobre la labor realizada por la (UTT) Unión de Trabajadores del Transporte de P.R. y Ramas Anexas, Inc., dentro del movimiento obrero de P.R. San Juan: UPR, 1969. M.A. thesis, Public Administration School, UPR. Very useful work. (CPR)

VII. 1955 and beyond

Agosto, Angel M. "La clase obrera, problemas y objetivos," in *Nueva Lucha*, 1:1, November 1970; "Objetivos del trabajo obrero del MPT," *Nueva Lucha*, 1:2, May 1971; *Trazando los nuevos rumbos de la clase obrera.* San Juan: Ed. El Proletario, 1972. Agosto is Labor & Union Affairs Secretary of Partido Socialista Puertorriqueno (PSP). (BP)

Andreu Iglesias, César. *El derecho a pensar en peligro.* San Juan: P.R. Printing & Pub. Co., 1955. Persecution of Communists. (BP)

Baiges Chapel, Pedro. "Las Leyes anti-obreras," in *Nueva Lucha, 1:2, May 1971.*

Congreso de Trabajadores Socialistas. *Actas.* San Juan: Ed. El Proletario, 1972. Organized by PSP. (BP)

Magazine *Chispa.* Vol. 1, 1970. Published by Labor and Union Affairs Secretariat of PSP. Articles on labor history as well as current struggles. (BP)

Morales, Gervasio. *La ley Taft-Hartley, camisa de fuerza del movimiento obrero.* San Juan: Ed. El Proletario, 1972. Based on articles by Baiges on anti-labor laws. (BP)

Moscoso, Teodoro. *El progreso técnico y los trabajadores.* San Juan: Gob. de P.R., 1958. (CPR volátil)

Muñoz Marín, Luis. *Función del movimiento obrero en la democracia puertorriqueña.* Speech at Labor Unity Congress. 1957. "Función" is to "cooperate with economic development" instrumented by government; hence, in the context, labor cooperation merely means "behave well." (CPR volátil)

Newspaper *Caliente.* (Official organ of Boilermakers Union). Vol. 1, 1971, monthly. This is one of the "International" unions that have done most for the rebirth of militant labor struggles. (BP)

Newspaper *Clamor.* San Juan: 1957. "Monthly of labor literature, education and culture." Independent. For labor unity. Edited by Tadeo Rodríguez García, important Afirmación Socialista leader in the 1930s. (BP)

Newspaper *Justicia.* Vol. 1, 1971. PIP organ for distribution in proletarian districts. (BP)

Newspaper *El Obrero.* Vol. 1, 1970. Published by PIP Committee in Bayamon. (BP)

Newspaper *Puerto Rico Obrero.* 1964. Independent but with PPD tendency. (CPR)

Newspaper *Salario*. 1966-71. FLT. Edited by Nicolás Nogueras Rivera. CPR has fairly complete collection.

Partido Independentista Puertorriqueño. *Independencia, Socialismo y Democracia: Unico camino, Programa del PIP*. San Juan: 1972. See section: "Sindicalismo y Problemas Laborales." (BP)

Partido Socialista Puertorriqueño. *La política obrera y sindical del PSP*. (Special number of *Chispa*. San Juan: 1973. See introduction to last part of this anthology.

P.R., Labor Department. *Junta de Relaciones del Trabajo*. CPR preserves good collection of this body's decisions.

Rottenberg, Simón. La administración de las uniones obreras. San Juan: UPR. (CPR volátil)

Server, O.B. "La degeneración del movimiento obrero en P.R.," in *La Escalera*. Summer 1967. (CPR)

Sierra Berdecia, Fernando. La emigración puertorriqueña, realidad y política pública. San Juan: DIP, 1956. (CPR) Author, PPD Secretary of Labor in early 1950s, sees collective bargaining as worker's panacea.